Fifth Workshop on Teaching NLP 2021

AA008074

Held online due to COVID-19

Mexico City, Mexico
10-11 June 2021

ISBN: 978-1-7138-3031-3

Printed from e-media with permission by:

Curran Associates, Inc.
57 Morehouse Lane
Red Hook, NY 12571

CURRAN ASSOCIATES INC.
proceedings.com

Some format issues inherent in the e-media version may also appear in this print version.

Copyright© (2021) by the Association for Computational Linguistics
All rights reserved.

Printed with permission by Curran Associates, Inc. (2021)

For permission requests, please contact the Association for Computational Linguistics at the address below.

Association for Computational Linguistics
209 N. Eighth Street
Stroudsburg, Pennsylvania 18360

Phone: 1-570-476-8006
Fax: 1-570-476-0860

acl@aclweb.org

Additional copies of this publication are available from:

Curran Associates, Inc.
57 Morehouse Lane
Red Hook, NY 12571 USA
Phone: 845-758-0400
Fax: 845-758-2633
Email: curran@proceedings.com
Web: www.proceedings.com

NAACL-HLT 2021

Teaching NLP

Proceedings of the Fifth Workshop

June 10 - 11, 2021
Mexico City (virtual)

©2021 The Association for Computational Linguistics

Introduction

Welcome to the Fifth Workshop on Teaching Natural Language Processing (NLP). This online workshop featured an exciting mix of papers, teaching material submissions, panels, talks, and participatory activities.

The field of NLP is growing rapidly, with new state-of-the-art methods emerging every year, if not sooner. As educators in NLP, we struggle to keep up. We need to make decisions about what to teach and how to teach it with every offering of a course, sometimes even as a course is being offered. The fast-paced nature of NLP brings unique challenges for curriculum design, and the immense growth of the field has lead to not just core NLP courses, but also to more specialized classes and seminars in subareas such as Natural Language Understanding, Computational Social Science, Machine Translation, and many more. We also have an increasing number of students interested in NLP, bringing with them a wide range of backgrounds and experiences.

We were happy to accept 13 long papers and 13 short papers on teaching materials. The latter were accompanied by exercises and assignments as Jupyter notebooks, software, slides, and teaching guidelines that will be made available via a repository created as result of the workshop. Both types of papers cover many topics: curriculum selection, teaching strategies, adapting to different student audiences, resources for assignments, and course or program design.

Our workshop also featured two panels, one on "What should we be teaching?" and another on "What does industry need?". The first panel featured Isabelle Augenstein (University of Copenhagen), Emily M. Bender (University of Washington), Yoav Goldberg (Bar Ilan University), and Dan Jurafsky (Stanford University). The second panel featured Lenny Bronner (The Washington Post), Delip Rao (Allen Institute for AI), Frank Rudzicz (University of Toronto), and Rachael Tatman (Rasa). We also had two amazing invited speakers, Ines Montani (Explosion) and Jason Eisner (Johns Hopkins University).

We thank the Program Committee, who thoughtfully reviewed these papers this year. We also appreciate the sponsorship funding we received from Google and Duolingo. Finally, we thank the workshop participants, whose interests in teaching allow us to establish and grow the next generation of NLP researchers and practitioners.

David Jurgens, Varada Kolhatkar, Lucy Li, Margot Mieskes, and Ted Pedersen (the co-organizers)

Organizing Committee

David Jurgens, University of Michigan

Varada Kolhatkar, University of British Columbia

Lucy Li, University of California, Berkeley

Margot Mieskes, Darmstadt University of Applied Sciences

Ted Pedersen, University of Minnesota, Duluth

Keynote Speakers

Jason Eisner, Johns Hopkins University

Ines Montani, Explosion

Panelists

Isabelle Augenstein, University of Copenhagen

Emily M. Bender, University of Washington

Lenny Bronner, The Washington Post

Yoav Goldberg, Bar-Ilan University

Dan Jurafsky, Stanford University

Delip Rao, Allen Institute for AI

Frank Rudzicz, University of Toronto

Rachael Tatman, Rasa

Program Committee

Benedikt Adelmann, University of Hamburg

Thomas Arnold, Technische Universität Darmstadt

Denilson Barbosa, University of Alberta

Austin Blodgett, Georgetown University

Su Lin Blodgett, Microsoft Research

Brendon Boldt, Carnegie Mellon University

Chris Brew, LivePerson

Julian Brooke, University of British Columbia

Paul Cook, University of New Brunswick

Carrie Demmans Epp, University of Alberta

Ivan Derzhanski, Bulgarian Academy of Sciences

Anna Feldman, Montclair State University

Alvin Grissom II, Haverford College

Bradley Hauer, University of Alberta

Marti A. Hearst, University of California, Berkeley
Katherine Keith, University of Massachusetts, Amherst
Grzegorz Kondrak, University of Alberta
Valia Kordoni, Humboldt University Berlin
Sandra Kübler, Indiana University
Vladislav Kubon, Charles University in Prague
James Kunz, Google / University of California, Berkeley
Lori Levin, Carnegie Mellon University
Deryle Lonsdale, Brigham Young University
Olga Lyashevskaya, HSE University
Christian M. Meyer, Technische Universitat Darmstadt
Bridget McInnes, Virginia Commonwealth University
Julie Medero, Harvey Mudd College
Gerald Penn, University of Toronto
Alexander Piperski, HSE University
Christopher Potts, Stanford University
Anoop Sarkar, Simon Fraser University
Nathan Schneider, Georgetown University
Alexandra Schofield, Harvey Mudd College
Melanie Siegel, Hochschule Darmstadt
Sowmya Vajjala, National Research Council
Gerhard Van Huyssteen, North-West University
Shira Wein, Georgetown University
Richard Wicentowski, Swarthmore College
Shuly Wintner, University of Haifa
Torsten Zesch, University of Duisburg-Essen
Heike Zinsmeister, University of Hamburg

Table of Contents

Workshop Program

Thursday, June 10, 2021

Poster Session 1

\+ ***Long Papers : Courses and Curricula***

Pedagogical Principles in the Online Teaching of Text Mining: A Retrospection
Rajkumar Saini, György Kovács, Mohamadreza Faridghasemnia, Hamam Mokayed, Oluwatosin Adewumi, Pedro Alonso, Sumit Rakesh and Marcus Liwicki

Teaching a Massive Open Online Course on Natural Language Processing
Ekaterina Artemova, Murat Apishev, Denis Kirianov, Veronica Sarkisyan, Sergey Aksenov and Oleg Serikov

Natural Language Processing 4 All (NLP4All): A New Online Platform for Teaching and Learning NLP Concepts
Rebekah Baglini and Hermes Hjorth

A New Broad NLP Training from Speech to Knowledge
Maxime Amblard and Miguel Couceiro

\+ ***Teaching Materials Short Papers : Courses and Curricula***

Applied Language Technology: NLP for the Humanities
Tuomo Hiippala

A Crash Course on Ethics for Natural Language Processing
Annemarie Friedrich and Torsten Zesch

A dissemination workshop for introducing young Italian students to NLP
Lucio Messina, Lucia Busso, Claudia Roberta Combei, Alessio Miaschi, Ludovica Pannitto, Gabriele Sarti and Malvina Nissim

\+ ***Teaching Materials Short Papers: Tools and Assignments***

MiniVQA - A resource to build your tailored VQA competition
Jean-Benoit Delbrouck

From back to the roots into the gated woods: Deep learning for NLP
Barbara Plank

Learning PyTorch Through A Neural Dependency Parsing Exercise
David Jurgens

Panel 1 : "What Should We Be Teaching?" Panelists : Isabelle Augenstein (U of Copenhagen), Emily M. Bender (U of Washington), Yoav Goldberg (Bar Ilan U), and Dan Jurafsky (Stanford U)

Poster Session 2

\+ ***Long Papers : Courses and Curricula***

A Balanced and Broadly Targeted Computational Linguistics Curriculum
Emma Manning, Nathan Schneider and Amir Zeldes

Gaining Experience with Structured Data: Using the Resources of Dialog State Tracking Challenge 2
Ronnie Smith

The Flipped Classroom model for teaching Conditional Random Fields in an NLP course
Manex Agirrezabal

\+ ***Teaching Materials Short Papers: Courses and Curricula***

Flamingos and Hedgehogs in the Croquet-Ground: Teaching Evaluation of NLP Systems for Undergraduate Students
Brielen Madureira

An Immersive Computational Text Analysis Course for Non-Computer Science Students at Barnard College
Adam Poliak and Jalisha Jenifer

Introducing Information Retrieval for Biomedical Informatics Students
Sanya Taneja, Richard Boyce, William Reynolds and Denis Newman-Griffis

Keynote Address : Ines Montani (Explosion)

Friday, June 11, 2021

Oral Presentations 2

\+ ***Long Papers : Courses and Curricula***

The Online Pivot: Lessons Learned from Teaching a Text and Data Mining Course in Lockdown, Enhancing online Teaching with Pair Programming and Digital Badges
Beatrice Alex, Clare Llewellyn, Pawel Orzechowski and Maria Boutchkova

Teaching NLP outside Linguistics and Computer Science classrooms: Some challenges and some opportunities
Sowmya Vajjala

Teaching NLP with Bracelets and Restaurant Menus: An Interactive Workshop for Italian Students
Ludovica Pannitto, Lucia Busso, Claudia Roberta Combei, Lucio Messina, Alessio Miaschi, Gabriele Sarti and Malvina Nissim

Panel 2 : "What Does Industry Need?" Panelists : Lenny Bronner (Washington Post), Delip Rao (AI2), Frank Rudzicz (U of Toronto), and Rachel Tatman (Rasa)

Keynote Address : Jason Eisner (Johns Hopkins University)

Pedagogical Principles in the Online Teaching of NLP: A Retrospection

György Kovács[1], Rajkumar Saini[1], Mohamadreza Faridghasemnia[2], Hamam Mokayed[1]
Tosin Adewumi[1], Pedro Alonso[1], Sumit Rakesh[1] and Marcus Liwicki[1]
[1]Luleå Tekniska Universitet / Luleå, Sweden-97187
[2]Örebro Universitet / Örebro, Sweden-70182
{gyorgy.kovacs, rajkumar.saini}@ltu.se
mohamadreza.farid@oru.se
{hamam.mokayed, oluwatosin.adewumi, pedro.alonso}@ltu.se
sumrak-0@student.ltu.se, marcus.liwicki@ltu.se

Abstract

The ongoing COVID-19 pandemic has brought online education to the forefront of pedagogical discussions. To make this increased interest sustainable in a post-pandemic era, online courses must be built on strong pedagogical foundations. With a long history of pedagogic research, there are many principles, frameworks, and models available to help teachers in doing so. These models cover different teaching perspectives, such as constructive alignment, feedback, and the learning environment. In this paper, we discuss how we designed and implemented our online Natural Language Processing (NLP) course following constructive alignment and adhering to the pedagogical principles of LTU. By examining our course and analyzing student evaluation forms, we show that we have met our goal and successfully delivered the course. Furthermore, we discuss the additional benefits resulting from the current mode of delivery, including the increased reusability of course content and increased potential for collaboration between universities. Lastly, we also discuss where we can and will further improve the current course design.

Keywords- *NLP, Constructive Alignment, LTU's Pedagogical Principles, Student Activation, Online Pedagogy, COVID19, Canvas, Blackboard, Zoom*

1 Introduction

With the COVID-19 pandemic, academic institutions were pushed to moving their education online (Gallagher and Palmer, 2020; Dick et al., 2020). Furthermore, even institutes that still allowed students on campus were more open to online alternatives. However, in order to solidify the results attained in online education (Ossiannilsson, 2021) in these extraordinary circumstances, it is crucial to demonstrate that this mode of education can be a viable alternative to presential education in terms of the underlying pedagogical fundamentals and the success of practical implementation. For this, in setting up our Natural Language Processing course, our goal was to do so based on constructive alignment and LTU's pedagogical principles. We hypothesized that adherence to both set of principles would be possible in an online version too. In this paper, by examining the design and implementation of the course and analyzing the student feedback, we will demonstrate the viability of our hypothesis.

The rest of the paper is organized as follows. First, we discuss the related literature in Section 1.1, followed by LTU's pedagogical principles in Section 1.2. Then in Section 2, we present the course design. That is followed by the Teaching and learning activities being discussed in Section 3. Next, we present the course evaluation result and the perspective of a volunteering student of the course in Section 4. Lastly, we conclude the paper and outline planned improvements in Section 5.

1.1 Related work

The teaching paradigm has been moving from a teacher-centered view to a more student-centered perspective (Kaymakamoglu, 2018). Meaning that instead of focusing on the role of the teacher, the focus is more and more on what the student should do, that is, process the material through deliberate practice, collaboration, and active reflection. To effectively support this process, teaching is planned and conducted with the student's disposition in mind, considering their prior knowledge, expectations, study skills, and other conditions. With the proper planning, design, and implementation of the course, active learning can then be achieved.

This active learning or student activation (Cook and Babon, 2017) is achieved when students are going into lectures and tutorials prepared to engage in the learning process, and they are not just passively trying to absorb information. Active learning encourages active cognitive processing of informa-

Proceedings of the Fifth Workshop on Teaching NLP, pages 1–12
June 10–11, 2021. ©2021 Association for Computational Linguistics

tion, and the concept is not a new one. Confucius is often quoted as saying: "Tell me and I will forget, show me and I may remember, involve me and I will learn". The use of student activation or active learning is well suited for presential learning. In an online setting, this type of learning has to be adapted to acquire the same knowledge from online activities. The main goal for students is to learn as well from online as in presential lectures.

Following levels from (Center for Teaching and Learning, 1990) might help to trigger student activation.

- To test the students' memory by asking questions related to specific facts, terms, principles, or theories.
- To utilize the students' knowledge to solve problems or analyze a situation.
- To exercise the informed judgment of the students.

Many pedagogical theories and frameworks have been developed to facilitate effective teaching covering different aspects of teaching (Kandlbinder, 2014; Chi and Wylie, 2014; Cook and Babon, 2017; Rust, 2002). However, with the advancement of technology and globalization, the traditional pedagogical models were evolved to make distance learning possible. Students can sit anywhere and learn online through the internet and connect with other students in the physical classroom or online.

Our designed course follows pedagogical principles to enhance learning outcomes. The course is segmented into 83 videos, given by eight lecturers of different expertise, coherent and harmonized. This well-balanced theory-practical course covers a broad range of applications and approaches.

1.2 LTU's Pedagogical Principles

To support the development of teaching practices and students developing the necessary skills required for them to become independent actors in their respective fields, LTU developed its pedagogical idea centering around nine important principles (Luleå University of Technology, University Pedagogy Center). These principles support Örebro University pedagogical principles (Örebro University), and we believe other courses, in other universities, should follow the same principles. Here, we briefly introduce these principles (along with feedback regarding the course) as a barometer for our course design.

1. **Emphasize relevant knowledge and skill,** is an important goal at university education to emphasize relevant skills and knowledge; that is to say, students should acquire the relevant theoretical knowledge, as well as the skills necessary to apply that knowledge.

2. **Encourage active cognitive processing,** so as students engage with the subject matter deliberately, contributing to long-term learning (Chi and Wylie, 2014).

3. **Choose forms of assessment that enhance learning.** The design of assessment has a great impact on student learning (Snyder, 1971; Wiiand, 1998; Ramsden, 2003), and thus it is important to choose the methods ("If you want to change student learning then change the methods of assessment" (Brown G., 1999)), frequency, and content of assessment in a way that would contribute to student learning. Naturally, active learning, and student activation discussed in more detail in Section refssec:related are crucial components of adherence to this principle.

4. **Ensure clarity in the course and task design,** an important principle to make sure students have a clear picture of the course and its requirements. One approach to achieve this is that of constructive alignment (Kandlbinder, 2014), making clear connections between the goals of the program, the intended learning outcomes of the course, the assessment methods, and the activities carried out through the course.

5. **Promote knowledge-enhancing feedback.** It is important that students receive feedback on their work beside the final assessment, which could guide their progress and inform them how close they are to learning outcomes (Elmgren and Henriksson, 2018). The impact of feedback is highest when it is in-time, personalized, and specific.

6. **Foster independence and self-awareness** is an important principle when we consider the current need for life-long learning and the goal of university education as enabling students to become independent actors in their respective fields.

7. **Be aware of your students' starting points,** as learning is more effective when the new information is either integrated into existing mental frameworks or said frameworks are reshaped by the new information. For this, however, it is crucial that we are aware of the current mental framework of students. Furthermore, being aware of the starting point of learners is also crucial to identify skill or knowledge gaps that should be filled.

8. **Communicate high, positive expectations,** so as to stimulate students for higher performance; a phenomenon widely known as the Pygmalion effect (Goddard, 1995).

9. **Create a supportive learning environment,** is a principle supporting all preceding principles. Since the proper environment is key to communicate not only high but positive expectations in a manner that encourages and not discourages students. Similarly, in a supportive environment, students are more open to discussing their experiences and receiving feedback.

As we consider adherence to them especially difficult in an online setting, we will give particular consideration to principles 2, 5, and 9. For example, in the absence of in-presence teaching, when in-person interaction between students and teacher and among students is not possible, it is especially challenging to create a supportive learning environment, and the opportunities to give feedback also diminish. Online learning management systems like Canvas and Blackboard provide the infrastructures to conduct courses online. However, similar to classrooms, it is up to teachers and course developers to fill them with content and utilize them effectively. We would discuss the learning management systems and how we used them to support the pedagogical principles in Section 3.3.

2 Course Design

In this section, we examine the course design based on LTU's pedagogical principles (see Section 1.2), the principle of constructive alignment, and other pedagogical considerations. We should note here that one may arrive at similar design patterns based solely on practical considerations as well. However, we consider it an integral part of our contribution that the design of the NLP course discussed here is rooted not only in pedagogical practices but also in pedagogical theories and research.

2.1 Objectives/Intended Learning Outcomes

In accordance with constructive alignment (Kandlbinder, 2014), course level objectives and Intended Learning Outcomes (ILOs) were set at the beginning of process of course design. For this, we were following the pedagogical principles, as well as ABCD and SMART techniques (Tullu et al., 2015; Smaldino et al., 2005; Doran et al., 1981). Based on these factors, the ILOs for the NLP course were as follows: *After passing the course, the student should be able to...*

- *...explain and use text preprocessing techniques*
- *...describe a text analytics system together with its components, optional and mandatory ones*
- *...explain how text could be analyzed*
- *...evaluate results of text analytics*
- *...analyze and reflect on the various techniques used in text analytics and the parameters needed as well as the problem solved*
- *...plan and execute a text analytics experiment*

2.2 Course description

The course contents were designed according to the ILOs discussed in Section 2.1. The syllabus and content of the course were designed after examining NLP courses, and other similar courses offered by different universities, as well as reviewing relevant literature (Agarwal, 2013; Hearst, 2005; Liddy and McCracken, 2005). Our NLP course consists of seven modules that provide motivation, tools, and techniques for solving NLP problems. This section explains the contents of the modules briefly to give the reader a better understanding of how the ILOs are reflected in the proposed contents.

The course starts at the first module with NLP applications, providing links to online API, chatbots, and dialog systems to motivate students. Then we discuss basic definitions and concepts in NLP, such as what a language is. The second module of this course is devoted to structure analysis of texts. Morphological analysis like n-grams and filtering (such as identifying missing values, tokenization, stemming & lemmatization, handling URLs, accents, contractions, typos, digits, etc.) is covered in the second module. Moreover, Part Of Speech (POS) is described, including its application and a more in-depth view into it. This module also describes the syntax and syntactic analysis of a text, followed by feature extraction and text representation; it starts with commonly used features in NLP and describes different encodings that can represent text to machines.

The third module of this course delivers the theory and practice of neural networks. It starts with the basics of neurons and network architectures, then training using backpropagation followed by vanishing gradients and over/under fitting problems. RNN, LSTM, GRU, and CNN layers are covered in depth. This module finishes by debugging neural networks, discussing regularizers, and covering common problems of neural networks.

Having the essential tools of NLP, the fourth module is more towards application, text classification, and how NLP problems can be solved using neural networks. This module starts in learning taxonomies, with a step-by-step design of an end-to-end neural network. It also discusses common choices for simple network architectures, learning taxonomies, multi-class, multi-label, and multi-task problems. After that, text classification is grounded to the problem of tagging in NLP, followed by transfer learning methods. At the end of this module, standard metrics in NLP are discussed.

The fifth module is dedicated to semantics, introducing semantics and symbols in NLP and possible ways to represent them. The theory of frames and synsets are discussed as the formal representation of semantics. Then, vector representations of semantics are discussed alongside different approaches to obtain them. Approaches like distributional hypothesis, statistical methods, and neural methods such as Word2vec are covered. At the end of this module, some of the state-of-the-art word embeddings are reviewed.

Sequence to sequence architectures, encoder-decoder architecture, attention, transformers, and Bert model are discussed in the next module. At the end, some different topics such as structured prediction, arc-standard transition parsing, and insights into dialog and chatbots, image captioning, and gender bias in NLP were discussed.

2.3 Video Clips

Our main challenge here is to deliver the material in a manner that still adheres to Principle 2 and encourages active cognitive processing. To achieve this goal, the design of the lecture format is one of the first consequences. For that, we split our material into short videos with a length of at most ten minutes. (McKeachie et al., 2006; Benjamin, 2002; Ozan and Ozarslan, 2016; Bordes et al., 2021). Delivering the course in short videos has the benefit of encouraging active cognitive processing of students among videos, as discussed in Section 1.

Another benefit of presenting our course content in short videos is the potential for the reusability of videos (Crame, 2016). Lastly, splitting all subjects into smaller topics facilitates sharing the workload among many presenters. It allowed us to organize the course in a joint setting, as discussed in more detail in Section 2.4.

2.4 Joint Course

Designing and developing a course for multiple initiatives requires a deep knowledge of the field, a broad range of knowledge in the field, and a deeper understanding of each topic. This requirement is not easy to be fulfilled by one lecturer. Thus, we make it a joint course between Örebro University (ORU) and LTU. This allows benefiting from multiple lecturers that let each deliver a specialized lecture. Load sharing is the other benefit of a joint course. However, designing and developing a joint course with multiple lecturers brought some difficulties, such as:

- Keeping harmony between lectures.
- Segmenting sub-topics to keep the lengths short.
- Distributing each subtopic between lecturers.
- Avoiding repetition in lectures.

To overcome these difficulties, lecturers from the two universities hold weekly meetings to design the course and distribute sub-topics among themselves. Lecturers created material by themselves, and then the material and the narratives are reviewed weekly. Moreover, after the course's first run, all materials are reviewed again to keep the outcome coherent and harmonic. This revision and harmonization of material should contribute to the clarity of course content (Principle 4).

2.5 Assessment and Assignments

To achieve desired students' activation, we designed the initial assignments and project tasks involving ready-to-use web API for various applications like hate speech, profanity filtering, image captioning. Later, the focus is on how these applications are developed using NLP. Therefore, we cover theoretical, numerical, and programming tasks in assignments and projects.

The course's assessment design is based on a quote by David Boud "students can escape bad teaching, but they cannot escape bad assessment". The forms of assessment in the joint NLP course were based on guiding the students towards achieving their learning outcomes. We avoid designing the assessment as a written exam at the end of the course as we are looking to engage the students with the course contents all the way till the end of the course (Principle 2, 3) (Luleå University of Technology, University Pedagogy Center). The assessment had been done in two stages which are practical project and oral discussion. The practical project is designed to follow the principle of the constructive alignment (Kandlbinder, 2014). The project's main objective is to lead the student to develop an actual NLP application (Principle 8) (Luleå University of Technology, University Pedagogy Center) but in the form of accumulative five tasks. The task will guide the students through the different levels of Bloom's cognitive domain (Bloom et al., 1956), namely *Remembering, Understanding, Applying, Analyzing, Evaluating and Creating*.

Each task is designed to match with the weekly delivered contents, so it will give real feedback on how the students understand and implement the concepts in practice (Principle 5) (Luleå University of Technology, University Pedagogy Center), and whether they can transfer the knowledge (theory) from one context to another context (Practical Implementation). Students have the flexibility to choose the programming language (however, Python is preferred), framework, or tool that they would like to use to reach the target. The provided flexibility will give a chance to find multiple approaches proposed by different students to sort out the problem (Principle 6, (Luleå University of Technology, University Pedagogy Center)). The sharing of different ideas among the class will add significant value to the course outcome. The final exam is an oral exam for each student. It is more like a discussion, and we assess each student based on that. An open discussion trying to mimic the understanding of a real problem related to NLP is conducted. The discussion starts with an asking about the general understanding of one of the known NLP applications, such as machine translation. All the consecutive questions are asked to evaluate the practical understanding of the problem and test the need in each stage to implement the solution. The examiner and examinee use the zoom's whiteboard to convey the questions and answers for better clarity.

3 Teaching and Learning Activities

The course is designed to maximize the intended learning outcomes. We refer to students some python programming tutorials available online to get familiarized with Python. This section describes this course's teaching and learning activities, which includes delivering lectures in short videos, live sessions, lab sessions, and our learning management system.

3.1 Live Sessions

The lectures are delivered through recorded videos on each module of the course. However, it is essential to take the students' questions, reflections and address their potential confusion after they have watched the video lectures. For this, we conducted weekly live sessions for each module. Students learned from the video lectures and discussed with the instructors in the live sessions, thus, aligned with flipped classroom learning. These live sessions where students had the opportunity to directly ask the instructors contributed toa supportive learning environment (Principle 9), and gave us the opportunity to provide the students with feedback (Principle 5).

The live sessions were delivered to address the queries regarding the theoretical concepts, practicals, contents, specific assignments, and other organizational queries. We addressed the immediate queries, and the queries asked in discussion threads in Canvas for the modules covered until a specific live session. However, there was a scope of queries related to the upcoming part of the course.

Live sessions are conducted online through zoom every week during the course. There are at least two instructors and one teaching assistant present during online live sessions. First, we took the queries asked in the learning management system. We have a follow-up discussion regarding those queries. Next, we have other questions related to the theory and practicals.

We encourage students to ask more and more questions/confusions to enhance their learning (Gibbs, 2005). In the end, we ask for regular feedback (Principle 5) (Luleå University of Technology, University Pedagogy Center) for each module, either in the live sessions or in learning management system.

3.2 Lab Sessions

Practical (lab) sessions make up student-centered teaching strategies for experiential courses (Moate and Cox, 2015). The lab sessions provide practical programming experience to the students, following Kolb's cycle and ICAP framework (Kolb, 2014; Chi and Wylie, 2014). Students watch or read a given experience (as concrete experience) and reflect on it (as reflective observation) before conceptualizing how to go about implementation through flowchart or pseudocode and finally active experimentation by writing and running the codes. Furthermore, in a lab session, students get to ask questions and get possible answers from their colleagues or the instructor. They also get formative feedback after the lab session (Principle 5) through online channels identified in this work, making it possible for them to improve their practical skills. They can work together in groups (using online collaborative tools), which is sometimes preferred. This makes it an interactive session, thereby achieving the interacting stage of the ICAP framework (Chi and Wylie, 2014). Assessment at the end of each lab session provides a good context and affects learning (Rust, 2002).

The technique is a vital element of pedagogy, which is the science of teaching (Lea, 2004). This approach fulfills the emerging trend of flipped classroom (Europass Teacher Academy, 2020), where students are responsible for their own learning before attending classes (Ng, 2018). The sessions help to bridge the gap in knowledge between students and the instructors. It was essential to be aware that not all the students had the same level of programming experience. Hence, it was essential to provide the practical sessions in stages that could address the beginner, intermediate and experienced developers. Students were given tasks that progressed from introductory programming with Python for text preprocessing to introduction to the Pytorch framework and, finally, an advanced machine translation (MT) task.

3.3 Learning Management Systems

The lack of in-person interaction between students and teachers did emphasize the framework through which the students were interacting with the course material and the teachers. The two universities offering the NLP course used different frameworks or Learning Management Systems (LMSs) for this task; however, the principles to bear in mind were the same. Most importantly, the course material had to be presented in the LMS in a way to make it clear for the student what their task is and how to proceed with their learning (Principle 4: ensure clarity in the course and task design). Another critical aspect of the LMS was to facilitate interaction between teachers and students, providing an open channel of communication (Principle 9: Create a supportive learning environment). Additionally, it was required that the LMS facilitates feedback (Principle 5: Promote knowledge-enhancing feedback) and supports the assessment methods to be used for the course (Principle 3: Choose forms of assessment that enhance learning). In the following sections, we will discuss how each LMS was used to achieve these goals.

3.3.1 Canvas and Blackboard

Both Canvas and Blackboard are cloud-based LMS used for courses at many educational institutes. Here, we will discuss (in numerical order) how we set up the course in them to support the above-listed pedagogical principles.

- Principle 3: Both Canvas and Blackboard enables the posting and evaluation of the assignment types we used (for more details, see Section 2.5). Moreover, they also enable students to assign peer feedback tasks for students automatically. This feature contributes to the adherence to Principle 6 (Foster independence and self-awareness) by encouraging students to reflect on others' learning and the requirements of each assignment.

- Principle 4: On the starting page (the entry point for students to the course room), the course syllabus is linked, and students can also find the course plan here, along with a weekly, thematical breakdown of the course. In this breakdown, we also provide links that allow students to access all materials allotted for the given weeks. Moreover, to further enhance the clarity in course design, the material was added weekly to direct students' attention to the current tasks. Another tool provided by Canvas and Blackboard that serves clarity is assignments page, where students can access all assignments in one place, enabling them to overview what assignments they have already fulfilled, what assignments are still due, and when due dates are coming up.

- Principle 5: The opportunity to provide knowledge-enhancing feedback was two-fold. For one, teachers could rate and comment on student assignments. Moreover, teachers could provide feedback through the various forums on the course's discussion page, also hosted on Canvas and Blackboard.

- Principle 9: The discussion page of the LMS used also served as an open communication channel among students and between students and teachers. This contributes to a high degree of interaction that is important for a supportive learning environment.

4 Results

The NLP course (7.5 credits) was a part of the one-year Data Science Masters program at LTU. There were 24 students enrolled in the NLP course. The students were from academia and industry both. Most students had a background in computer science or engineering and thus had at least an introductory course in programming. Some students, however, had no programming background.

4.1 A student's perspective of the course

This section is the work of a student who took the course and gave his comments, as discussed below.

Keeping in mind that students need to be prepared for both the industry and research front. Students need to focus on using tools and methods that are most widely used. When there are so many tools to deal with, students get overburdened. Here, the instructor needs to follow a suitable pathway to let students understand the concept and implement an executable project for demonstration. The class contains students with both programming and non-programming backgrounds. Python was used in the project assignments. The students without a programming background may not feel confident using Python. Therefore, there should be an alternative to that.

Text Preprocessing is an essential step in NLP that various libraries exist for that. The main attention of lecturers was on applying preprocessing (such as identifying missing values, tokenization, lemmatization, etc.) on a text file. It did not seem easy to apply those on Pandas dataframes. Specially applying regular expressions on Pandas dataframe for a beginner seemed to be daunting. Though the instructors have done their job of both concepts and practicalities, students felt less confident to carry the instructor's work and stuck using libraries. So, one needs to develop a clear strategy or steps for being selective in using libraries that are more helpful for carrying real project development. It helps to form the proper foundations for the student. Therefore students would feel more confident to carry forward the concepts taught by the lecturers in a class. Similarly, when using libraries such as Tensorflow and Pytorch.

Some students had high expectations towards the instructors that instructors should have supported them in building a web-based or desktop NLP application, i.e., taking the NLP course project to technology readiness level 7. However, this was beyond this course.

Another difficulty students were facing was understanding the speech patterns in the videos recorded by lecturers coming from different backgrounds, and having different accents. Moreover, there were many technical terms and idioms in the course that are hard to capture at the first sight. A neat solution to this can be subtitles. Adding subtitles to recorded lectures improve speech understanding, and helps students to capture new technical terms.

This course came with various interesting points from students' perspectives. Such as:

- Efficient knowledge transfer.

- To make the student feel confident at the end of the course by applying theoretical and practical aspects learned in the course.

- Removing the barrier for students coming from different cultures, different backgrounds.

- In initial stages, sticking to most widely used programming language and libraries and ecosystem in NLP. At the same time, being selective in libraries, which are more useful in day-to-day project/coding implementations.

- Motivating students to build their own models, and its customization.

4.2 Course evaluation by students

The department surveys each course. Students are asked to give a rating on a scale of 1-6 (1: strongly disagree, 6: strongly agree). Students are encouraged to provide feedback; however, it is up to them if they want to give the feedback or not. Here, we discuss the students' reflections we received after the course. In total, eight students gave their responses in the course evaluation report out of the twenty-four students taking the course. The survey consists of six sections: self-assessment, course aims and content, quality of teaching, course materials, examination, and overall assessment.

Table 1 shows the stats of students′ self-assessment. It can be noticed that many students did not spend sufficient effort. In a way, we failed in motivating students to put their efforts into the course. It may be due to students' other commitments. However, the fact remains that we could not manage students to put enough effort into the course. Thus, we need to think about how we can improve more in this regard.

The following questions (Table 2) were asked regarding ILOs of the course, to ensure that the course design and implementation adhere to one aspect of the principle of constructive alignment (i.e. the teaching and learning activities support the ILOs), as well as that Principles 1 (Emphasize relevant knowledge and skill) and 4 (Ensure clarity in course design) were at least partially fulfilled. While the last question partially reflected in Principle 9 as well (Create a supportive learning environment). The average scores for these statements are between 4.25 and 4.9, suggesting that students on average agree with the given statements, thus we have managed to achieve these goals in the design and delivery of the course. The lowest agreement was given for the third statement, thus our main objective for the upcoming installment of the course will be to ensure that the study guide provides better guidance for the students.

Another set of questions were asked for the evaluation of course delivery, and the exam conducted (see Table 3). For one, these questions measure another aspect of the constructive alignment (i.e. the alignment of assessment with ILOs - Question 3.5). Moreover, it is also measured here, how well adherence to some of LTUs principles was implemented. It can once again be noted here that all average values are above 3.5, thus students are more inclined to agree with the given statements than they are to disagree with them. In particular, they rate the alignment between the examination and ILOs (and thus the adherence to constructive alignment) quite high. The second highest score was given for the technical support and communication, suggesting that this aspect of creating a supportive learning environment (Principle 9) was rather successful. The score given for the rewarding nature of theoretical teaching and learning activities was only one decimal lower, which suggests that in this aspect, we were successful in emphasizing relevant knowledge and skill (Principle 1). However, the score concerning the practical aspects of teaching and learning activities was considerably lower (though still closer to six than one), suggesting that there is more room for improvement in terms of practical tasks and assignments, as some comments also confirmed. Another way to address the score is to communicate more clearly towards students that building a complete web-based or desktop NLP application is beyond the scope of this introductory course. Another area where there is more room for improvement is regarding the input of instructors supporting student learning (Question 3.1).

Lastly, the overall assessment of the course by students is shown in Table 4. While, the overall scores are encouraging for us (in particular the question regarding the overall impression of students about the course - Question 4.3), there is still scope for improvement in all sections, and our goal for future installments of the course is to achieve even higher student satisfaction scores.

5 Conclusion and Improvements planned for the future versions of the course

Here, we discuss the course and the improvements we plan for the future course.

5.1 Conclusion

This paper discusses how the course was designed, organized, and delivered online at the university. We followed the pedagogy principles in all these phases of the course. We argue that we can deliver the course fully online even after the pandemic as we delivered the course up to a satisfactory level. To be precise, we hypothesized that our course

Table 1: Students' self-assessment regarding the NLP course

No.	Question	Average score
1.1	< 5h 0% 6h-15h 50% 16-25h 37.5% 26-35h 12.5% 36-45h 0% >46h 0% How many hours of study have you in average dedicated to this course per week, including both scheduled and non-scheduled time?	
1.2	I am satisfied with my efforts during the course.	4.5
1.3	have participated in all the teaching and learning activities in the course.	4.0
1.4	I have prepared myself prior to all teaching and learning activities.	3.3

Table 2: Evaluation of achieving ILOs and aim of the conducted NLP course

No.	Question	Average score
2.1	The intended learning outcomes of the course have been clear.	4.9
2.2	The contents of the course have helped me to achieve the ILOs of the course	4.5
2.3	The course planning and the study guide have provided good guidance	4.25

Table 3: Evaluation of the course delivery and the exam of the conducted NLP course

No.	Question	Average score
3.1	The teacher's input has supported my learning.	4.0
3.2	The teaching and learning activities of the theoretical nature have been rewarding	4.6
3.3	The practical/creative teaching and learning activities of the course e.g. labs, field trips, teaching practice, placements/internships, project work have been rewarding.	4.0
3.4	The technical support for communication, e.g. learning platform, e-learning resources, has been satisfactory.	4.7
3.5	The examination was in accordance with the ILOs of the course.	5.0

Table 4: Overall assessment of the NLP course by the students

No.	Question	Average score
4.1	The workload of the course is appropriate for the number of credits given.	4.3
4.2	Given the aims of the course the level of work required has been appropriate	4.1
4.3	My overall impression is that this has been a good course	4.6

would adhere to the LTU's pedagogical principles and other pedagogical theories refereed in this paper and delivered online at the same time. This could be verified from the students' response report; The average scores (Table 4) greater than 4 support our hypothesis. In fact the scores in Tables 2, and 3 also support our hypothesis. However, there is always room for improvement. We figured out many things to improve even before the course was finished. The students' response report gave us a clear idea of where to put more energy to improve the course, e.g., as observed from Table 3, we will improve on teachers' efforts and projects related activities. The planned improvements are listed below.

5.2 Improvements planned

Here we discuss the improvements planned for future iterations of the course based on student feedback and pedagogical principles.

5.2.1 Two-layered course

Our course design started to be for multiple initiatives, for people from the industry and people from academia, people with no background in AI and maths, and people with a strong background. This ended up in designing a general course that can be used for all people with different backgrounds and goals. One track of 3 credits for industrial students and one track of 7.5 credits for academic students. Although this idea never came to real life, we would like to mention our final thoughts of it as one of the possible future works.

Students from the industry most often have different backgrounds, limited knowledge in mathematics, and stronger motivation, looking for specific applications. On the other hand, academic students have a better knowledge of mathematics. They have sufficient background in the field and are interested in learning a broad range of applications and topics.

Thus, we designed the course to cover theories, concepts, applications, and their implementation. For example, for a topic like neural networks, the materials should include mathematical background, practical usage, and possible tweaks and configurations. The choice of two tracks will be taking theoretical subtopics only for academics and practicalities for both. In the end, all who finish the course have a broad understanding of various applications in NLP that should satisfy their interests.

5.2.2 Other Improvements

- Better naming convention of the videos for clarity
- Adding subtitles to the videos for better understanding (the video lectures are delivered in English, but none of the lecturers are native speakers).
- Adding quizzes between videos for better student activation and learning.
- Removing handwritten notes from the lecture videos and slides, as in some cases students found that difficult to read.
- Multiple practical tasks with different levels of difficulty can be provided to cater to the students' different levels of programming experience, so each student can pick the task applicable to them.
- Splitting the project into subtasks aligned with the NLP pipeline.
- More live sessions to support students' learning.
- Giving more to the point references to the content related to the theory and project implementation.
- A tutorial on specific libraries to use during the course and their setup.
- Additional tutorial on building a usable web app, e.g., for Hate speech detection, where anyone can feed a text and classify it.

We hope that future versions of the course will be better in all aspects (planning, designing, organizing, and conducting) and perspectives.

References

Apoorv Agarwal. 2013. Teaching the basics of nlp and ml in an introductory course to information science. In *Proceedings of the Fourth Workshop on Teaching NLP and CL*, pages 77–84.

L.T. Benjamin. 2002. Lecturing. In S.F. Davis and W. Buskist, editors, *The Teaching of psychology: Essays in honor of Wilbert J. McKeachie and Charles L. Brewer*, pages 57–67.

B. S. Bloom, M. B. Engelhart, E. J. Furst, W. H. Hill, and D. R. Krathwohl. 1956. *Taxonomy of educational objectives. The classification of educational goals. Handbook 1: Cognitive domain*. Longmans Green, New York.

Stephen J. Bordes, Donna Walker, Louis Jonathan Modica, Joanne Buckland, and Andrew K. Sobering. 2021. Towards the optimal use of video recordings to support the flipped classroom in medical school basic sciences education. *Medical Education Online*, 26(1):1841406. PMID: 33119431.

Atkins M. Brown G. 1999. *Effective teaching in higher education*. Routledge.

Center for Teaching and Learning. 1990. Improving multiple choice questions. *For your consideration... suggestions and reflections on Teaching and Learning*, (8).

Michelene TH Chi and Ruth Wylie. 2014. The ICAP framework: Linking cognitive engagement to active learning outcomes. *Educational psychologist*, 49(4):219–243.

Brian Robert Cook and Andrea Babon. 2017. Active learning through online quizzes: better learning and less (busy) work. *Journal of Geography in Higher Education*, 41(1):24–38.

Cynthia J. Crame. 2016. Effective educational videos: Principles and guidelines for maximizing student learning from video content. *CBE life sciences education*, 15(4).

Geoffrey Dick, Asli Yagmur Akbulut, and Vic Matta. 2020. Teaching and learning transformation in the time of the coronavirus crisis. *Journal of Information Technology Case and Application Research*, 22(4):243–255.

George T. Doran et al. 1981. There's a SMART way to write management's goals and objectives. *Management review*, 70(11):35–36.

Maya Elmgren and Ann-Sofie Henriksson. 2018. *Academic Teaching*. Studentlitteratur AB.

Europass Teacher Academy. 2020. Flipped classroom. online. Accessed on: March 08, 2021.

Sean Gallagher and Jason Palmer. 2020. The pandemic pushed universities online. the change was long overdue.

Graham Gibbs. 2005. *Improving the quality of student learning*. University of South Wales (United Kingdom).

R. W. Goddard. 1995. The pygmalion effect. *Personnel Journal*, 64(6):10–16.

Marti A Hearst. 2005. Teaching applied natural language processing: Triumphs and tribulations. In *Proceedings of the Second ACL Workshop on Effective Tools and Methodologies for Teaching NLP and CL*, pages 1–8.

Peter Kandlbinder. 2014. Constructive alignment in university teaching. *HERDSA News*, 36(3):5–6.

Sibel Ersel Kaymakamoglu. 2018. Teachers' beliefs, perceived practice and actual classroom practice in relation to traditional (teacher-centered) and constructivist (learner-centered) teaching (note 1). *Journal of Education and Learning*, 7(1):29–37.

David A Kolb. 2014. *Experiential learning: Experience as the source of learning and development*. FT press.

Mary R Lea. 2004. Academic literacies: A pedagogy for course design. *Studies in higher education*, 29(6):739–756.

Elizabeth D Liddy and Nancy J McCracken. 2005. Hands-on nlp for an interdisciplinary audience.

Luleå University of Technology, University Pedagogy Center. LTU's pedagogical principles. `https://ltu.instructure.com/courses/8692/files/1364701/download?wrap=1`.

W.J. McKeachie, M. Svinicki, M.D. Svinicki, B.K. Hofer, and R.M. Suinn. 2006. *McKeachie's Teaching Tips: Strategies, Research, and Theory for College and University Teachers*. College teaching series. Houghton Mifflin.

Randall M Moate and Jane A Cox. 2015. Learner-centered pedagogy: Considerations for application in a didactic course. *Professional Counselor*, 5(3):379–389.

Eugenia MW Ng. 2018. Integrating self-regulation principles with flipped classroom pedagogy for first year university students. *Computers & Education*, 126:65–74.

Ledningsstaben Örebro University. Örebro University basic pedagogical view. `https://www.oru.se/om-universitetet/vision-strategi-och-regelverk/pedagogisk-grundsyn/`.

Ebba Ossiannilsson. 2021. The new normal: Post covid-19 is about change and sustainability. *Near East University Online Journal of Education*, 4(1):72–77.

Ozlem Ozan and Yasin Ozarslan. 2016. Video lecture watching behaviors of learners in online courses. *Educational Media International*, 53(1):27–41.

P. Ramsden. 2003. *Learning to Teach in Higher Education*. RoutledgeFalmer.

Chris Rust. 2002. The impact of assessment on student learning: how can the research literature practically help to inform the development of departmental assessment strategies and learner-centred assessment practices? *Active learning in higher education*, 3(2):145–158.

S.E. Smaldino, J.D. Russell, and R. Heinich. 2005. *Instructional Technology and Media for Learning*. Pearson/Merrill/Prentice Hall.

B.R. Snyder. 1971. *The Hidden Curriculum*. Borzoi book. Knopf.

Milind S Tullu, Sandeep B Bavdekar, and Nirmala N Rege. 2015. Educational (learning) objectives: Guide to teaching and learning. *The Art of Teaching Medical Students-E-Book*, page 89.

Towe Wiiand. 1998. Examinationen i fokus : högskolestudenters lärande och examination : en litteraturöversikt.

Teaching a Massive Open Online Course on Natural Language Processing

Ekaterina Artemova[1,2]*, Murat Apishev [1], Veronika Sarkisyan [1], Sergey Aksenov[1], Denis Kirjanov[3], Oleg Serikov [1,4]

[1] HSE University, Moscow, Russia
[2] Huawei Noah's Ark lab, Moscow, Russia
[3] SberDevices, Sberbank, Moscow, Russia
[4] DeepPavlov, MIPT, Dolgoprudny, Russia

`https://openedu.ru/course/hse/TEXT/`

Abstract

This paper presents a new Massive Open Online Course on Natural Language Processing, targeted at non-English speaking students. The course lasts 12 weeks; every week consists of lectures, practical sessions, and quiz assignments. Three weeks out of 12 are followed by Kaggle-style coding assignments.

Our course intends to serve multiple purposes: (i) familiarize students with the core concepts and methods in NLP, such as language modeling or word or sentence representations, (ii) show that recent advances, including pretrained Transformer-based models, are built upon these concepts; (iii) introduce architectures for most demanded real-life applications, (iv) develop practical skills to process texts in multiple languages. The course was prepared and recorded during 2020, launched by the end of the year, and in early 2021 has received positive feedback.

1 Introduction

The vast majority of recently developed online courses on Artificial Intelligence (AI), Natural Language Processing (NLP) included, are oriented towards English-speaking audiences. In non-English speaking countries, such courses' audience is unfortunately quite limited, mainly due to the language barrier. Students, who are not fluent in English, find it difficult to cope with language issues and study simultaneously. Thus the students face serious learning difficulties and lack of motivation to complete the online course. While creating new online courses in languages other than English seems redundant and unprofitable, there are multiple reasons to support it. First, students may find it easier to comprehend new concepts and problems in their native language. Secondly, it may be easier to build a strong online learning community if students can express themselves fluently. Finally, and more specifically to NLP, an NLP course aimed at building practical skills should include language-specific tools and applications. Knowing how to use tools for English is essential to understand the core principles of the NLP pipeline. However, it is of little use if the students work on real-life applications in the non-English industry.

In this paper, we present an overview of an online course aimed at Russian-speaking students. This course was developed and run for the first time in 2020, achieving positive feedback. Our course is a part of the HSE university's online specialization on AI and is built upon previous courses in the specialization, which introduced core concepts in calculus, probability theory, and programming in Python. Outside of the specialization, the course can be used for additional training of students majoring in computer science or software engineering and others who fulfill prerequisites.

The main contributions of this paper are:

- We present the syllabus of a recent wide-scope massive open online course on NLP, aimed at a broad audience;
- We describe methodological choices made for teaching NLP to non-English speaking students;
- In this course, we combine recent deep learning trends with other best practices, such as topic modeling.

The remainder of the paper is organized as follows: Section 2 introduces methodological choices made for the course design. Section 3 presents the course structure and topics in more details. Section 4 lists home works. Section 5 describes the hosting platform and its functionality.

2 Course overview

The course presented in this paper is split into two main parts, six weeks each, which cover (i) core

*Corresponding author, email: elartemova@hse.ru

Proceedings of the Fifth Workshop on Teaching NLP, pages 13–27
June 10–11, 2021. ©2021 Association for Computational Linguistics

NLP concepts and approaches and (ii) main applications and more sophisticated problem formulations. The first six weeks' main goal is to present different word and sentence representation methods, starting from bag-of-words and moving to word and sentence embeddings, reaching contextualized word embeddings and pre-trained language models. Simultaneously we introduce basic problem definitions: text classification, sequence labeling, and sequence-to-sequence transformation. The first part of the course roughly follows Yoav Goldberg's textbook (Goldberg, 2017), albeit we extend it with pre-training approaches and recent Transformer-based architectures.

The second part of the course introduces BERT-based models and such NLP applications as question answering, text summarization, and information extraction. This part adopts some of the explanations from the recent draft of "Speech and Language Processing" (Jurafsky and Martin, 2000). An entire week is devoted to topic modeling, and BigARTM (Vorontsov et al., 2015), a tool for topic modeling developed in MIPT, one of the top Russian universities and widely used in real-life applications. Overall practical sessions are aimed at developing text processing skills and practical coding skills.

Every week comprises both a lecture and a practical session. Lectures have a "talking head" format, so slides and pre-recorded demos are presented, while practical sessions are real-time coding sessions. The instructor writes code snippets in Jupyter notebooks and explains them at the same time. Overall every week, there are 3-5 lecture videos and 2-3 practical session videos. Weeks 3, 5, 9 are extended with coding assignments.

Weeks 7 and 9 are followed by interviews. In these interviews, one of the instructors' talks to the leading specialist in the area. Tatyana Shavrina, one of the guests interviewed, leads an R&D team in Sber, one of the leading IT companies. The second guest, Konstantin Vorontsov, is a professor from one of the top universities. The guests are asked about their current projects and interests, career paths, what keeps them inspired and motivated, and what kind of advice they can give.

The final mark is calculated according to the formula:

$$\textit{\# of accepted coding assignment} \\ +0.7\texttt{mean}(\textit{quiz assignment mark})$$

Coding assignments are evaluated on the binary scale (accepted or rejected), and quiz assignments are evaluated on the 10 point scale. To earn a certificate, the student has to earn at least 4 points.

In practical sessions, we made a special effort to introduce tools developed for processing texts in Russian. The vast majority of examples, utilized in lectures, problems, attempted during practical sessions, and coding assignments, utilized datasets in Russian. The same choice was made by Pavel Braslavski, who was the first to create an NLP course in Russian in 2017 (Braslavski, 2017). We utilized datasets in English only if Russian lacks the non-commercial and freely available datasets for the same task of high quality.

Some topics are intentionally not covered in the course. We focus on written texts and do not approach the tasks of text-to-speech and speech-to-text transformations. Low-resource languages spoken in Russia are out of the scope, too. Besides, we almost left out potentially controversial topics, such as AI ethics and green AI problems. Although we briefly touch upon potential biases in pre-trained language models, we have to leave out a large body of research in the area, mainly oriented towards the English language and the US or European social problems. Besides, little has been explored in how neural models are affected by those biases and problems in Russia.

The team of instructors includes specialists from different backgrounds in computer science and theoretical linguists. Three instructors worked on lectures, two instructors taught practical sessions, and three teaching assistants prepared home assignments and conducted question-answering sessions in the course forum.

3 Syllabus

Week 1. Introduction. The first introductory **lecture** consists of two parts. The first part overviews the core tasks and problems in NLP, presents the main industrial applications, such as search engines, Business Intelligence tools, and conversational engines, and draws a comparison between broad-defined linguistics and NLP. To conclude this part, we touch upon recent trends, which can be grasped easily without the need to go deep into details, such as multi-modal applications (Zhou et al., 2020), cross-lingual methods (Feng et al., 2020; Conneau et al., 2020) and computational humor (Braslavski et al., 2018; West and

Horvitz, 2019). Throughout this part lecture, we try to show NLP systems' duality: those aimed at understanding language (or speech) and those aimed at generating language (or speech). The most complex systems used for machine translation, for example, aim at both. The second part of the lecture introduces such basic concepts as bag-of-words, count-based document vector representation, `tf-idf` weighting. Finally, we explore bigram association measures, `PMI` and `t-score`. We point out that these techniques can be used to conduct an exploratory analysis of a given collection of texts and prepare input for machine learning methods.

Practical session gives an overview of text prepossessing techniques and simple count-based text representation models. We emphasize how prepossessing pipelines can differ for languages such as English and Russian (for example, what is preferable, stemming or lemmatization) and give examples of Python frameworks that are designed to work with the Russian language (pymystem3 (Segalovich), pymorphy2 (Korobov, 2015)). We also included an intro to regular expressions because we find this knowledge instrumental both within and outside NLP tasks.

During the first weeks, most participants are highly motivated, we can afford to give them more practical material, but we still need to end up with some close-to-life clear examples. We use a simple sentiment analysis task on Twitter data to demonstrate that even the first week's knowledge (together with understanding basic machine learning) allows participants to solve real-world problems. At the same time, we illustrate how particular steps of text prepossessing can have a crucial impact on the model's outcome.

Week 2. Word embeddings. **The lecture** introduces the concepts of distributional semantics and word vector representations. We familiarize the students with early models, which utilized singular value decomposition (SVD) and move towards more advanced word embedding models, such as `word2vec` (Mikolov et al., 2013) and `fasttext` (Bojanowski et al., 2017). We briefly touch upon the hierarchical softmax and the hashing trick and draw attention to negative sampling techniques. We show ways to compute word distance, including Euclidean and cosine similarity measures.

We discuss the difference between `word2vec` and `GloVe` (Pennington et al., 2014) models and emphasize main issues, such as dealing with out-of-vocabulary (OOV) words and disregarding rich morphology. `fasttext` is then claimed to address these issues. To conclude, we present approaches for intrinsic and extrinsic evaluation of word embeddings. Fig. 1 explains the difference between bag-of-words and bag-of-vectors.

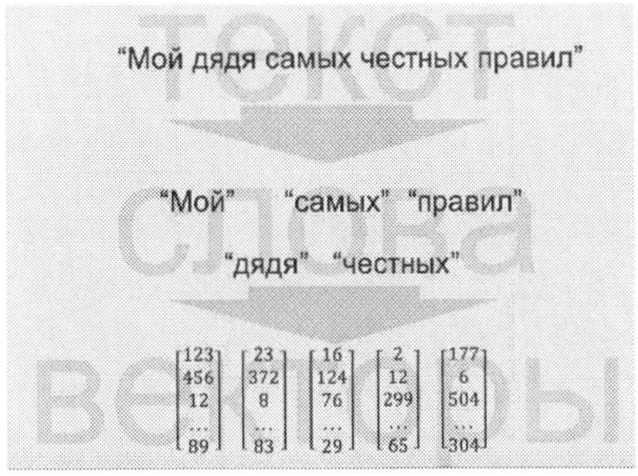

Figure 1: One slide from Lecture 2. Difference between raw texts (top line), bag-of-words (middle line), and bag-of-vectors (bottom line). Background words: text, words, vectors.

In **practical session** we explore only advanced word embedding models (`word2vec`, `fasttext` and `GloVe`) and we cover three most common scenarios for working with such models: using pre-trained models, training models from scratch and tuning pre-trained models. Giving a few examples, we show that `fasttext` as a character-level model serves as a better word representation model for Russian and copes better with Russian rich morphology. We also demonstrate some approaches of intrinsic evaluation of models' quality, such as solving analogy tasks (like well known "king - man + woman = queen") and evaluating semantic similarity and some useful techniques for visualization of word embeddings space.

This topic can be fascinating for students when supplemented with illustrative examples. Exploring visualization of words clusters on plots or solving analogies is a memorable part of the "classic" NLP part of most students' course.

Week 3. Text classification. The **lecture** considers core concepts for supervised learning. We begin by providing examples for text classification applications, such as sentiment classification and spam filtering. Multiple problem statements, such as binary, multi-class, and multi-label classification, are stated. To introduce ML algorithms, we start with logistic regression and move towards neural methods for text classification. To this end, we introduce `fasttext` as an easy, out-of-the-box solution. We introduce the concept of sentence (paragraph) embedding by presenting `doc2vec` model (Le and Mikolov, 2014) and show how such embeddings can be used as input to the classification model. Next, we move towards more sophisticated techniques, including convolutional models for sentence classification (Kim, 2014). We do not discuss backpropagation algorithms but refer to the DL course of the specialization to refresh understanding of neural network training. We show ways to collect annotated data on crowdsourcing platforms and speed up the process using active learning (Esuli and Sebastiani, 2009). Finally, we conclude with text augmentation techniques, including SMOTE (Chawla et al., 2002) and EDA (Wei and Zou, 2019).

In the **practical session** we continue working with the text classification on the IMDb movies reviews dataset. We demonstrate several approaches to create classification models with different word embeddings. We compare two different ways to get sentence embedding, based on any word embedding model: by averaging word vectors and using `tf-idf` weights for a linear combination of word vectors. We showcase `fasttext` tool for text classification using its built-in classification algorithm.

Additionally, we consider use `GloVe` word embedding model to build a simple Convolutional Neural Network for text classification. In this week and all of the following, we use PyTorch [1] as a framework for deep learning.

Week 4. Language modeling. The **lecture** focuses on the concept of language modelling. We start with early count-based models (Song and Croft, 1999) and create a link to Markov chains. We refer to the problem of OOV words and show the `add-one` smoothing method, avoiding more sophisticated techniques, such as Knesser-Ney smoothing (Kneser and Ney, 1995), for the sake of time. Next, we introduce neural language models. To this end, we first approach Bengio's language model (Bengio et al., 2003), which utilizes fully connected layers. Second, we present recurrent neural networks and show how they can be used for language modeling. Again, we remind the students of backpropagation through time and gradient vanishing or explosion, introduced earlier in the DL course. We claim, that LSTM (Hochreiter and Schmidhuber, 1997) and GRU (Chung et al., 2014) cope with these problems. As a brief revision of the LSTM architecture is necessary, we utilize Christopher Olah's tutorial (Olah, 2015). We pay extra attention to the inner working of the LSTM, following Andrej Karpathy's tutorial (Karpathy, 2015). To add some research flavor to the lecture, we talk about text generation (Sutskever et al., 2011), its application, and different decoding strategies (Holtzman et al., 2019), including beam search and nucleus sampling. Lastly, we introduce the sequence labeling task (Ma and Hovy, 2016) for part-of-speech (POS) tagging and named entity recognition (NER) and show how RNN's can be utilized as sequence models for the tasks.

The **practical session** in this week is divided into two parts. The first part is dedicated to language models for text generation. We experiment with count-based probabilistic models and RNN's to generate dinosaur names and get familiar with perplexity calculation (the task and the data were introduced in Sequence Models course from DeepLearning.AI [2]). To bring things together, students are asked to make minor changes in the code and run it to answer some questions in the week's quiz assignment.

The second part of the session demonstrates the application of RNN's to named entity recognition. We first introduce the BIO and BIOES annotation schemes and show frameworks with pre-trained NER models for English (Spacy [3]) and Russian (Natasha[4]) languages. Further, we move on to CNN-biLSTM-CRF architecture described in the lecture and test it on CoNLL 2003 shared task data (Sang and De Meulder, 2003).

Week 5. Machine Translation. This **lecture** starts with referring to the common experience of using machine translation tools and a historical overview of the area. Next, the idea of encoder-decoder (seq2seq) architecture opens the technical part of the lecture. We start with RNN-based seq2seq models (Sutskever et al., 2014) and introduce the concept of attention (Bahdanau et al., 2015). We show how attention maps can be used for "black box" interpretation. Next, we reveal the core architecture of modern NLP, namely, the

[1] `https://pytorch.org/`

[2] `https://www.coursera.org/learn/nlp-sequence-models`

[3] `https://spacy.io`

[4] `https://natasha.github.io`

Transformer model (Vaswani et al., 2017) and ask the students explicitly to take this part seriously. Following Jay Allamar's tutorial (Alammar, 2015), we decompose the transformer architecture and go through it step by step. In the last part of the lecture, we return to machine translation and introduce quality measures, such as WER and BLEU (Papineni et al., 2002), touch upon human evaluation and the fact that BLEU correlates well with human judgments. Finally, we discuss briefly more advanced techniques, such as non-autoregressive models (Gu et al., 2017) and back translation (Hoang et al., 2018). Although we do not expect the student to comprehend these techniques immediately, we want to broaden their horizons so that they can think out of the box of supervised learning and autoregressive decoding.

In the first part of **practical session** we solve the following task: given a date in an arbitrary format transform it to the standard format "dd-mm-yyyy" (for example, "18 Feb 2018", "18.02.2018", "18/02/2018" → "18-02-2018"). We adopt the code from PyTorch machine translation tutorial [5] to our task: we use the same RNN encoder, RNN decoder, and its modification - RNN encoder with attention mechanism - and compare the quality of two decoders. We also demonstrate how to visualize attention weights.

The second part is dedicated to the Transformer model and is based on the Harvard NLP tutorial (Klein et al., 2017) that decomposes the article "Attention is All You Need" (Vaswani et al., 2017). Step by step, like in the lecture, we go through the Transformer code, trying to draw parallels with a simple encoder-decoder model we have seen in the first part. We describe and comment on every layer and pay special attention to implementing the attention layer and masking and the shapes of embeddings and layers.

Week 6. Sesame Street I. The sixth **lecture** and the next one are the most intense in the course. The paradigm of pre-trained language models is introduced in these two weeks. The first model to discuss in detail is ELMo (Peters et al., 2018). Next, we move to BERT (Devlin et al., 2019) and introduce the masked language modeling and next sentence prediction objectives. While presenting BERT, we briefly revise the inner working of Transformer blocks. We showcase three scenarios to fine-tune BERT: (i) text classification by using different pooling strategies (`[CLS]`, `max` or `mean`), (ii) sentence pair classification for paraphrase identification and for natural language inference, (iii) named entity recognition. SQuAD-style question-answering, at which BERT is aimed too, as avoided here, as we will have another week for QA systems. Next, we move towards GPT-2 (Radford et al.) and elaborate on how high-quality text generation can be potentially harmful. To make the difference between BERT's and GPT-2's objective more clear, we draw parallels with the Transformer architecture for machine translation and show that BERT is an encoder-style model, while GPT-2 is a decoder-style model. We show Allen NLP (Gardner et al., 2018) demos of how GPT-2 generates texts and how attention scores implicitly resolve coreference.

Figure 2: To spice up the lectures, the lecturer is dressed in an ELMo costume

In this week, we massively rely on Jay Allamar's (Alammar, 2015) tutorial and adopt some of these brilliant illustrations. One of the main problems, though, rising in this week is the lack of Russian terminology, as the Russian-speaking community has not agreed on the proper ways to translate such terms as "contextualized encoder" or "fine-tuning". To spice up this week, we were dressed in Sesame Street kigurumis (see Fig. 2).

The main idea of the **practical session** is to demonstrate ELMo and BERT models, considered

[5] https://pytorch.org/tutorials/intermediate/seq2seq_translation_tutorial.html

earlier in the lecture. The session is divided into two parts, and in both parts, we consider text classification, using ELMo and BERT models, respectively.

In the first part, we demonstrate how to use ELMo word embeddings for text classification on the IMBdb dataset used in previous sessions. We use pre-trained ELMo embeddings by AllenNLP (Gardner et al., 2018) library and implement a simple recurrent neural network with a GRU layer on top for text classification. In the end, we compare the performance of this model with the scores we got in previous sessions on the same dataset and demonstrate that using ELMo embeddings can improve model performance.

The second part of the session is focused on models based on Transformer architecture. We use huggingface-transformers library (Wolf et al., 2020) and a pre-trained BERT model to build a classification algorithm for Google play applications reviews written in English. We implement an entire pipeline of data preparation, using a pre-trained model and demonstrating how to fine-tune the downstream task model. Besides, we implement a wrapper for the BERT classification model to get the prediction on new text.

Week 7. Sesame Street II. To continue diving into the pre-trained language model paradigm, the **lecture** first questions, how to evaluate the model. We discuss some methods to interpret the BERT's inner workings, sometimes referred to as BERTology (Rogers et al., 2021). We introduce a few common ideas: BERT's lower layers account for surface features, lower to middle layers are responsible for morphology, while the upper-middle layers have better syntax representation (Conneau and Kiela, 2018). We talk about ethical issues (May et al., 2019), caused by pre-training on raw web texts. We move towards the extrinsic evaluation of pre-trained models and familiarize the students with GLUE-style evaluations (Wang et al., 2019b,a). The next part of the lecture covers different improvements of BERT-like models. We show how different design choices may affect the model's performance in different tasks and present RoBERTa (Liu et al., 2019), and ALBERT (Lan et al., 2019) as members of a BERT-based family. We touch upon the computational inefficiency of pre-trained models and introduce lighter models, including DistillBERT (Sanh et al., 2019). To be solid, we touch upon other techniques to compress pre-trained models, including pruning (Sajjad et al., 2020) and quantization (Zafrir et al., 2019), but do not expect the students to be able to implement these techniques immediately. We present the concept of language transferring and introduce multilingual Transformers, such as XLM-R (Conneau et al., 2020). Language transfer becomes more and more crucial for non-English applications, and thus we draw more attention to it. Finally, we cover some of the basic multi-modal models aimed at image captioning and visual question answering, such as the unified Vision-Language Pre-training (VLP) model (Zhou et al., 2020).

In the **practical session** we continue discussing BERT-based models, shown in the lectures. The session's main idea is to consider different tasks that may be solved by BERT-based models and to demonstrate different tools and approaches for solving them. So the practical session is divided into two parts. The first part is devoted to named entity recognition. We consider a pre-trained cross-lingual BERT-based NER model from the DeepPavlov library (Burtsev et al., 2018) and demonstrate how it can be used to extract named entities from Russian and English text. The second part is focused on multilingual zero-shot classification. We consider the pre-trained XLM-based model by HuggingFace, discuss the approach's key ideas, and demonstrate how the model works, classifying short texts in English, Russian, Spanish, and French.

Week 8. Syntax parsing. The **lecture** is devoted to computational approaches to syntactic parsing and is structured as follows. After a brief introduction about the matter and its possible applications (both as an auxiliary task and an independent one), we consider syntactic frameworks developed in linguistics: dependency grammar (Tesnière, 2015) and constituency grammar (Bloomfield, 1936). Then we discuss only algorithms that deal with dependency parsing (mainly because there are no constituency parsers for Russian), so we turn to graph-based (McDonald et al., 2005) and transition-based (Aho and Ullman, 1972) dependency parsers and consider their logics, structure, sorts, advantages, and drawbacks. Afterward, we familiarize students with the practical side of parsing, so we introduce syntactically annotated corpora, Universal Dependencies project (Nivre et al., 2016b) and some parsers which perform for Russian well (UDPipe (Straka and Straková, 2017),

DeepPavlov Project (Burtsev et al., 2018)). The last part of our lecture represents a brief overview of the problems which were not covered in previous parts: BERTology, some issues of web-texts parsing, latest advances in computational syntax (like enhanced dependencies (Schuster and Manning, 2016)).

The **practical session** starts with a quick overview of CoNLL-U annotation format (Nivre et al., 2016a): we show how to load, parse and visualize such data on the example from the SynTagRus corpus [6]. Next, we learn to parse data with pre-trained UDPipe models (Straka et al., 2016) and Russian-language framework Natasha. To demonstrate some practical usage of syntax parsing, we first understand how to extract subject-verb-object (SVO) triples and then design a simple template-based text summarization model.

Week 9. Topic modelling The focus of this **lecture** is topic modeling. First, we formulate the topic modeling problem and ways it can be used to cluster texts or extract topics. We explain the basic probabilistic latent semantic analysis (PLSA) model (HOFMANN, 1999), that modifies early approaches, which were based on SVD (Dumais, 2004). We approach the PLSA problem using the Expectation-Minimization (EM) algorithm and introduce the basic performance metrics, such as perplexity and topic coherence.

As the PLSA problem is ill-posed, we familiarize students with regularization techniques using Additive Regularization for Topic Modeling (ARTM) model (Vorontsov and Potapenko, 2015) as an example. We describe the general EM algorithm for ARTM and some basic regularizers. Then we move towards the Latent Dirichlet Allocation (LDA) model (Blei et al., 2003) and show that the maximum a posteriori estimation for LDA is the special case of the ARTM model with a smoothing or sparsing regularizer (see Fig. 3 for the explanation snippet). We conclude the lecture with a brief introduction to multi-modal ARTM models and show how to generalize different Bayesian topic models based on LDA. We showcase classification, word translation, and trend detection tasks as multi-modal models.

In **practical session** we consider the models discussed in the lecture in a slightly different order. First, we take a closer look at Gensim realization

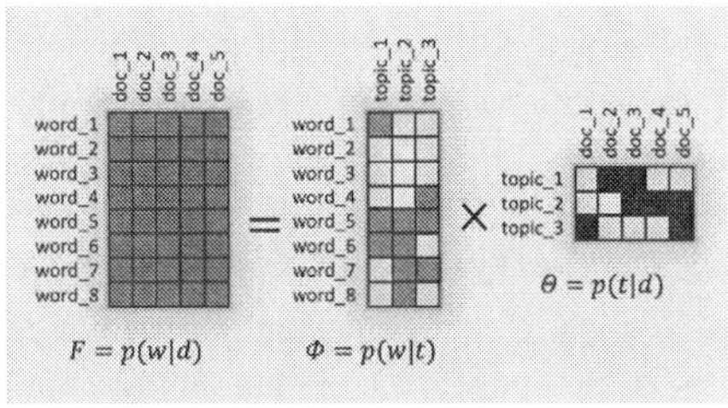

Figure 3: One slide from Lecture 9. Sparsification of an ARTM model explained.

of the LDA model (Řehůřek and Sojka, 2010), pick up the model's optimal parameters in terms of perplexity and topic coherence, and visualize the model with pyLDAvis library. Next, we explore BigARTM (Vorontsov et al., 2015) library, particularly LDA, PLSA, and multi-modal models, and the impact of different regularizers. For all experiments, we use a corpus of Russian-language news from Lenta.ru [7] which allows us to compare the models to each other.

Week 10. In this **lecture** we discussed mono-lingual seq2seq problems, text summarization and sentence simplification. We start with extractive summarization techniques. The first approach introduced is TextRank (Mihalcea and Tarau, 2004). We present each step of this approach and explain that any sentence or keyword embeddings can be used to construct a text graph, as required by the method. Thus we refer the students back to earlier lectures, where sentence embeddings were discussed. Next, we move to abstractive summarization techniques. To this end, we present performance metrics, such as ROUGE (Lin, 2004) and METEOR (Banerjee and Lavie, 2005) and briefly overview pre-Transformer architectures, including Pointer networks (See et al., 2017). Next, we show recent pre-trained Transformer-based models, which aim at multi-task learning, including summarization. To this end, we discuss pre-training approaches of T5 (Raffel et al., 2020) and BART (Lewis et al., 2020), and how they help to improve the performance of mono-lingual se2seq tasks. Unfortunately, when this lecture was created, multilingual versions of these models were not available, so they are left out of the scope. Finally, we talk about sentence simplification task (Coster and Kauchak, 2011; Alva-Manchego et al., 2020) and its social impact. We present SARI (Xu et al., 2016) as a

[6] `https://universaldependencies.org/treebanks/ru_syntagrus/index.html`

[7] `https://github.com/yutkin/Lenta.Ru-News-Dataset`

metric for sentence simplification performance and state, explain how T5 or BART can be utilized for the task.

The **practical session** is devoted to extractive summarization and TextRank algorithm. We are urged to stick to extractive summarization, as Russian lacks annotated datasets, but, at the same time, the task is demanded by in industry—extractive summarization compromises than between the need for summarization techniques and the absence of training datasets. Nevertheless, we used annotated English datasets to show how performance metrics can be used for the task. The CNN/DailyMail articles are used as an example of a dataset for the summarization task. As there is no standard benchmark for text summarization in Russian, we have to use English to measure different models' performance. We implement the TextRank algorithm and compare it with the algorithm from the NetworkX library (Hagberg et al., 2008). Also, we demonstrate how to estimate the performance of the summarization by calculating the ROUGE metric for the resulting algorithm using the PyRouge library[8]. This practical session allows us to refer back the students to sentence embedding models and showcase another application of sentence vectors.

Week 11. The penultimate **lecture** approaches Question-Answering (QA) systems and chat-bot technologies. We present multiple real-life industrial applications, where chat-bots and QA technologies are used, ranging from simple task-oriented chat-bots for food ordering to help desk or hotline automation. Next, we formulate the core problems of task-oriented chat-bots, which are intent classification and slot-filling (Liu and Lane, 2016) and revise methods, to approach them. After that, we introduce the concept of a dialog scenario graph and show how such a graph can guide users to complete their requests. Without going deep into technical details, we show how ready-made solutions, such as Google Dialogflow[9], can be used to create task-oriented chat-bots. Next, we move towards QA models, of which we pay more attention to information retrieval-based (IR-based) approaches and SQuAD-style (Rajpurkar et al., 2016) approaches. Since natural language generation models are not mature enough (at least for Russian) to be used in free dialog, we explain how IR-based techniques imitate a conversation with a user. Finally, we show how BERT can be used to tackle the SQuAD problem. The lecture is concluded by comparing industrial dialog assistants created by Russian companies, such as Yandex.Alisa or Mail.ru Marusya.

In the **practical session** we demonstrate several examples of using Transformer-based models for QA task. Firstly, we try to finetune Electra model (Clark et al., 2020) on COVID-19 questions dataset [10] and BERT on SQuAD 2.0 (Rajpurkar et al., 2018) (we use code from hugginface tutorial [11] for the latter). Next, we show an example of usage of pretrained model for Russian-language data from DeepPavlov project. Finally, we explore how to use BERT for joint intent classification and slot filling task (Chen et al., 2019).

Week 12. The last **lecture** wraps up the course by discussing knowledge graphs (KG) and some of their applications for QA systems. We revise core information extraction problems, such as NER and relation detection, and show how they can be used to extract a knowledge graph from unstructured texts (Paulheim, 2017). We touch upon the entity linking problem but do not go deep into details. To propose to students an alternative view to information extraction, we present machine reading comprehension approaches for NER (Li et al., 2019a) and relation detection (Li et al., 2019b), referring to the previous lecture. Finally, we close the course by revising all topics covered. We recite the evolution of text representation models from bag-of-words to BERT. We show that all the problems discussed throughout the course fall into one of three categories: (i) text classification or sentence pair classification, (ii) sequence tagging, (iii) sequence-to-sequence transformation. We draw attention to the fact that the most recent models can tackle all of the problem categories. Last but not least we revise, how all of these problem statements are utilized in real-life applications.

The **practical session** in this week is dedicated to information extraction tasks with Stanford CoreNLP library (Manning et al., 2014). The session's main idea is to demonstrate using the tool for constructing knowledge graphs based on natural text. We consider different ways of using the

[8]urlhttps://github.com/andersjo/pyrouge

[9]https://cloud.google.com/dialogflow

[10]https://github.com/xhlulu/covid-qa

[11]https://huggingface.co/transformers/custom_datasets.html#question-answering-with-squad-2-0

library and experimented with using the library to solve different NLP tasks that were already considered in the course: tokenization, lemmatization, POS-tagging, and dependency parsing. The library includes models for 53 languages, so we consider examples of solving these tasks for English and Russian texts. Besides, relation extraction is considered using the Open Information Extraction (OpenIE) module from the CoreNLP library.

4 Home works

The course consists of multiple ungraded quiz assignments, 11 graded quiz assignments, three graded coding assignments. Grading is performed automatically in a Kaggle-like fashion.

4.1 Quiz Assignments

Every video lecture is followed by an ungraded quiz, consisting of 1-2 questions. A typical question address the core concepts introduced:

- What kind of vectors are more common for word embedding models?
  A1: dense (true), A2: sparse (false)

- What kind of layers are essential for GPT-2 model?
  A1: transformer stacks (true), A2: recurrent layers (false), A3: convolutional layers (false), A4: dense layers (false)

A graded test is conducted every week, except the very last one. It consists of 12-15 questions, which we tried to split into three parts, being more or less of the same complexity. First part questions about main concepts and ideas introduced during the week. These questions are a bit more complicated than after video ones:

- What part of an encoder-decoder model solves the language modeling problem, i.e., the next word prediction?
  A1: encoder (false), A2: decoder (true)

- What are the BPE algorithm units?
  A1: syllables (false), A2: morphemes (false), A3: $n-$grams (true), A4: words (false)

Second part of the quiz asks the students to conduct simple computations by hand:

- Given a detailed description of an neural architecture, compute the number of parameters;

- Given a gold-standard NER annotation and a system output, compute token-based and span-based micro F_1.

The third part of the quiz asks to complete a simple programming assignment or asks about the code presented in practical sessions:

- Given a pre-trained language model, compute perplexity of a test sentence

- Does DeepPavlov cross-lingual NER model require to announce the language of the input text?

For convenience and to avoid format ambiguity, all questions are in multiple-choice format. For questions, which require a numerical answer, we provided answer options in the form of intervals, with one of the endpoints excluded.

Each quiz is estimated on a 10 point scale. All questions have equal weights.

The final week is followed by a comprehensive quiz covering all topics studied. This quiz is obligatory for those students who desire to earn a certificate.

4.2 Coding assignments

There are three coding assignments concerning the following topics: (i) text classification, (ii) sequence labeling, (iii) topic modeling. Assignments grading is binary. Text classification and sequence labeling assignments require students to beat the score of the provided baseline submission. Topic modeling assignment is evaluated differently.

All the coding tasks provide students with the starter code and sample submission bundles. The number of student's submissions is limited. Sample submission bundles illustrate the required submission format and could serve as the random baseline for each task. Submissions are evaluated using the Moodle[12] (Dougiamas and Taylor, 2003) CodeRunner[13] (Lobb and Harlow, 2016) plugin.

4.2.1 Text classification and sequence labeling coding assignments

Text classification assignment is based on the Harry Potter and the Action Prediction Challenge from Natural Language dataset (Vilares and Gómez-Rodríguez, 2019), which uses fiction fantasy texts. Here, the task is the following: given

[12]https://moodle.org/

[13]https://coderunner.org.nz/

some text preceding a spell occurrence in the text, predict this spell name. Students are provided with starter code in Jupyter notebooks (Pérez and Granger, 2007). Starter code implements all the needed data pre-processing, shows how to implement the baseline Logistic Regression model, and provides code needed to generate the submission.

Students' goal is to build three different models performing better than the baseline. The first one should differ from the baseline model by only hyperparameter values. The second one should be a Gradient Boosting model. The third model to build is a CNN model. All the three models' predictions on the provided testing dataset should be then submitted to the scoring system. Submissions, where all the models beat the baseline models classification F1-score, are graded positively.

Sequence labeling Sequence labeling assignment is based on the LitBank data (Bamman et al., 2019). Here, the task is to given fiction texts, perform a NER labeling. Students are provided with a starter code for data pre-processing and submission packaging. Starter code also illustrates building a recurrent neural model using the PyTorch framework, showing how to compose a single-layer unidirectional RNN model.

Students' goal is to build a bidirectional LSTM model that would outperform the baseline. Submissions are based on the held-out testing subset provided by the course team.

4.2.2 Topic modeling assignment

Topic modeling assignment motivation is to give students practical experience with LDA (Blei et al., 2003) algorithm. The assignment is organized as follows: first, students have to download and preprocess Wikipedia texts.

Then, the following experiment should be conducted. The experiment consists of training and exploring an LDA model for the given collection of texts. The task is to build several LDA models for the given data: models differ only in the configured number of topics. Students are asked to explore the obtained models using the pyLDAvis (Sievert and Shirley, 2014) tool. This stage is not evaluated. Finally, students are asked to submit the topic labels that LDA models assign to words provided by the course team. Such a prediction should be performed for each of the obtained models.

5 Platform description

The course is hosted on OpenEdu [14] - an educational platform created by the Association "National Platform for Open Education", established by leading Russian universities. Our course and all courses on the platform are available free of charge so that everyone can access all materials (including videos, practical Jupyter notebooks, tests, and coding assessments). The platform also provides a forum where course participants can ask questions or discuss the material with each other and lecturers.

6 Expected outcomes

First of all, we expect the students to understand basic formulations of the NLP tasks, such as text classification, sentence pair modeling, sequence tagging, and sequence-to-sequence transformation. We expect the students to be able to recall core terminology and use it fluently. In some weeks, we provide links to extra materials, mainly in English, so that the students can learn more about the topic themselves. We hope that after completing the course, the students become able to read those materials. Secondly, we anticipate that after completing the course, the students are comfortable using popular Python tools to process texts in Russian and English and utilize pre-trained models. Thirdly, we hope that the students can state and approach their tasks related to NLP, using the knowledge acquired, conducting experiments, and evaluating the results correctly.

7 Feedback

The early feedback we have received so far is positive. Although the course has only been advertised so far to a broader audience, we know that there are two groups interested in the course. First, some students come to study at their own will. Secondly, selected topics were used in offline courses in an inverse classroom format or as additional materials. The students note that our course is a good starting point for studying NLP and helps navigate a broad range of topics and learn the terminology. Some of the students note that it was easy for them to learn in Russian, and now, as they feel more comfortable with the core concepts, they can turn to read detailed and more recent sources. Unfortunately, programming assignments turn out to be our weak

[14] `https://npoed.ru/`

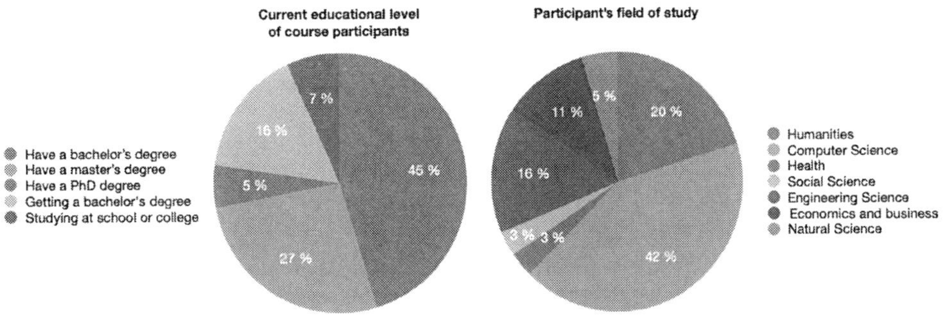

Figure 4: The results of survey among course participants. Left: current educational level. Right: professional area.

spot, as there are challenging to complete, and little feedback on them can be provided.

We ask all participants to fill in a short survey after they enroll in the course. So far, we have received about 100 responses. According to the results, most students (78%) have previously taken online courses, but only 24% of them have experience with courses from foreign universities. The average age of course participants is 32 years; most of them already have or are getting a higher education (see Fig. 4 for more details). Almost half of the students are occupied in Computer Science area, 20% have a background in Humanities, followed by Engineering Science (16%).

We also ask students about their motivation in the form of a multiple-choice question: almost half of them (46%) stated that they want to improve their qualification either to improve at their current job (33%) or to change their occupation (13%), and 20% answered they enrolled the course for research and academic purposes. For the vast majority of the student, the reputation of HSE university was the key factor to select this course among other available.

8 Conclusion

This paper introduced and described a new massive open online course on Natural Language Processing targeted at Russian-speaking students. This twelve-week course was designed and recorded during 2020 and launched by the end of the year. In the lectures and practical session, we managed to document a paradigm shift caused by the discovery and widespread use of pre-trained Transformer-based language models. We inherited the best of two worlds, showing how to utilize both static word embeddings in a more traditional machine learning setup and contextualized word embeddings in the most recent fashion. The course's theoretical outcome is understanding and knowing core concepts and problem formulations, while the practical outcome covers knowing how to use tools to process text in Russian and English.

Early feedback we got from the students is positive. As every week was devoted to a new topic, they did not find it difficult to keep being engaged. The ways we introduce the core problem formulations and showcase different tools to process texts in Russian earned approval. What is more, the presented course is used now as supplementary material in a few off-line educational programs to the best of our knowledge.

Further improvements and adjustments, which could be made for the course, include new home works related to machine translation or monolingual sequence-to-sequence tasks and the development of additional materials in written form to support mathematical calculations, avoided in the video lecture for the sake of time.

References

Alfred V Aho and Jeffrey D Ullman. 1972. The theory of parsing, translation, and compiling.

Jay Alammar. 2015. The illustrated transformer. *Jay Alammar blog*.

Fernando Alva-Manchego, Carolina Scarton, and Lucia Specia. 2020. Data-driven sentence simplification: Survey and benchmark. *Computational Linguistics*, 46(1):135–187.

Dzmitry Bahdanau, Kyung Hyun Cho, and Yoshua Bengio. 2015. Neural machine translation by jointly learning to align and translate. In *3rd International Conference on Learning Representations, ICLR 2015*.

David Bamman, Sejal Popat, and Sheng Shen. 2019. An annotated dataset of literary entities. In *Proceedings of the 2019 Conference of the North American Chapter of the Association for Computational Linguistics: Human Language Technologies, Volume 1 (Long and Short Papers)*, pages 2138–2144.

Satanjeev Banerjee and Alon Lavie. 2005. Meteor: An automatic metric for mt evaluation with improved correlation with human judgments. In *Proceedings of the acl workshop on intrinsic and extrinsic evaluation measures for machine translation and/or summarization*, pages 65–72.

Yoshua Bengio, Réjean Ducharme, Pascal Vincent, and Christian Janvin. 2003. A neural probabilistic language model. *The journal of machine learning research*, 3:1137–1155.

David M Blei, Andrew Y Ng, and Michael I Jordan. 2003. Latent dirichlet allocation. *the Journal of machine Learning research*, 3:993–1022.

Leonard Bloomfield. 1936. Language or ideas? *Language*, pages 89–95.

Piotr Bojanowski, Edouard Grave, Armand Joulin, and Tomas Mikolov. 2017. Enriching word vectors with subword information. *Transactions of the Association for Computational Linguistics*, 5:135–146.

Pavel Braslavski. 2017. Nlp – how will it be in russian? *Habr blog*.

Pavel Braslavski, Vladislav Blinov, Valeria Bolotova, and Katya Pertsova. 2018. How to evaluate humorous response generation, seriously? In *Proceedings of the 2018 Conference on Human Information Interaction & Retrieval*, pages 225–228.

Mikhail Burtsev, Alexander Seliverstov, Rafael Airapetyan, Mikhail Arkhipov, Dilyara Baymurzina, Nickolay Bushkov, Olga Gureenkova, Taras Khakhulin, Yurii Kuratov, Denis Kuznetsov, et al. 2018. Deeppavlov: Open-source library for dialogue systems. In *Proceedings of ACL 2018, System Demonstrations*, pages 122–127.

Nitesh V Chawla, Kevin W Bowyer, Lawrence O Hall, and W Philip Kegelmeyer. 2002. Smote: synthetic minority over-sampling technique. *Journal of artificial intelligence research*, 16:321–357.

Qian Chen, Zhu Zhuo, and Wen Wang. 2019. BERT for joint intent classification and slot filling. *CoRR*, abs/1902.10909.

Junyoung Chung, Caglar Gulcehre, Kyunghyun Cho, and Yoshua Bengio. 2014. Empirical evaluation of gated recurrent neural networks on sequence modeling. In *NIPS 2014 Workshop on Deep Learning, December 2014*.

Kevin Clark, Minh-Thang Luong, Quoc V. Le, and Christopher D. Manning. 2020. ELECTRA: Pre-training text encoders as discriminators rather than generators. In *ICLR*.

Alexis Conneau, Kartikay Khandelwal, Naman Goyal, Vishrav Chaudhary, Guillaume Wenzek, Francisco Guzmán, Édouard Grave, Myle Ott, Luke Zettlemoyer, and Veselin Stoyanov. 2020. Unsupervised cross-lingual representation learning at scale. In *Proceedings of the 58th Annual Meeting of the Association for Computational Linguistics*, pages 8440–8451.

Alexis Conneau and Douwe Kiela. 2018. Senteval: An evaluation toolkit for universal sentence representations. In *Proceedings of the Eleventh International Conference on Language Resources and Evaluation (LREC 2018)*.

William Coster and David Kauchak. 2011. Simple english wikipedia: a new text simplification task. In *Proceedings of the 49th Annual Meeting of the Association for Computational Linguistics: Human Language Technologies*, pages 665–669.

Jacob Devlin, Ming-Wei Chang, Kenton Lee, and Kristina Toutanova. 2019. Bert: Pre-training of deep bidirectional transformers for language understanding. In *Proceedings of the 2019 Conference of the North American Chapter of the Association for Computational Linguistics: Human Language Technologies, Volume 1 (Long and Short Papers)*, pages 4171–4186.

Martin Dougiamas and Peter Taylor. 2003. Moodle: Using learning communities to create an open source course management system.

Susan T Dumais. 2004. Latent semantic analysis. *Annual review of information science and technology*, 38(1):188–230.

Andrea Esuli and Fabrizio Sebastiani. 2009. Active learning strategies for multi-label text classification. In *European Conference on Information Retrieval*, pages 102–113. Springer.

Fangxiaoyu Feng, Yinfei Yang, Daniel Cer, Naveen Arivazhagan, and Wei Wang. 2020. Language-agnostic bert sentence embedding. *arXiv preprint arXiv:2007.01852*.

Matt Gardner, Joel Grus, Mark Neumann, Oyvind Tafjord, Pradeep Dasigi, Nelson F Liu, Matthew Peters, Michael Schmitz, and Luke Zettlemoyer. 2018. Allennlp: A deep semantic natural language processing platform. In *Proceedings of Workshop for NLP Open Source Software (NLP-OSS)*, pages 1–6.

Yoav Goldberg. 2017. Neural network methods for natural language processing. *Synthesis lectures on human language technologies*, 10(1):1–309.

Jiatao Gu, James Bradbury, Caiming Xiong, Victor OK Li, and Richard Socher. 2017. Non-autoregressive neural machine translation. *arXiv preprint arXiv:1711.02281*.

Aric Hagberg, Pieter Swart, and Daniel S Chult. 2008. Exploring network structure, dynamics, and function using networkx. Technical report, Los Alamos National Lab.(LANL), Los Alamos, NM (United States).

Vu Cong Duy Hoang, Philipp Koehn, Gholamreza Haffari, and Trevor Cohn. 2018. Iterative back-translation for neural machine translation. In *Proceedings of the 2nd Workshop on Neural Machine Translation and Generation*, pages 18–24.

Sepp Hochreiter and Jürgen Schmidhuber. 1997. Long short-term memory. *Neural computation*, 9(8):1735–1780.

T HOFMANN. 1999. Probabilistic latent semantic analysis. In *Proc. Conf. on Uncertainty in Artificial Intelligence (UAI), 1999*, pages 289–296.

Ari Holtzman, Jan Buys, Li Du, Maxwell Forbes, and Yejin Choi. 2019. The curious case of neural text degeneration. In *International Conference on Learning Representations*.

Daniel Jurafsky and James H Martin. 2000. Speech and language processing: An introduction to natural language processing, computational linguistics, and speech recognition.

Andrej Karpathy. 2015. The unreasonable effectiveness of recurrent neural networks. *Andrej Karpathy blog*, 21:23.

Yoon Kim. 2014. Convolutional neural networks for sentence classification. *CoRR*, abs/1408.5882.

Guillaume Klein, Yoon Kim, Yuntian Deng, Jean Senellart, and Alexander M. Rush. 2017. Opennmt: Open-source toolkit for neural machine translation. In *Proc. ACL*.

Reinhard Kneser and Hermann Ney. 1995. Improved backing-off for m-gram language modeling. In *1995 international conference on acoustics, speech, and signal processing*, volume 1, pages 181–184. IEEE.

Mikhail Korobov. 2015. Morphological analyzer and generator for russian and ukrainian languages. In *International Conference on Analysis of Images, Social Networks and Texts*, pages 320–332. Springer.

Zhenzhong Lan, Mingda Chen, Sebastian Goodman, Kevin Gimpel, Piyush Sharma, and Radu Soricut. 2019. Albert: A lite bert for self-supervised learning of language representations. In *International Conference on Learning Representations*.

Quoc Le and Tomas Mikolov. 2014. Distributed representations of sentences and documents. In *International conference on machine learning*, pages 1188–1196. PMLR.

Mike Lewis, Yinhan Liu, Naman Goyal, Marjan Ghazvininejad, Abdelrahman Mohamed, Omer Levy, Veselin Stoyanov, and Luke Zettlemoyer. 2020. Bart: Denoising sequence-to-sequence pre-training for natural language generation, translation, and comprehension. In *Proceedings of the 58th Annual Meeting of the Association for Computational Linguistics*, pages 7871–7880.

Xiaoya Li, Jingrong Feng, Yuxian Meng, Qinghong Han, Fei Wu, and Jiwei Li. 2019a. A unified mrc framework for named entity recognition. *arXiv preprint arXiv:1910.11476*.

Xiaoya Li, Fan Yin, Zijun Sun, Xiayu Li, Arianna Yuan, Duo Chai, Mingxin Zhou, and Jiwei Li. 2019b. Entity-relation extraction as multi-turn question answering. In *Proceedings of the 57th Annual Meeting of the Association for Computational Linguistics*, pages 1340–1350.

Chin-Yew Lin. 2004. Rouge: A package for automatic evaluation of summaries. In *Text summarization branches out*, pages 74–81.

Bing Liu and Ian Lane. 2016. Attention-based recurrent neural network models for joint intent detection and slot filling. *Interspeech 2016*, pages 685–689.

Yinhan Liu, Myle Ott, Naman Goyal, Jingfei Du, Mandar Joshi, Danqi Chen, Omer Levy, Mike Lewis, Luke Zettlemoyer, and Veselin Stoyanov. 2019. Roberta: A robustly optimized bert pretraining approach. *arXiv preprint arXiv:1907.11692*.

Richard Lobb and Jenny Harlow. 2016. Coderunner: A tool for assessing computer programming skills. *ACM Inroads*, 7(1):47–51.

Xuezhe Ma and Eduard Hovy. 2016. End-to-end sequence labeling via bi-directional lstm-cnns-crf. In *Proceedings of the 54th Annual Meeting of the Association for Computational Linguistics (Volume 1: Long Papers)*, pages 1064–1074.

Christopher D Manning, Mihai Surdeanu, John Bauer, Jenny Rose Finkel, Steven Bethard, and David McClosky. 2014. The stanford corenlp natural language processing toolkit. In *Proceedings of 52nd annual meeting of the association for computational linguistics: system demonstrations*, pages 55–60.

Chandler May, Alex Wang, Shikha Bordia, Samuel Bowman, and Rachel Rudinger. 2019. On measuring social biases in sentence encoders. In *Proceedings of the 2019 Conference of the North American Chapter of the Association for Computational Linguistics: Human Language Technologies, Volume 1 (Long and Short Papers)*, pages 622–628.

Ryan McDonald, Koby Crammer, and Fernando Pereira. 2005. Online large-margin training of dependency parsers. In *Proceedings of the 43rd Annual Meeting of the Association for Computational Linguistics (ACL'05)*, pages 91–98.

Rada Mihalcea and Paul Tarau. 2004. Textrank: Bringing order into text. In *Proceedings of the 2004 conference on empirical methods in natural language processing*, pages 404–411.

Tomas Mikolov, Ilya Sutskever, Kai Chen, Greg Corrado, and Jeffrey Dean. 2013. Distributed representations of words and phrases and their compositionality. In *Proceedings of the 26th International Conference on Neural Information Processing Systems-Volume 2*, pages 3111–3119.

Joakim Nivre, Marie-Catherine de Marneffe, Filip Ginter, Yoav Goldberg, Jan Hajič, Christopher D. Manning, Ryan McDonald, Slav Petrov, Sampo Pyysalo, Natalia Silveira, Reut Tsarfaty, and Daniel Zeman. 2016a. Universal Dependencies v1: A multilingual treebank collection. In *Proceedings of the Tenth International Conference on Language Resources and Evaluation (LREC'16)*, pages 1659–1666, Portorož, Slovenia. European Language Resources Association (ELRA).

Joakim Nivre, Marie-Catherine De Marneffe, Filip Ginter, Yoav Goldberg, Jan Hajic, Christopher D Manning, Ryan McDonald, Slav Petrov, Sampo Pyysalo, Natalia Silveira, et al. 2016b. Universal dependencies v1: A multilingual treebank collection. In *Proceedings of the Tenth International Conference on Language Resources and Evaluation (LREC'16)*, pages 1659–1666.

Christopher Olah. 2015. Understanding lstm networks. *Christopher Olah blog*.

Kishore Papineni, Salim Roukos, Todd Ward, and Wei-Jing Zhu. 2002. Bleu: a method for automatic evaluation of machine translation. In *Proceedings of the 40th annual meeting of the Association for Computational Linguistics*, pages 311–318.

Heiko Paulheim. 2017. Knowledge graph refinement: A survey of approaches and evaluation methods. *Semantic web*, 8(3):489–508.

Jeffrey Pennington, Richard Socher, and Christopher D Manning. 2014. Glove: Global vectors for word representation. In *Proceedings of the 2014 conference on empirical methods in natural language processing (EMNLP)*, pages 1532–1543.

Fernando Pérez and Brian E. Granger. 2007. IPython: a system for interactive scientific computing. *Computing in Science and Engineering*, 9(3):21–29.

Matthew E Peters, Mark Neumann, Mohit Iyyer, Matt Gardner, Christopher Clark, Kenton Lee, and Luke Zettlemoyer. 2018. Deep contextualized word representations. In *Proceedings of NAACL-HLT*, pages 2227–2237.

Alec Radford, Jeffrey Wu, Rewon Child, David Luan, Dario Amodei, and Ilya Sutskever. Language models are unsupervised multitask learners.

Colin Raffel, Noam Shazeer, Adam Roberts, Katherine Lee, Sharan Narang, Michael Matena, Yanqi Zhou, Wei Li, and Peter J Liu. 2020. Exploring the limits of transfer learning with a unified text-to-text transformer. *Journal of Machine Learning Research*, 21:1–67.

Pranav Rajpurkar, Robin Jia, and Percy Liang. 2018. Know what you don't know: Unanswerable questions for squad. *CoRR*, abs/1806.03822.

Pranav Rajpurkar, Jian Zhang, Konstantin Lopyrev, and Percy Liang. 2016. Squad: 100,000+ questions for machine comprehension of text. In *Proceedings of the 2016 Conference on Empirical Methods in Natural Language Processing*, pages 2383–2392.

Radim Řehůřek and Petr Sojka. 2010. Software Framework for Topic Modelling with Large Corpora. In *Proceedings of the LREC 2010 Workshop on New Challenges for NLP Frameworks*, pages 45–50, Valletta, Malta. ELRA. `http://is.muni.cz/publication/884893/en`.

Anna Rogers, Olga Kovaleva, and Anna Rumshisky. 2021. A primer in bertology: What we know about how bert works. *Transactions of the Association for Computational Linguistics*, 8:842–866.

Hassan Sajjad, Fahim Dalvi, Nadir Durrani, and Preslav Nakov. 2020. Poor man's bert: Smaller and faster transformer models. *arXiv preprint arXiv:2004.03844*.

Erik Tjong Kim Sang and Fien De Meulder. 2003. Introduction to the conll-2003 shared task: Language-independent named entity recognition. In *Proceedings of the Seventh Conference on Natural Language Learning at HLT-NAACL 2003*, pages 142–147.

Victor Sanh, Lysandre Debut, Julien Chaumond, and Thomas Wolf. 2019. Distilbert, a distilled version of bert: smaller, faster, cheaper and lighter. *arXiv preprint arXiv:1910.01108*.

Sebastian Schuster and Christopher D Manning. 2016. Enhanced english universal dependencies: An improved representation for natural language understanding tasks. In *Proceedings of the Tenth International Conference on Language Resources and Evaluation (LREC'16)*, pages 2371–2378.

Abigail See, Peter J Liu, and Christopher D Manning. 2017. Get to the point: Summarization with pointer-generator networks. In *Proceedings of the 55th Annual Meeting of the Association for Computational Linguistics (Volume 1: Long Papers)*, pages 1073–1083.

Ilya Segalovich. A fast morphological algorithm with unknown word guessing induced by a dictionary for a web search engine.

Carson Sievert and Kenneth Shirley. 2014. Ldavis: A method for visualizing and interpreting topics. In *Proceedings of the workshop on interactive language learning, visualization, and interfaces*, pages 63–70.

Fei Song and W Bruce Croft. 1999. A general language model for information retrieval. In *Proceedings of the eighth international conference on Information and knowledge management*, pages 316–321.

Milan Straka, Jan Hajič, and Jana Straková. 2016. UDPipe: Trainable pipeline for processing CoNLL-U files performing tokenization, morphological analysis, POS tagging and parsing. In *Proceedings of the Tenth International Conference on Language Resources and Evaluation (LREC'16)*, pages 4290–4297, Portorož, Slovenia. European Language Resources Association (ELRA).

Milan Straka and Jana Straková. 2017. Tokenizing, pos tagging, lemmatizing and parsing ud 2.0 with udpipe. In *Proceedings of the CoNLL 2017 Shared Task: Multilingual Parsing from Raw Text to Universal Dependencies*, pages 88–99.

Ilya Sutskever, James Martens, and Geoffrey E Hinton. 2011. Generating text with recurrent neural networks. In *ICML*.

Ilya Sutskever, Oriol Vinyals, and Quoc V Le. 2014. Sequence to sequence learning with neural networks. *Advances in Neural Information Processing Systems*, 27:3104–3112.

Lucien Tesnière. 2015. *Elements of Structural Syntax*. John Benjamins Publishing Company.

Ashish Vaswani, Noam Shazeer, Niki Parmar, Jakob Uszkoreit, Llion Jones, Aidan N Gomez, Łukasz Kaiser, and Illia Polosukhin. 2017. Attention is all you need. In *Proceedings of the 31st International Conference on Neural Information Processing Systems*, pages 6000–6010.

David Vilares and Carlos Gómez-Rodríguez. 2019. Harry Potter and the action prediction challenge from natural language. In *Proceedings of the 2019 Conference of the North American Chapter of the Association for Computational Linguistics: Human Language Technologies, Volume 1 (Long and Short Papers)*, pages 2124–2130, Minneapolis, Minnesota. Association for Computational Linguistics.

Konstantin Vorontsov, Oleksandr Frei, Murat Apishev, Peter Romov, and Marina Dudarenko. 2015. Bigartm: Open source library for regularized multimodal topic modeling of large collections. In *International Conference on Analysis of Images, Social Networks and Texts*, pages 370–381. Springer.

Konstantin Vorontsov and Anna Potapenko. 2015. Additive regularization of topic models. *Machine Learning*, 101(1):303–323.

Alex Wang, Yada Pruksachatkun, Nikita Nangia, Amanpreet Singh, Julian Michael, Felix Hill, Omer Levy, and Samuel R Bowman. 2019a. Superglue: A stickier benchmark for general-purpose language understanding systems. *Advances in Neural Information Processing Systems*, 32.

Alex Wang, Amanpreet Singh, Julian Michael, Felix Hill, Omer Levy, and Samuel R Bowman. 2019b. Glue: A multi-task benchmark and analysis platform for natural language understanding. In *7th International Conference on Learning Representations, ICLR 2019*.

Jason Wei and Kai Zou. 2019. Eda: Easy data augmentation techniques for boosting performance on text classification tasks. In *Proceedings of the 2019 Conference on Empirical Methods in Natural Language Processing and the 9th International Joint Conference on Natural Language Processing (EMNLP-IJCNLP)*, pages 6383–6389.

Robert West and Eric Horvitz. 2019. Reverse-engineering satire, or "paper on computational humor accepted despite making serious advances". In *Proceedings of the AAAI Conference on Artificial Intelligence*, volume 33, pages 7265–7272.

Thomas Wolf, Lysandre Debut, Victor Sanh, Julien Chaumond, Clement Delangue, Anthony Moi, Pierric Cistac, Tim Rault, Rémi Louf, Morgan Funtowicz, Joe Davison, Sam Shleifer, Patrick von Platen, Clara Ma, Yacine Jernite, Julien Plu, Canwen Xu, Teven Le Scao, Sylvain Gugger, Mariama Drame, Quentin Lhoest, and Alexander M. Rush. 2020. Transformers: State-of-the-art natural language processing. In *Proceedings of the 2020 Conference on Empirical Methods in Natural Language Processing: System Demonstrations*, pages 38–45, Online. Association for Computational Linguistics.

Wei Xu, Courtney Napoles, Ellie Pavlick, Quanze Chen, and Chris Callison-Burch. 2016. Optimizing statistical machine translation for text simplification. *Transactions of the Association for Computational Linguistics*, 4:401–415.

Ofir Zafrir, Guy Boudoukh, Peter Izsak, and Moshe Wasserblat. 2019. Q8bert: Quantized 8bit bert. *arXiv preprint arXiv:1910.06188*.

Luowei Zhou, Hamid Palangi, Lei Zhang, Houdong Hu, Jason Corso, and Jianfeng Gao. 2020. Unified Vision-language Pre-training for Image Captioning and VQA. In *Proceedings of the AAAI Conference on Artificial Intelligence*, volume 34, pages 13041–13049.

Natural Language Processing 4 All (NLP4All): A New Online Platform for Teaching and Learning NLP Concepts

Anonymous NAACL-HLT 2021 submission

Abstract

Natural Language Processing offers new insights into language data across almost all disciplines and domains, and allows us to corroborate and/or challenge existing knowledge. The primary hurdles to widening participation in and use of these new research tools are, first, a lack of coding skills in students across K-16, and in the population at large, and second, a lack of knowledge of how NLP-methods can be used to answer questions of disciplinary interest outside of linguistics and/or computer science. To broaden participation in NLP and improve NLP-literacy, we introduced a new tool web-based tool called Natural Language Processing 4 All (NLP4All). The intended purpose of NLP4All is to help teachers facilitate learning with and about NLP, by providing easy-to-use interfaces to NLP-methods, data, and analyses, making it possible for non- and novice-programmers to learn NLP concepts interactively.

1 Introduction

An emerging body of work has explored ways of lowering the threshold for people to work with AI and ML-technologies, specifically in educational contexts. Much of this work has focused on making AI "explainable" (Gunning, 2017) by visualizing the underlying math, or visualizing how machines make decisions. However, NLP has been largely absent from these efforts so far. To address this gap, we developed a new educational tool called NaturalLanguageProcessing4All (NLP4All), which allows teachers to interactively introduce applications of statistical NLP to students without any coding skills.

NLP4All[1] is a web-based interface for teaching and learning NLP concepts, designed with flexibility and accessibility in mind. It is an open source application built in Python on top of the Flask framework, and can therefore be easily extended with existing Python-based NLP- and ML-packages. The first prototype of NLP4All is designed to work with tweets only, but we are currently expanding to be able to work with any kind of text, bringing NLP tools to a wider array of disciplines and student populations.

We first present the design of the tool and its current capabilities, and then briefly describe two different real-world settings in which we have used NLP4All.

2 Teaching text classification with NLP4All

NLP4All provides two different user types: teachers and students. Whereas teachers can see data from all students and can create new projects, students' activities are more limited in the system.

The system is organized into **user groups**, **projects**, and **analyses**. To better describe how the system, we will briefly outline how each of these work.

2.1 User Groups

User groups provide an easy way to organize groups of students. A group will consist of students who are doing the same activities, and simply act as an easy way to add students to projects. They will typically consist of students in one class. User groups can be created by a teacher and associated with a unique sign-up link to be distributed to the intended recipient group.

2.2 Projects

Projects in NLP4All offer teachers a way to organize a lesson by selecting some texts of interest, and tying them to a user group. A project consists of a title, a description, a user group (of students), and a set corpora that will be included in the project. Teachers create projects with associated datasets

[1] A demo version of NLP4All can be accessed here: http://86.52.121.12:5000/, pre-loaded with the data and analysis described in this paper.

Proceedings of the Fifth Workshop on Teaching NLP, pages 28–33
June 10–11, 2021. ©2021 Association for Computational Linguistics

prior to classroom sessions; they can either choose to use several pre-loaded datasets (Tweets from the accounts of different American and Danish politicians or political parties) or upload their own texts in .csv or .json format.

Figure 1: Teacher view displaying Projects interface.

2.3 Analyses

Inside a project, both teachers and students can create a new analysis. An analysis is NLP4All's name for an untrained model and all data associated with training it. Students can create a new analysis if they think that they have trained their old model poorly and want to start from scratch. Students can only create personal analyses - i.e. analyses that are unique to their account, and not shared among other members of the user group. Teachers, in contrast, can create analyses that are shared between all members of a user group.

There are two different ways in which an analysis can be shared (Fig. 2): the teacher can choose to just share the texts that students hand-label, or they can choose to share an underlying model. For the former case, the teacher can specify a number of texts from each category, and NLP4All will create a mini-corpus of just those texts for students to work with. For the latter case, students work with the whole corpus of the texts present in the project, but all train the same underlying model as they hand label texts.

NLP4All also supports text annotation, but we do not discuss this functionality here.

3 Example: Teaching classification with NLP4All

The initial version of NLP4All features interactive tools for a curriculum module on **text classification** with Naïve Bayes and Logistic Regression models. In this section, we walk through an example of how NLP4All could be used in the classroom

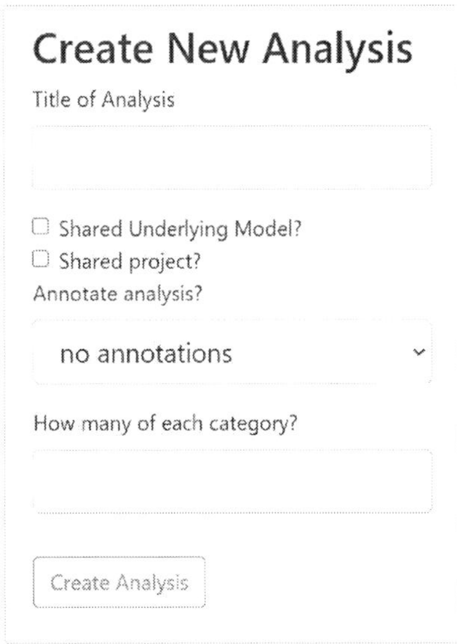

Figure 2: New Analysis interface.

to introduce Naïve Bayes text classification using a corpus of posts from the Twitter accounts of Joe Biden and Bernie Sanders collected in the run-up to the 2020 Democratic Primaries.

Upon logging in, students see a landing page which lists all projects that the student is currently part of, as determined by the instructor (Fig. 3).

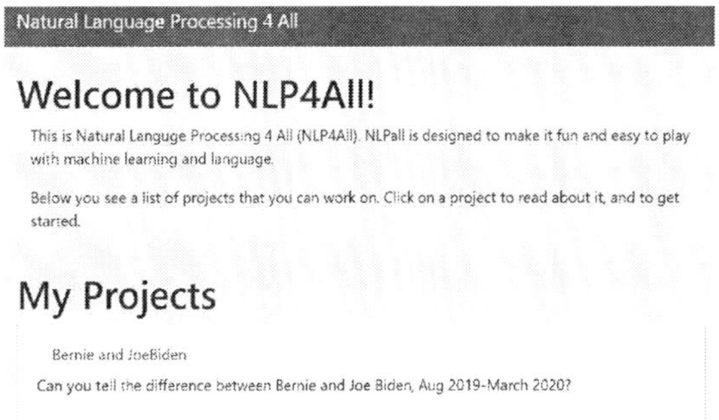

Figure 3: Landing page for students.

3.1 Hand labeling: The Tweet View

The current implementation of NLP4All has a special view called the Tweet View, where students hand label Twitter data, as seen in Fig. 4. At the bottom of the page, it shows the tweet currently being labeled. Students label each tweet by dragging the Twitter bird to whichever side of the circle represents the category that they think the it belongs to. For example, by dragging the bird to the green part of the circle, a student would label the tweet in Fig. 4 as having been written by Bernie Sanders. All

Tweets in this dataset were pre-processed so that mentions, hashtags, and links were replaced with mention, #hashtag, and http://link, respectively.

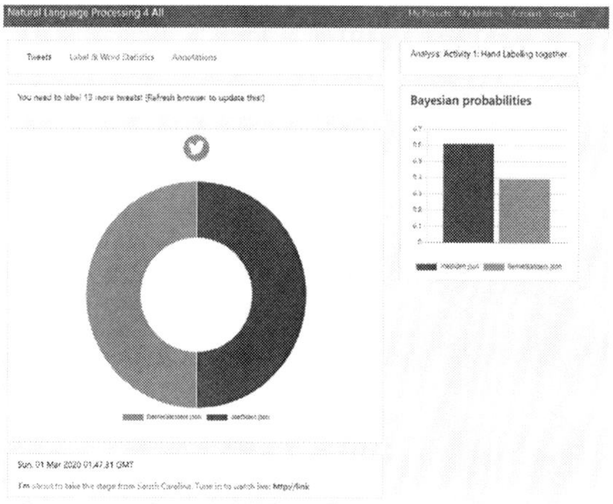

Figure 4: The Tweet View interface.

In the top right corner Fig. 4, the Tweet View also shows the model's best estimate of who wrote the tweet, based on the data that it has been trained on so far. For the current tweet, the model estimates that Biden wrote the tweet with around .63 and that Bernie wrote it with the remaining .37. By making the classification explicit to students, we hope to achieve two different goals. First, we want students to understand how each word contributes to the overall classification. Second, we want students to critically reflect on whether they agree with the model's assessment. It is, of course, important when working with ML to not always trust your model. By giving students a clear idea of how the model reaches its conclusions, we hope that students can learn not only to be skeptical of ML models in a general sense, but that they can begin to understand why particular features or combinations of features may confuse a model, and through this get a better sense of what can go wrong when ML makes classifications. Finally, at the top of the page, students are shown how many more tweets this student needs to hand label before they are done with all tweets.

4 Using label and word statistics to facilitate learning

Clicking the *Label & Word Statistics* link at the top of the page gives an overview of all tweets that students in this shared analysis have labeled, how many labeled them correctly, and how many labeled them incorrectly.

The purpose of this view is for the teacher to be able to discuss with students which tweets are hard to classify (i.e. the ones that many hand label incorrectly), which ones are easy, to foster discussion in the classroom what we know about these data. The screenshot below shows us this list, sorted by correct-% in ascending order. Here, we see that 22 out of 23 students mislabeled the tweet with the text, "FLORIDA: Today is the LAST DAY to register for the Democratic primary. You must register as a Democrat to vote in the March 17th primary at http://link Let's win this together! http://link". This is not surprising, given how generic this tweet is given the choice between two democratic candidates competing in the same primaries.

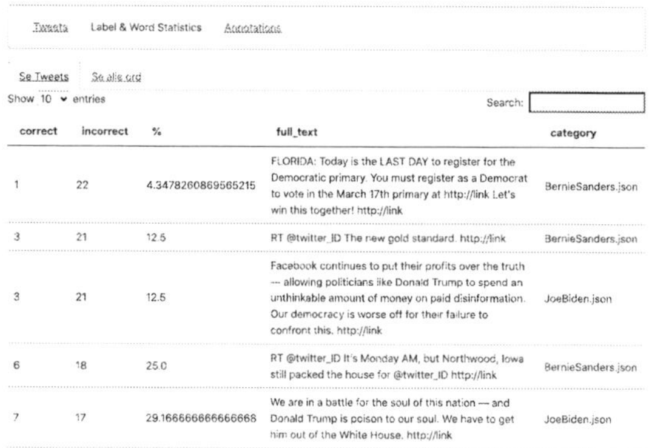

correct	incorrect	%	full_text	category
1	22	4.3478260869565215	FLORIDA: Today is the LAST DAY to register for the Democratic primary. You must register as a Democrat to vote in the March 17th primary at http://link Let's win this together! http://link	BernieSanders.json
3	21	12.5	RT @twitter_ID The new gold standard. http://link	BernieSanders.json
3	21	12.5	Facebook continues to put their profits over the truth — allowing politicians like Donald Trump to spend an unthinkable amount of money on paid disinformation. Our democracy is worse off for their failure to confront this. http://link	JoeBiden.json
6	18	25.0	RT @twitter_ID It's Monday AM, but Northwood, Iowa still packed the house for @twitter_ID http://link	BernieSanders.json
7	17	29.166666666666668	We are in a battle for the soul of this nation — and Donald Trump is poison to our soul. We have to get him out of the White House. http://link	JoeBiden.json

Figure 5: Label & Word Statistics view. After students participate in hand labeling data, this view can be used to facilitate discussion.

Sorting the list in descending order of correct-%, we can see the tweets that all or most students labeled correctly. For instance, the tweet "We will not defeat Donald Trump with a candidate who, instead of holding the crooks on Wall Street accountable, blamed the end of racist policies such as redlining for the financial crisis." was seemingly easily recognizable as a Bernie-tweet (23/23 students labeled it correctly.) Similarly, "We need a leader who will be ready on day one to pick up the pieces of Donald Trump's broken foreign policy and repair the damage he has caused around the world. http://link" was easily recognizable by 23 students as having been written by the Biden team. (The wrong guess was from the teacher demonstrating the system to students.)

The *See all words* link brings up a table of all words present in tweets that have been labeled so far. This list shows how many times each word

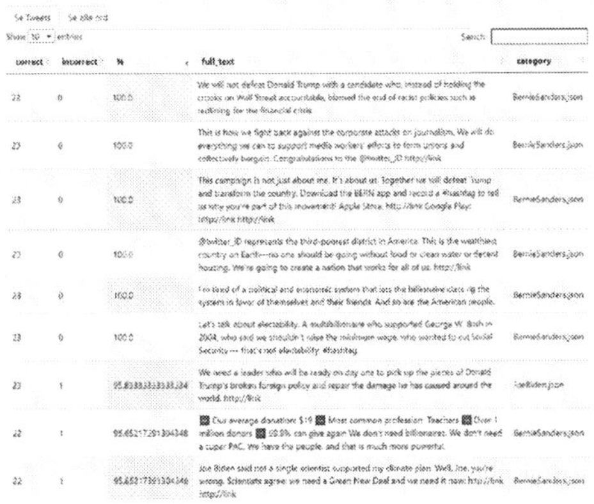

Figure 6: Label & Word Statistics view, sorted by % correctly labeled.

has appeared in the set of labeled tweets, and to which extent each word predicts each of the categories in the project, here Joe Biden and Bernie Sanders. For instructional purposes, this list can be used to discuss a variety of questions: In the screenshot above, the list is sorted by how many times a word appears. Since the texts have not been filtered, this can act as a point of entry to a discussion of why only some words are meaningful when it comes to distinguishing between different classes. The teacher may choose this moment to introduce students to the concept of stop words, or even to the notion of statistical power laws behind word frequency (Zipf's law).

Figure 7: Word statistics, sorted by frequency.

4.1 Model training and evaluation

NLP4All also lets students create their own Naïve Bayes models by specifying a set search terms to train their model on. Asterisks work as wildcards, and can be placed anywhere in a word, including at the front or back. Importantly, for the purpose of reflection and classroom discussions, students are prompted to also state a reason why they think this would be a good word feature for distinguishing between the categories of text in the project. In the screenshot in Fig. 8 we see how one student has added four different terms and their reasons for inclusion.

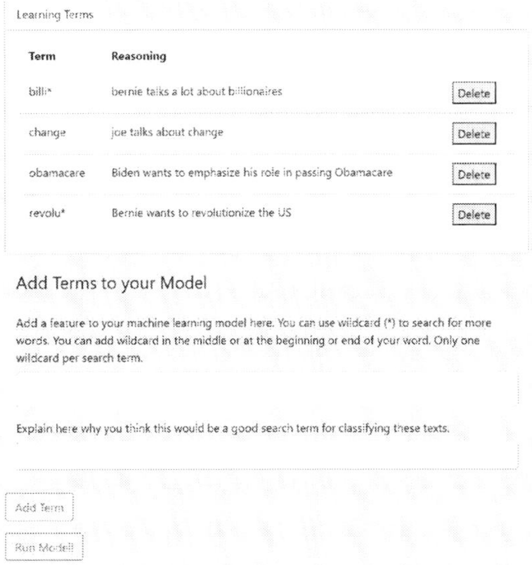

Figure 8: Student-defined word features

By clicking *Run Model* button at the bottom, NLP4All finds all words that match the search terms (including wild cards) and trains a Naïve Bayes model based on them. It returns the screen shown in the example screenshot in Fig. 9.

Here, the user is shown a table with information on each word found from their set of search terms: which category the model predicts based on the training set, how accurately that word was for predicting tweets in the test set, and how many tweets contain the word ('targeted') in the test set.

In this particular case, we see that the word 'billionaire' is the most predictive term: based on the training set, the model predicts that a tweet containing 'billionaire' is written by Bernie Sanders, and this was the case in every single one of the 54 tweets containing this word in the test set. Finally, each search term earns a score. This provides a "gamified" element of NLP4All that can be ignored, but that has been found to be motivating and fun to many students. Students can iterative improve their models by adding or removing search

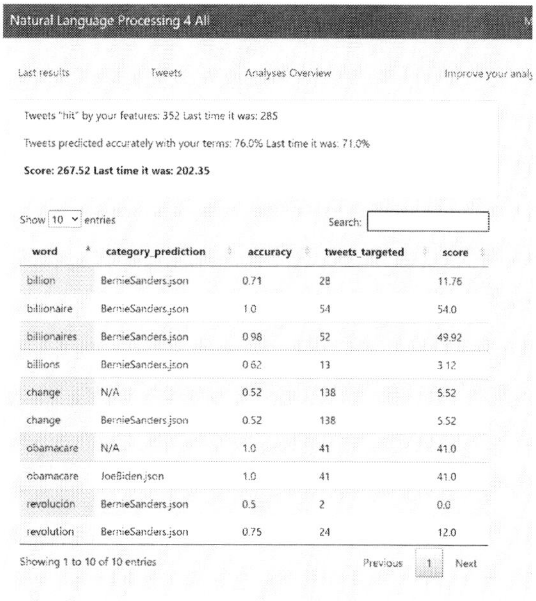

Figure 9: Feedback on model performance

terms, and running these analyses until they are happy with the terms they have found.

NLP4All users can also view confusion matrices for any of their trained models, as illustrated in Fig. 10.

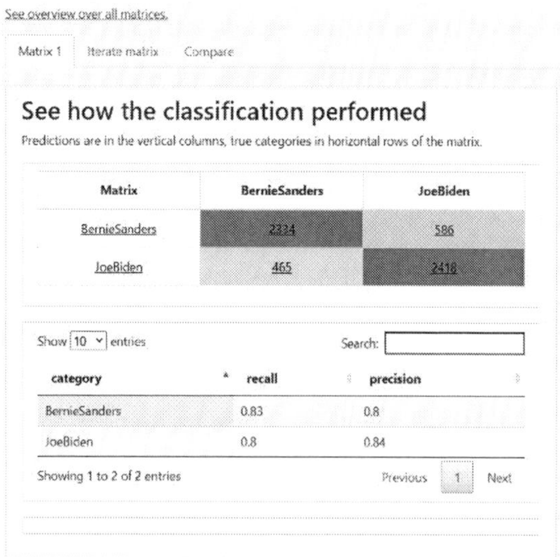

Figure 10: Viewing a confusion matrix

5 NLP4All in the classroom: Case studies

5.1 Introducing text classification to MA students in the Humanities

Recent revisions to the national study regulations for humanities students in Denmark place an emphasis on digitization and digital literacy. This poses a challenge, however, as students in these programs typically have little background or interest in math, statistics, or programming and some lack even basic computer skills.

Working with a faculty member in at a major Danish university, we developed a classroom module on Classification as part of a introductory course on Computational Linguistics. The students in the class were second semester masters students in Linguistics and Cognitive Semiotics. Only one out of 22 students had any background in programming, and none had taken a specialization in math or science in high school. Student prepared for the two-week module by reading an introductory textbook chapter on Document Classification (Dickinson et al., 2012).

In a post-classroom evaluation of students (n=20), 100% agreed that 'the in-class exercises using NLP4All were effective for learning' and that the exercises 'improved my understanding of text classification'. In additional comments, several students reported that they enjoyed the gamified and competitive aspect of NLP4All, while others mentioned that they liked the opportunity to work with real-world social media data.

5.2 Facilitating social studies discussion in a Danish high school

We tested NLP4All in a Social Studies high school classroom. In collaboration with a social studies teacher, we developed a 6-hour learning unit on language, ideology and political parties. The unit was designed to address one of learning goals of our national learning standards, specifying that students should learn about the different policy positions of political parties (we have 13 in our national parliament.) In other words, the purpose was not to teach NLP, but to teach with NLP, and to offer NLP-methods as a way of analyzing larger amounts of text than is otherwise possible.

24 2nd year (sophomore) Danish high school students participated, with roughly equal numbers of girls and boys. In a survey sent out to students prior to our test, none of these students self-reported as having any programming experience, and 20 out of

24 reported no or low interest in computer science or machine learning. All had self-selected into "A-level" Social Studies, a 3-year elective class. About one third of students had immigrant backgrounds, slightly above the national average.

The teacher and students used NLP4All to discuss tweets from pairs of Danish political parties. First, students had to label tweets and a model to tell a socialist and a nationalist party apart. Then, students did the same with the same socialist party, and a libertarian party.

We cannot report on more concrete findings or analyses of learning data at present, as these results are currently under review at another venue. However, in evaluations the students reported enjoying being able to provide concrete evidence for their analyses. To them, purely qualitative analyses sometimes feel fluffy, but by showing that their analyses were backed up by hundreds or thousands of tweets made them feel more comfortable making claims during classroom discussions.

6 Comparison to Prior Work

We have found two systems that are similar to NLP4All in certain ways, though also different in others. GATE (Cunningham, 2002) is a combined Java API and graphical interface that makes it easy to create NLP pipelines without writing all code from scratch. While it was originally made for researchers, it has also been used in teaching contexts (Bontcheva et al., 2002) because it makes it easy for novice programmers to implement more sophisticated NLP methods than they could do on their own. However, presumably because GATE was made for researchers, it is not made for classroom contexts, and does not offer interfaces on data that would be useful for teachers during the teaching situation. Light et al. (2005) present a web interface that lets novices process text with common models and methods like NLTK's PoS tagger and grammar parser. The web interface lets novices combine these models when processing text and visualizes output. However, similar to GATE, this interface does not provide views on data that are relevant to the teaching context. Additionally, the modules are black boxed to the students and do not provide any information on how the models work, how they are trained, or how they make predictions.

7 Conclusion

At present, NLP4All provides support for teaching the following technical topics, without requiring any programming on the part of teachers or students:

- Classification algorithms
  - Naive Bayes
  - Logistic regression
- Feature selection
- Supervised machine learning, test and train sets
- Model evaluation
  - Precision, recall, f-measure
  - Confusion matrices

With a grant received in Spring 2021, the platform will be extended to support new learning modules on tf-idf, vector-based representations of texts, topic modeling, and word embeddings.

References

Kalina Bontcheva, Hamish Cunningham, Valentin Tablan, Diana Maynard, and Oana Hamza. 2002. Using GATE as an Environment for Teaching NLP. In *Proceedings of the ACL-02 Workshop on Effective tools and methodologies for teaching natural language processing and computational linguistics*, pages 54–62.

Hamish Cunningham. 2002. GATE: A framework and graphical development environment for robust NLP tools and applications. In *Proc. 40th annual meeting of the association for computational linguistics (ACL 2002)*, pages 168–175.

Markus Dickinson, Chris Brew, and Detmar Meurers. 2012. *Language and computers*. John Wiley & Sons.

David Gunning. 2017. Explainable artificial intelligence (xai). *Defense Advanced Research Projects Agency (DARPA), nd Web*, 2(2).

Marc Light, Robert Arens, and Xin Lu. 2005. Web-based interfaces for natural language processing tools. In *Proceedings of the Second ACL Workshop on Effective Tools and Methodologies for Teaching NLP and CL*, pages 28–31.

A New Broad NLP Training from Speech to Knowledge

Maxime Amblard and **Miguel Couceiro**
LORIA, UMR 7503, Université de Lorraine, Inria and CNRS
{maxime.amblard, miguel.couceiro}@univ-lorraine.fr

Abstract

In 2018, the Master Sc. in NLP[1] opened at the IDMC[2], Université de Lorraine - Nancy, France. Far from being a creation ex-nihilo, it is the product of a history and many reflections on the field and its teaching. This article proposes epistemological and critical elements on the opening and maintainance of this so far new master's program in NLP.

1 Introduction

This article discusses the epistemological background of the creation of the Master of Science program in natural language processing (NLP) at the University of Lorraine in 2018. It puts forward a critical analysis of the environment, of the methodology chosen to produce this program, and it highlights the salient elements for the teaching of NLP.

Currently, the master's degree is taught at the IDMC of the University de Lorraine. It is accessible to students trained within the undergraduate program of the institute or to students that successfully apply to the program. A jury from the pedagogical team evaluates the adequacy of the candidates' profile with the requirements and expectations of the training. For the detailed description of the master's degree in NLP, please visit our dedicated website[3].

We propose a singular training at the French level, and probably at the international level. It is a Master's degree that gives the tools and methods to carry out language data processing. If NLP is at the heart of the training, we have opened up to speech and knowledge processing. The objective is to train tomorrow's professionals in both the economic and academic fields for language data processing.

[1]Natural Language Processing

[2]Institut des Sciences du Digital, du Management et de la Cognition https://idmc.univ-lorraine.fr/

[3]https://idmc.univ-lorraine.fr/idmc-master-degree-in-natural-language-processing/

In this article we present the Master's degree in NLP at the IDMC. We start by reviewing the historical background that is important to the current NLP Master's program, before presenting the approach explaining the constitution of the program. We will then return to the program itself and discuss some structural aspects. Finally, we put forward some elements of analysis.

2 History

The Department of Mathematics and Computer Science at the University of Nancy 2 pursued a policy of opening up both of these disciplines to human and social sciences. At the beginning of the 2000s, the department proposed a training program based on these aspects by integrating economics and business management. Following this interdisciplinary view, the pedagogical team created a bachelor's degree program in cognitive sciences. Several thematic openings were made, in particular, towards psychology, biology, linguistics and neurosciences. The dynamics was successful and paved the way to the opening of a complete master's program in Cognitive Sciences (two years). The core of the training has clearly been cognitive sciences.

2.1 Research environment

The French higher education and research implies that research and teaching are carried out in different components. Thus, the teachers carry out their research in a different research laboratory. In Nancy (France), two laboratories are particularly concerned: LORIA[4] and ATILF[5]. These two laboratories are mixed research units, i.e., university laboratories co-accredited by a research center. This co-accreditation makes it possible to integrate staff who only have research duties. It appears as a quality label for the research carried out. ATILF

[4]https://www.loria.fr/en/

[5]https://www.atilf.fr//

Proceedings of the Fifth Workshop on Teaching NLP, pages 34–45
June 10–11, 2021. ©2021 Association for Computational Linguistics

is co-accredited by the CNRS[6], and LORIA is co-accredited by the CNRS and Inria[7]. The two laboratories ensure a sustained research activity in the field in Nancy. ATILF is organized with three themes: lexicons; corpora and knowledge; and dynamic aspects of language. Atilf is known for the *Trésor de la Langue Française Informatisé*, a large online dictionary of French.

Research in computer science is carried out jointly by LORIA and the Inria Nancy Grand-Est center. Beyond institutional issues, the researchers work jointly on all computer science domains. In particular, LORIA is organised into research departments, one of which is the largest and entirely devoted to NLP research. The department gathers about fifty permanent staff members in eight teams of different sizes (Cello, Team K, Multispeech, Orpailleur, Read, SMarT, Sémagramme, Synalp).

2.2 Creation of a training program in NLP

The dynamics of the teaching of mathematics and computer science open to other disciplines, and the strong research activity in Nancy have proven to be a favorable ground for the creation of a training program in NLP. In the early 2000s, the Master's degree in Cognitive Science integrated language-related issues into some of its courses. A DESS, an applied training program at the master's level, was also opened for a few years under the direction of Fiammetta Nammer and Yannick Toussaint. However, as the people in charge were not in the teaching component and the theme was not yet explicitly recognized by the French industry, this attempt had to be stopped quickly. It nevertheless established the possibility of developing a curriculum in NLP.

It was in 2005 that the main turning point took place. At that time, the dynamic was set up, embodied by Patrick Blackburn and Guy Perrier. The latter was a university professor in computer science and set up a training program integrating students from computer science programs with linguistics programs within the Master's degree in Cognitive Science. During this time, Patrick Blackburn was working on the creation of the Erasmus Mundus Language and Communication Technologies consortium, of which Nancy would be the french partner.

The Erasmus Mundus master's program on Language and Communication Technologies[8] is a joint master's program between seven European Universities. This is an excellence program supported by European Union, which offers appealing grants to students each year. The recipients are selected at the international level and based on selection criteria[9] that take into account the qualitiy of their trainning and their motivation. Some students integrate the program as self-funded. Each student of the program spends a full year in two partner university of the consortium. They also share activities and events all together during the year.

In 2009, Maxime Amblard took over the responsibility of the Master's program on Cognitive Sciences (SC), institutionalizing the existence of the NLP theme in the university. From that moment on, he has been in charge of the NLP theme, first as head of the SC Master's program from 2009 to 2012[10], and then as head of the M2 TAL[11] speciality from 2010 to 2012 and from 2015 to 2018. He carried out two years of sabatical leave[12] fully dedicated to research. He was then the project leader for the creation of the Master's program in NLP that was opened in 2018. He was the creator and organizor of the teaching from 2009 to today, both in Cognitive Sciences and in NLP. The responsibilities of 2nd year of the NLP program were assumed by Fabienne Venant in 2009-2010, Laure Buhry in 2013-14, then Miguel Couceiro from 2018. The coordination of the Erasmus Mundus LCT at the Université de Lorraine has been carried out by Miguel Couceiro since 2015.

2.3 Other contextual elements

In addition to the synergy between the cognitive science and NLP courses, it is worth noting the presence of other important training factors. On the one hand, there is a Master's degree in Language Sciences as well as a second Erasmus Mundu program specialized in Lexicology: EMLEX[13]. This program works very differently because the classes share semesters together on a given campus. The students are therefore not systematically present in Nancy. In all cases, they are also international students selected for their results and motivation.

[6]Centre National pour la Recherche Scientifique https://www.cnrs.fr/

[7]Institut National de la Recherche en Informatique et Automatique https://inria.fr/

[8]https://lct-master.org/

[9]See https://lct-master.org/

[10]The responsibility of the SC master has since been assumed by Manuel Rebuschi

[11]"Traitement automatique des langues" that then became NLP.

[12]*délégation*

[13]https://www.emlex.phil.fau.eu/

In addition, the Université de Lorraine integrates engineering schools into its structure. In particular, the Ecole des Mines de Nancy. This engineering training is recognized as being of high quality in France. However, students from this type of training rarely go on to complete a PhD, despite their qualities. For those who are interested in this type of opening, it is traditional to offer double courses with Master's programs. Thus we have set up an exchange protocol that allows students from the Ecole des Mines to join the Master's program during the last year of the program.

All these elements made the Université de Lorraine a suitable environment for developing the master's program in NLP.

3 Definition of the NLP program

The first question is to decide to whom the program is intended. To do this we went back to the ambition we wanted to give to the program. Once the objective was clarified, we were able to work on defining the content of the program.

3.1 Program's objectives

The first observation made in 2016 was that there was an effective increase in the need for NLP, both for industrial issues and for the development of research. At that time, a very strong dynamic was already in place, driven by AI and deep learning.

We realized that the training we had developed until then was attached to a more traditional definition of NLP, rooted in computer science and linguistics. Its objectives being mainly to accompany students towards research, this was not very surprising, but it proved to be out of step with scientific and societal evolutions.

The project took shape in the idea of considering that students should leave the Master's program for industry as much as for research. We already considered that a significant part of the companies concerned were also concerned with research issues. This shift towards more applicative issues also seemed necessary to us to be able to integrate more students into the training.

Moreover, our experience with the second year of the Master's program showed us that the students who successfully completed the program could have very heterogeneous profiles. The challenge for us was more to define the type of profile that we wanted to find at the end of the training and to propose paths to bring the students there. This being the case, in view of the size of the classes, it was not possible to multiply the paths and above all, it seemed important to us that the profiles be built in interaction with each other. To achieve this, we need to have a precise vision of the type of training we can accept.

We have therefore chosen to build a training program centered on computer science and mathematics for the NLP that is as open to research issues as it is to applications.

3.2 Methodology

To build the program, a project manager was appointed in 2015 by the teaching component in the person of Maxime Amblard with the task of designing a project to be presented to the university in June 2016. Some examples were used, such as (Bender et al., 2008).

The project manager made the choice to start from scratch, considering that the contents present at that time needed to be renovated. He set up a working group gathering members of the LORIA and ATILF teams working on language data who wanted to invest in the new training. The aim was to integrate new colleagues, new views and possibly new themes/issues.

A shared space was set up online allowing all parties to access the working material as it became available. The working group started with 13 people and ended up with 25 people. It was decided to meet the equivalent of once a month until July 2026. After each meeting, the leader wrote a report that was sent to all members, as well as a doodle to choose the date of the next meeting and the agenda of this meeting. The participants thus had the agenda well in advance, which allowed them to prepare the meeting as well as possible or to send their points of view and their work in case of absence. This methodology ensured that no information was lost and that the work dynamic was maintained throughout the year. In addition, meeting times were strictly adhered to. In the end, this procedure worked well in a complicated context. All the proposals made were heard and discussed. Some less committed participants naturally withdrew from the project. The vast majority of the participants stayed until the end and others were really committed to the project. We did not need to change the methodology during the process. The most difficult element to manage was to maintain a focus with the group and synthesize all the proposals as we went along. We return to the major orientations in the following section.

Higher education and research are undergoing numerous transformations. This is obviously the case in France. In particular, at that time, major programs were being launched and it was important to position training in this ecosystem. In the end, we quickly dismissed this issue, considering that the constitution of a scientifically solid program would always be easier to defend.

After several discussion sessions, we came to some important conclusions:

- the environment has many competences as well in data processing as in linguistics, which moreover with habits of work in common;
- the Erasmus Mundus LCT obliged us to teach in English, which is not always easy in France, but this should be a strength for the recruitment of international students;
- we had a scientific positioning neither in computer science nor in linguistics, clearly based on mathematics and computer science;
- it is now possible to award a French diploma in NLP;
- the needs in both the industrial and the academic worlds are important.

We have also considered two hypotheses on the organization of the training: the non-opening of the training to distance learning because it requires another type of organization that we cannot propose for now, and the possibility of carrying out the training in alternation. This program is a French specificity which allows students to study while being employed by a company. Thus, the training alternates (in the literal sense) periods of training at the institute and periods of work in a company.

One important aspect is to have concluded that if we have many strengths in the field of NLP, we have the specificity of covering a wider field of language data processing. If we are not the only ones in France, we wanted to make a specificity of our mathematic and computer science positioning in the field of language data processing. We have therefore decided to offer a curriculum entitled "Computer Science, Speech, Text and Knowledge". Thus, the new program deals with speech processing, NLP and knowledge. It is obvious that the reconciliation of formal and statistics tools operated in the last ten years facilitates this closeness.

3.3 Broad Program Directions

We have therefore chosen to integrate students whose initial training is either in computer science or linguistics, with an appetite for formalization, programming and mathematics. A single pathway is proposed through the training that brings together these different profiles. The objective is to bring all students to the same exit point. Beyond this declaration of intent, it is obvious that we cannot transform in two years linguists who have never done programming into operational computer scientists, just as we cannot transform computer scientists into linguists in the same time. On the other hand, students must be comfortable enough to overcome the paralysis of working in a new field, to go beyond naive approaches and above all to be able to discuss the different aspects precisely with specialists in the other field. To achieve this, there is nothing better than to mix these profiles throughout the training.

This mixing adds entropy to the construction of individual paths. To compensate for this, we have proposed a very legible and regular architecture in the training. This apparently very rigid organization allows students to build their path together.

Moreover, as we have already mentioned, the aim is to offer a course with a strong research component, while at the same time offering numerous applications.

It was therefore decided that the first year would serve as a substrate to establish the background by opening up to long-term prospects. The second year would focus on NLP topics, with many more applications and especially a significant amount of time devoted to an internship either in a laboratory or in a company. The training is given over two years, i.e. 4 semesters:

- two semesters of the first year of 260 effective teaching hours each - 30 credits each
- one long semester of the second year of 350 effective hours of teaching each - 30 credits
- one internship of at least 5 months (one semester) - 30 credits

The architecture of each of the three semesters is the same with 5 teaching units of equal importance in the validation of the training. The organization of studies in France implies that each semester validates 30 credits (ECTS).

3.4 Renewal of Teaching Practices

As we have already mentioned, we did not want to transform our teaching practices by switching to distance learning, especially because we thought it was important to have different profiles working together. It is difficult to measure this at a distance.

However, we questioned these practices to propose more applied teaching or with effective data manipulation, as well as the implementation of group work, in particular in the form of projects.

Concerning the discovery of research, we propose a project in groups of 2 to 4 students, called "supervised project". This is a project carried out during the first year, at the initiative of a researcher, and which leads to the writing of two reports. The first part of the year is a bibliographic work. It consists of taking the time to read and understand scientific articles on the state of the art and to put them in perspective with the proposed project. The work is synthesized in a bibliographic report which opens to the second part of the work which is a more classical realization part. The students produce a report, which is a first experience of long writing before their final report of master, as well as a defense of 20 minutes in front of a jury and the presentation of a poster. The objective is to have them carry out a research project over a long period of time, with links to the literature on the one hand and actual achievements on the other, and also to master the codes of scientific presentation. This work often leads to publications in international conference workshops.

As an example, here are some titles of projects carried out in recent years on different themes: Speaker Adaptation Techniques for Automatic Speech Recognition, Testing Greenberg's Linguistic Universals on the Universal Dependencies Corpora using a Graph Rewriting tool, Does my question answer your answer, Anomaly detection with deep learning models, ...

The counterpart of this work is the realization of an applied group project throughout the first semester of the second year of the program. It is carried out by groups of 3 to 4 students. The initiative is left to the students, who are nevertheless supervised by two teachers. Once the application is identified, the students implement the concepts they have encountered in their training to produce an application. The functional and deployable applications are put online to showcase the work done. The students also produce a report explaining their approach and their achievement, and they make a defense. Here some examples of realization subjects:

- GECko+ is built on top of two Artificial Intelligence models in order to correct spelling and grammar mistakes, and tackling discourse fallacies with BERT (Devlin et al., 2018).
- Askme is a Question Answering model built on the Stanford Question Answering Dataset (SQuAD) with a fine-tuned BERT. Askme is able to automatically answer factual questions without being aware of the context.
- IGrander Essay: Automated Essay Grading systems provide an easy and time-efficient solution to essay scoring.
- Multilingual multispeaker expressive Text-to-speech system: The main goal of this work is from text input to be able to generate speech with expressivity for multiple languages, which are currently French and English, with an end-to-end multilingual text-to-speech (TTS) system.

The first experiences have shown that both formats are very formative. It is common for groups of students to go from very enthusiastic to overwhelmed phases. Thanks to the mentoring process, all projects are completed by the end of the semester. In both cases, although very different from each other, the situation allows them to better understand where the interests of NLP are and especially where the difficulties are. Working over a long period of time shows them the importance of anticipating problems in both research and development. We make sure that the groups are mixed in terms of profiles to avoid the pitfall of groups stuck on IT developments, as well as groups missing out on linguistic issues. We note that an additional exercise is paper writing in the format of the main conferences in the field.

3.5 Support for internationalization

As part of the development of French universities, the gouvernment has set up the development of major projects, under the name Project Investment of the Future (PIA). The Université de Lorraine benefits from a major project of this type called Lorraine University of Excellence (LUE). This project covers several themes around systems engineering. The training program has benefited from financial support from this program to support internationalization. For this purpose, we are translating the presentation documents into several languages, in particular into Russian, Persian, Greek and Turkish. The objective is to accompany as effectively as possible the arrival of students in the training.

In addition, we have made a promotional film for international students to highlight the necessary complementarity between computer science and linguistics that is achieved within our training. The production was made in a professional way by relying on the students and their profile. Once again, the aim is to highlight the diversity and quality of the students' profiles.

4 Program Design

4.1 Education

We do not want to propose an advertising brochure of the training, also we do not give explicitly the titles of each teaching sub-unit. This being said, the training is thought to put forward continuum between the semesters, as much as possible on the whole training, at least between the semesters. It is this dynamic that we put forward. We invite the readers to refer to the descriptions of the training for more details. We have the three semesters with regular teaching. Units of the first semester are numbered 70X, ones of the second semester with 80X and those of the last semester with 90X, where X takes its value in $\{1, 2, 3, 4, 5\}$. In each semester, the students follow all the units. For now, the programm has no optional course.

The **first units** described in Table 1 gather the fundamental background in mathematics and computer science. For these units, the continuum is natural: on one side probabilities and statistics - machine learning - neural networks, and on the other one programming - semantic web - data mining/recommendation.

The **second units**, see Table 2, gathers the teachings around corpora and formal tools[14].

The **third units**, see Table 3 gathers the teaching on software engineering and data sciences.

The linguistics units are the one ending by 4, see Table 4.

Finally, the **fifth units**, see Table 5, is the project-based teaching that we have detailed above, to which we add language teaching (French for non-French speakers, English for the others). In the second year, we add opening lessons, in particular around ethical issues.

Students are evaluated on the acquisition of targeted skills, identified for the Sc. Master.

To compensate for the differences in levels, the technical courses of the first semester are accompanied by a refresher course. After several years of courses, we notice that the difference in level is not caught up between the different audiences. We have decided to change the organization of some courses as of the next academic year. For example, for Python programming, two courses will be offered, one for beginners and an advanced course, shared with cognitive science students.

The teachers are free to choose the teaching methods they follow, within the general perspective of the program. We clearly share the objectives for the end of the program where students are autonomous in dealing with the scientific literature and in participating to produce new results.

4.2 Example of a course

It is obviously not possible to describe the all courses of the training and it is not the object of this article. We want to highlight one course in particular which allows us to put forward the principle of training by project by mixing profiles.

This is **Methods4NLP** given in unit 704. It is one of the very first courses introducing NLP to students. The teaching is divided into several sequences: a first one allowing to set up a common culture around NLP, a second academic one presenting the basic formalizations that they will develop throughout the two years of training, and the setting up of a project.

The first phase can be divided into three parts:

- a seminar to set the spectrum of NLP, from linguistic aspects to technical developments. This teaching allows to give a common culture to the students at the beginning of the program by positioning NLP in relation to the challenges of AI.

- apprehension of the concepts by experimentation with unplugged activities (Bell et al., 2009)(Romero et al., 2018): one simulating machine learning with a machine playing Nim's game, the other on Huffman coding with groundhogs. The students meet the two paradigms of NLP in an intuitive way.

[14]For units two and three in the second year, we make sure to offer state of the art teaching applied to language data.

701	Probabilities, Statistics and Algorithms for AI: The course deals with fundamental mathematical tools, particularly statistical and algorithmic tools, which are necessary to define and resolve an artificial intelligence problem. The course unit stresses a case study approach in order to ensure the acquisition of theoretical aspects and practical application (Elementary mathematics tools, propabilities and statistics; and Python programming, both for beginners and advanced users)
801	Machine Learning and Semantic Web: This course takes on the fundamental principles of Machine Learning, of data mining and knowledge extraction. All the notions are illustrated through practical applications on real data (Machine learning theory and Web Semantics)
901	Deep Learning and Data Mining: The objective of this course unit is to acquire machine learning tools, mainly deep neural networks and factorisation matrices, to be able to manipulate these tools when considering practical applications (tweets, traces of e-learning), as well as to expand the students' knowledge in semantic web and the extensions of analysis of formal concepts for textual and relational data processing (Neural Networks, Deep Neural Networks; Data mining (structured data and text); and Collaborative filtering)

Table 1: Description of the teaching units of block 1

702	Design and Acquisition of corpus: This course aims to introduce techniques of construction, structuring, annotating and archival of textual oral or multimodal corpora, which play an essential role in the analysis of the structure of spoken and written language, and on the other hand in the training and evaluation of NLP algorithms. This subject is complex as it is necessary that (1) the corpora be restricted to a reasonable size in order to guarantee the proper collection of corresponding data and that (2) this data sufficiently represents the phenomena studied (Written Corpora; and Spoken Corpora).
802	Formal Tools: This course unit is dedicate to the introduction to theoretical frameworks and logic used in symbolic approaches to the modeling of language. It consists of mathematical logic and of formal languages. The objective is to familiarize the students with these formal models, their properties, the demonstration techniques associated with them, and the notions of calculability and complexity.
902	Text and Speech Processing: Automatic processing of texts and speeches involves different methods of machine learning. This class will introduce these methods and illustrate their use through examples and practical application using tools developed (Speech processing, Processing Textual Data, Terminology and ontology).

Table 2: Description of the teaching units of block 2

703	Software Engineering: Collection, analysis and formalization of customers' needs (Software design and; Functional analysis; specifications; and Project management)
803	Data Science: This course unit introduces fundamental techniques for the extraction, storage, cleaning, visualisation and analysis of data. We give a practical introduction to the tools and software libraries which allows the processing of data. We combine theoretical sessions with programming exercises which allows students to put into practice the software and concepts taught during the course.
903	Natural Language and Discourse: This course unit gathers courses which deal with discursive and semantic processing of language (Application to texts; Computational semantics; and Discourse and Dialog modelling)

Table 3: Description of the teaching units of block 3

704	Linguistics for NLP-1: This course takes on one hand the fundamental elements of NLP and on the other hand the phonological and morphological elements, which are studied through a language sciences based approach (Methods for Natural Language Processing; Phonology; and Morphology)
804	Linguistics for NLP-2: This course takes up where the previous teachings of linguistics left off, wherein the content and methodologies of the courses are, however, independent from these prior teachings. The courses are concentrated on syntax and semantics, as well as lexicology. In this context, the focus is put on the question of formalisation of linguistic rules (Lexicology: lexical units and phraseology; Syntax; and Semantics)
904	Lexicon and Grammars for NLP: This course introduces advanced tools for the computational modeling of different types of linguistic information which describe lexical units (lexical resources) or the rules of organisation of larger units (grammar) (Diachronic and synchronic lexicology; Lexical resources; and Syntactic framework)

Table 4: Description of the teaching units of block 4

705	This course unit is composed of the first part of the year-long supervised project (which will be finalized in the second semester), as well as language classes. The project consists of group work (in pairs), which is supervised by researchers, in which the students will carry out the bibliographic part of the final report. Language classes will allow non-anglophone students to become more familiar with scientific english, the language in which all courses are conducted, whereas the french classes will facilitate non-francophone students' social and cultural integration. The course allows students to test their first skills acquired during the semester while synthesizing the different research issues concerned by a more open research topic. Students are evaluated on the acquisition of targeted skills, identified for the Sc. Master.
805	This course unit is made up of language classes as well as the second part of the year-long supervised project (UE 705) which is finalized during the second semester. The second part of the year-long project begins by following through with the procedure introduced in the first semester groupwork, and leads up to the presentation at the end of the year, explaining the implementation of the project, which puts to test all of the skills the student acquires during the first year of the program. The language classes allow students to become more comfortable with the knowledge of scientific english.
905	Projects and Foreign Language: This course unit gathers many teaching including the project and language classes (Software project; Law and ethics; Research methods; Professional integration; Foreign language courses (French or English))

Table 5: Description of the teaching units of block 5

- first experiments to highlight the possibility of getting results with few developments with two labs: one on FastText (Bojanowski et al., 2016)(Joulin et al., 2016) and the one on Scikit Learn (Pedregosa et al., 2011), are proposed. The objective is to make all students aware of the ease of manipulating data without understanding what is behind it, and the difficulty of confronting how to improve the results.

The second phase is carried out in two parallel parts: project and lectures.

For the project part, the students form groups of 4 in a balanced way between the profiles. It is requested that the students of the same nationality do not stay together and especially that all the groups have explicit different profiles (linguist and computer scientist). The groups choose the subject of their development. They are only required to explicitly include NLP aspects in their project (POS tagging, Named Entity recognition, Machine learning, etc.).

This project is shared with another course that deals with written corpora. For this course, the project must contain the constitution of a corpus, its normalization, as much as possible its annotation with study of the quality of the annotation, and thus implementation in a defined context. Thus, the themes of the projects are more naturally related to NLP than to speech processing, or even to knowledge processing.

For information, here are a few topics chosen by the students: Gender bias in young targeted literature: 19th century vs. early 21st century, Author Identification for Philosophers, Song Lyrics Generator, Autonomous Vocabulary Assistant, ...

It is interesting to let the students choose a topic that interests them. Sometimes we see students with very specific subjects, letting them work on them allows us to build on their engagement. If the subject is not relevant, it allows us to put them back into a more appropriate training perspective. There is no such thing as a bad topic. The different topics make students aware of the difference between the desire to achieve a development and the possibility of achieving it. In general, we see that some groups prefer to stay close to a very classical topic and often regret not having explored more diversity of topics. Moreover, a recurrent element appears on the question of the evaluation of development. This practice makes them aware of the significance of anticipating the implementation of the evaluation in order to measure the quality of the final project.

Students are monitored weekly. They have to make a 1 minute presentation of the progress of their developments in front of the whole class. They may not have made any progress, what is important is that all students follow the progress of all groups. During the Covid-19 period, the follow-up was done by video-conference and it was difficult to share this experience with the whole class. During the semester, students submit 3 progress reports, the first ones being only a few pages long. They are used to document problems, issues and progress. The final report is due before the exam period during which a defense is organized.

Finally, the last part consists of more academic teaching that takes up the two main paradigms of NLP and defines them explicitly (Agarwal, 2013). The first part deals with out-of-context grammars and automata. These concepts are often known by students more or less well. This allows on the one hand to bring everyone up to speed and on the other hand to show how basic concepts in computer science find links with linguistics. This is done by looking at Turing's work on abstract machines, or through Chomsky's hierarchy. Then the course highlights the use of statistical techniques by explaining Bayes' models and automatic classification as done by Jurafsky (Jurafsky and Martin, 2018). Finally, the last part explains dynamic programming by focusing on the syntax with the algorithm of CKY (Kozen, 1977). This part of the course is carried out in a traditional way with plenary teaching and tutorials.

This course is the course which launches the training. Indeed, if it begins with a phase requiring little knowledge a priori, it continues with a phase that requires the mobilization of technical knowledge delivered in the other courses, as well as linguistic knowledge. The fact of leaving the choice of the theme allows to motivate the students, while showing them the need to be autonomous and proactive in the training. In addition, a very traditional part of the course allows students to establish common ground by building epistemological bridges between computer science and linguistics.

5 Analysis of student profiles

After having presented the structure, the organization and the stakes of the training, we propose to come back on quantitative elements concerning the

	# applicants.	# students	Comp.	Mixed	ling	Fr	Eu	non-EU
2015-16 M2	35	17	41	24	35	24	12	65
2016-17 M2	20	6	67	17	17	67	0	33
2017-18 M2	33	17	47	18	29	41	0	59
Mean	29,33	13,33	51,66	19,66	27	44	4	52,33
2018-19 M1	47	16	25	38	38	50	13	38
M2	21	7	57	29	14	29	14	57
2019-20 M1	65	20	30	25	45	35	30	35
M2	32	20	45	20	35	30	0	70
2020-21 M1	117	33	45	18	36	36	12	52
M2	33	27	48	19	33	26	15	59
Mean M1	76,33	23	33,33	27	39,66	40,33	18,33	41,66
Mean M2	28,66	18	50	22,66	27,33	28,33	9,66	62
Mean	52,5	20,5	41,66	24,83	33,5	34,33	14	51,83

Table 6: Distribution of students in the training over the last 6 years: number of candidates, number of students, then distribution of students in percentage (%) between the 3 profiles (CS, mixed and L), then according to their nationality (France, Europe and non-EU).

disciplinary profile of the students, the diversity of their origin and their success. In order to give a little more perspective to these elements, we rely on the data of the Master's since 2018, that is to say 3 academic years, as well as on the M2 TAL speciality over the 3 previous years.

Before the definition of the program, we had made a study on the 2008-2017 classes. We noted that 36% of the students were French, 45% from another European country and 19% from a non-European country, which is proof of a good diversity of origin. Of those who continued their studies after the course, 40% joined a company, 33% were doing a thesis and 27% had an academic post.

Table 6 presents the evolution of the number of candidates and students in the training before the creation of the Master (3 years) and for the first 3 years of the training. It also contains the distribution of students according to the profiles (Fosler-Lussier, 2008): computer science, mixed or linguistics. Figure 1a shows the evolution of the data over time. We observe that the distribution is homogeneous over the different years of training, with an average of 41.6% computer scientists over the first three years of the Master's program for 33.5% linguists. This good distribution makes it possible to build balanced work groups. Moreover, we observe that the opening as a Master has significantly increased the average number of this profile from 27 to 33.5. This implies reinforcing the course for this type of profile and increasing the means implemented on their programming skills.

Another interesting element that appears in this table, put foward in Figure 1b, is the increase in the number of candidates, with 117 candidates for the M1 year in 2020-21. It should be noted that this number of applicants does not include students trained within the IDMC or Erasmus Mundus LCT students who are selected through another process. For M2 students, only a few students are selected, the majority coming from the first year of training. Our experience leads us to limit even more the number of students entering the second year directly, because on the one hand these students have gaps that they are unable to fill, and on the other hand they have difficulties integrating the class. These elements must of course be put into perspective because the effects of the health crisis must also be taken into account.

Finally, the other axis of analysis proposed is to look at the nationalities of the students. It can be seen that the average number of French students has decreased significantly, from 44% to 34.5%. This decrease did not affect the rate of oversea students, keeping their number slightly above 50.

Finally, an important element is to analyze the profiles at entry with the success at the end of the Master's degree. The first element is that the students who follow the two years of training have better results and rankings. This supports the idea that the training has singular characteristics that are difficult to catch up on. This is understandable because it is necessary to master concepts in computer science and linguistics, and moreover it is

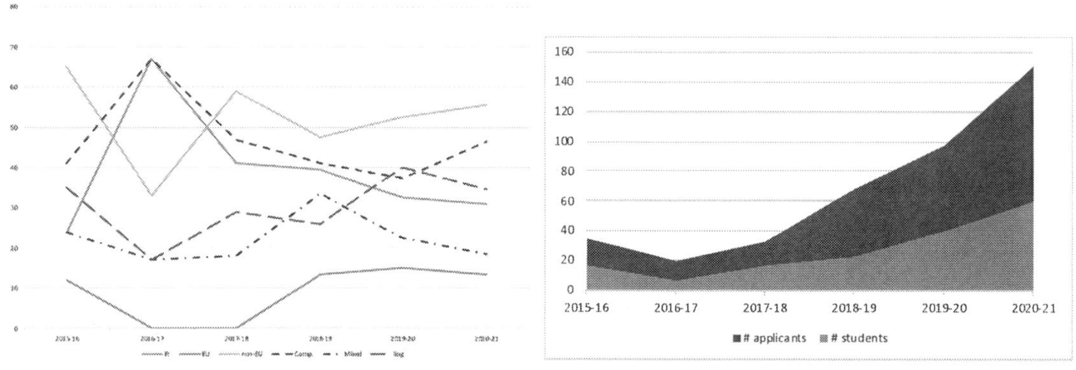

(a) Origin and background of the students.

(b) Number of applicants and students.

Figure 1: Data of the program from 2015 to 2020.

necessary to master the tools and methods of AI, which are specific and rather abstract.

One should not believe that a profile at the entrance would be privileged in this type of training. The ringleader or the first ones of the promotions do not have *a priori* determined profiles. They may come from traditional computer science or linguistics. What seems to make the difference is, in addition to their aptitude at entry, their investment in the training throughout the two years. This reassures us that the aim is to bring together the profiles, while respecting their original specificities.

6 Conclusion and perspectives

We highlighted the process of creating the Master's degree in NLP at the IDMC. This training is unique in that it delivers a French diploma in NLP. Students who enter the program have a background either in computer science or in linguistics. The training aims to give them strong skills to train future professionals in language data processing.

We have integrated collaborations with several components in our environment (Erasmus Mundus LCT, EMLEX, Ecole des Mines, etc.). The training is attractive and has good results. Students trained in this way are currently making choices between different possible careers, rather than being affected by the economic and sanitary situation due to the health crisis, that impacted negatively the job market.

Over the different years observed, we noticed that the number of internship proposals on the one hand and the number of job offers on the other hand, are constantly increasing. We see the search for profiles explicitly in NLP. Moreover, our opening towards more applied profiles has not been at the expense of the relationship with the academic world. Out of the first class that followed the 2 years of the training, 7 are pursuing a thesis which is very positive. These two dynamics reinforce our commitment to the development of the program.

Since the beginning of the program, we have asked for oral and written evaluations from the students on both the teaching and the organization of the training. This feedback has allowed us to improve the content while remaining within the same general framework. The integration of the students at the end of the training confirms us in the belief of the interest of the training that we have. The accreditation we have obtained is coming to an end and we must now prepare a proposal for a general evolution for 2023. The Master is now considered mature and can benefit from more autonomy.

For the future, we want to consolidate the training by slightly increasing the flow of students until we reach 40 students per year, especially with students from the European area. In addition, we are working on developing opportunities for research, which would allow us to offer training courses of very good quality towards PhD.

Acknowledgments

We truly want to thank the anonymous reviewers for their helpful comments and insights. This work was supported partly by the french PIA project "Lorraine Universite d'Excellence", reference ANR-15-IDEX-04-LUE.

References

Apoorv Agarwal. 2013. Teaching the basics of NLP and ML in an introductory course to information science. In *Proceedings of the Fourth Workshop on Teaching NLP and CL*, pages 77–84, Sofia, Bulgaria. Association for Computational Linguistics.

Tim Bell, Jason Alexander, Isaac Freeman, and Mick Grimley. 2009. Computer science unplugged: School students doing real computing without computers. *The New Zealand Journal of Applied Computing and Information Technology*, 13(1):20–29.

Emily M Bender, Fei Xia, and Erik Bansleben. 2008. Building a flexible, collaborative, intensive master's program in computational linguistics. In *Proceedings of the Third Workshop on Issues in Teaching Computational Linguistics*, pages 10–18.

Piotr Bojanowski, Edouard Grave, Armand Joulin, and Tomas Mikolov. 2016. Enriching word vectors with subword information. *arXiv preprint arXiv:1607.04606*.

Jacob Devlin, Ming-Wei Chang, Kenton Lee, and Kristina Toutanova. 2018. Bert: Pre-training of deep bidirectional transformers for language understanding. *arXiv preprint arXiv:1810.04805*.

Eric Fosler-Lussier. 2008. Strategies for teaching "mixed" computational linguistics classes. In *Proceedings of the Third Workshop on Issues in Teaching Computational Linguistics*, pages 36–44.

Armand Joulin, Edouard Grave, Piotr Bojanowski, and Tomas Mikolov. 2016. Bag of tricks for efficient text classification. *arXiv preprint arXiv:1607.01759*.

Daniel Jurafsky and James H Martin. 2018. Speech and language processing (draft). *Chapter A: Hidden Markov Models (Draft of September 11, 2018). Retrieved March*, 19:2019.

Dexter C Kozen. 1977. The cocke–kasami–younger algorithm. In *Automata and Computability*, pages 191–197. Springer.

F. Pedregosa, G. Varoquaux, A. Gramfort, V. Michel, B. Thirion, O. Grisel, M. Blondel, P. Prettenhofer, R. Weiss, V. Dubourg, J. Vanderplas, A. Passos, D. Cournapeau, M. Brucher, M. Perrot, and E. Duchesnay. 2011. Scikit-learn: Machine learning in Python. *Journal of Machine Learning Research*, 12:2825–2830.

Margarida Romero, Benjamin Lille, Thierry Viéville, Marie Duflot-Kremer, Cindy de Smet, and David Belhassein. 2018. Analyse comparative d'une activité d'apprentissage de la programmation en mode branché et débranché. In *Educode-Conférence internationale sur l'enseignement au numérique et par le numérique*.

Applied Language Technology: NLP for the Humanities

Tuomo Hiippala
Department of Languages, University of Helsinki
P.O. Box 24, Unioninkatu 40 B.
00014 University of Helsinki, Finland
tuomo.hiippala@helsinki.fi

Abstract

This contribution describes a two-course module that seeks to provide humanities majors with a basic understanding of language technology and its applications using Python. The learning materials consist of interactive Jupyter Notebooks and accompanying YouTube videos, which are openly available with a Creative Commons licence.

1 Introduction

Language technology is increasingly applied in the humanities (Hinrichs et al., 2019). This contribution describes a two-course module named *Applied Language Technology*, which seeks to provide humanities majors with a basic understanding of language technology and practical skills needed to apply language technology using Python. The module is intended to *empower* the students by showing that language technology is both accessible and applicable to research in the humanities.

2 Pedagogical Approach

The learning materials seek to address two major pedagogical challenges. The first challenge concerns terminology: in my experience, the greatest hurdle in teaching language technology to humanities majors is not 'technophobia' (Öhman, 2019, 480), but the technical jargon that acts as a gatekeeper to knowledge in the field (cf. Maton, 2014). This issue is fundamental to teaching students with no previous experience of programming. To exemplify, beginners in my class occasionally interpret the term 'code' in phrases such as "Write your code here" as a numerical code needed to unlock an exercise, as opposed to a command written in a programming language. For this reason, the learning materials introduce concepts in Python and language technology in layperson terms and gradually build up the vocabulary needed to advance beyond the learning materials.

The second challenge involves the diversity of the humanities, which covers a broad range of disciplines with different epistemological and methodological standpoints. This results in considerable differences in previous knowledge among the students: linguistics majors may be more likely to be exposed to computational methods and tools than their counterparts majoring in philosophy or art history. Some students may have taken an introductory course in Java or Python, whereas others have never used a command line interface before. To address this issue, the learning materials are based on Jupyter Notebooks, which provide an environment familiar to most students – a web browser – for interactive programming. The command line is used for interacting with GitHub, which is used to distribute the learning materials and exercises.

The module also emphasises peer and collaborative learning: 20% of the course grade is awarded for activity on the course discussion forum hosted on GitHub. All activity – both asking and answering questions – counts positively towards the final grade. This allows the students with previous knowledge to help onboard newcomers. According to student feedback, this also fosters a sense of community. The discussion forum is also used to discuss weekly readings, which focus on ethics (e.g. Hovy and Spruit, 2016; Bird, 2020) and the relationship between language technology and humanities (e.g. Kuhn, 2019; Nguyen et al., 2020). These discussions are guided by questions that encourage the students to draw on their disciplinary backgrounds, which exposes them to a wide range of perspectives to language technology and the humanities.

3 Learning Materials

The learning materials cover two seven-week courses.

The first course starts by introducing rich, plain and structured text and character encodings, fol-

Proceedings of the Fifth Workshop on Teaching NLP, pages 46–48
June 10–11, 2021. ©2021 Association for Computational Linguistics

lowed by file input/output in Python, common data structures for manipulating textual data and regular expressions. The course then exemplifies basic NLP tasks, such as tokenisation, part-of-speech tagging, syntactic parsing and sentence segmentation by using the spaCy 3.0 natural language processing library (Honnibal et al., 2020) to process examples in the English language. This is followed by an introduction to basic metrics for evaluating the performance of language models. The course concludes with a brief tour of the pandas library for storing and manipulating data (McKinney, 2010).

The second course begins with an introduction to processing diverse languages using the Stanza library (Qi et al., 2020), shows how Stanza can interfaced with spaCy, and how the resulting annotations can be searched for linguistic patterns using spaCy. The course then introduces word embeddings to provide the students with a general understanding of this technique and its role in modern NLP, which is also increasingly applied in research on the humanities. The course finishes with an exploration of discourse-level annotations in the Georgetown University Multilayer Corpus (Zeldes, 2017), which showcases the CoNLL-U annotation schema.

To what extent the students meet the learning objectives is measured in weekly exercises. The weekly assignments are distributed through GitHub Classroom and automatically graded using *nbgrader*[1], which allows generating feedback files with comments that are then pushed back to the student repositories on GitHub. The exercises are also revisited in weekly walkthrough sessions to allow the students to ask questions about the assignments. The students are also required to complete a final assignment for both courses: the first course concludes with a group project that involves preparing a set of data for further analysis, whereas the second course finishes with a longer individual assignment.

All learning materials are openly available with a Creative Commons 4.0 CC-BY licence at the addresses provided in the following section. Access to the weekly exercises is available on request.

4 Technical Stack

The learning materials are based on Jupyter Notebooks (Kluyver et al., 2016) hosted in their own GitHub repository.[2] This repository constitutes a submodule of a separate repository for the website, which is hosted on ReadTheDocs.[3] The notebooks containing the learning materials are rendered into HTML using the Myst-NB parser from the Executable Books project.[4] This allows keeping the learning materials synchronised, and enables the users to clone the notebooks without the source code for the website. Myst-NB also adds links to Binder (Project Jupyter et al., 2018) to each notebook on the ReadTheDocs website, which enables anyone to execute and explore the code.

The Jupyter Notebooks provide a familiar environment for interactively exploring Python and the various libraries used, whereas the ReadTheDocs website is meant to be used as a reference work. Both media embed videos from a YouTube channel associated with the courses.[5] These short explanatory videos exploit the features of the underlying audiovisual medium, such as overlaid arrows, animations and other modes of presentation to explain the topics.

5 Conclusion

This contribution has introduced a two-course module that aims to teach humanities majors to apply language technology using Python. Targeted at a student population with diverse disciplinary backgrounds and levels of previous experience, the learning materials use multiple media and layperson terms to build up the vocabulary needed to engage with Python and language technology, complemented by the use of a familiar environment – a web browser – for interactive programming using Jupyter Notebooks.

References

Steven Bird. 2020. Decolonising speech and language technology. In *Proceedings of the 28th International Conference on Computational Linguistics*, pages 3504–3519.

Erhard Hinrichs, Marie Hinrichs, Sandra Kübler, and Thorsten Trippel. 2019. Language technology for digital humanities: introduction to the special issue.

[1] https://nbgrader.readthedocs.io

[2] https://github.com/Applied-Language-Technology/notebooks

[3] https://applied-language-technology.readthedocs.io

[4] https://executablebooks.org

[5] https://www.youtube.com/c/AppliedLanguageTechnology

Language Resources and Evaluation, 53(4):559–563.

Matthew Honnibal, Ines Montani, Sofie Van Landeghem, and Adriane Boyd. 2020. spaCy: Industrial-strength Natural Language Processing in Python. DOI: 10.5281/zenodo.1212303.

Dirk Hovy and Shannon L. Spruit. 2016. The social impact of natural language processing. In *Proceedings of the 54th Annual Meeting of the Association for Computational Linguistics (Volume 2: Short Papers)*, pages 591–598. Association for Computational Linguistics.

Thomas Kluyver, Benjamin Ragan-Kelley, Fernando Pérez, Brian Granger, Matthias Bussonnier, Jonathan Frederic, Kyle Kelley, Jessica Hamrick, Jason Grout, Sylvain Corlay, Paul Ivanov, Damián Avila, Safia Abdalla, Carol Willing, and Jupyter development team. 2016. Jupyter Notebooks – a publishing format for reproducible computational workflows. In *Positioning and Power in Academic Publishing: Players, Agents and Agendas*, pages 87–90, Netherlands. IOS Press.

Jonas Kuhn. 2019. Computational text analysis within the humanities: How to combine working practices from the contributing fields? *Language Resources and Evaluation*, 53(4):565–602.

Karl Maton. 2014. *Knowledge and Knowers: Towards a Realist Sociology of Education*. Routledge, New York and London.

Wes McKinney. 2010. Data structures for statistical computing in Python. In *Proceedings of the 9th Python in Science Conference*, pages 51–56.

Dong Nguyen, Maria Liakata, Simon DeDeo, Jacob Eisenstein, David Mimno, Rebekah Tromble, and Jane Winters. 2020. How we do things with words: Analyzing text as social and cultural data. *Frontiers in Artificial Intelligence*, 3.

Emily Öhman. 2019. Teaching computational methods to humanities students. In *Proceedings of the Digital Humanities in the Nordic Countries 4th Conference*, volume 2364 of *CEUR Workshop Proceedings*, pages 479–494.

Project Jupyter, Matthias Bussonnier, Jessica Forde, Jeremy Freeman, Brian Granger, Tim Head, Chris Holdgraf, Kyle Kelley, Gladys Nalvarte, Andrew Osheroff, M Pacer, Yuvi Panda, Fernando Perez, Benjamin Ragan Kelley, and Carol Willing. 2018. Binder 2.0 – Reproducible, interactive, sharable environments for science at scale. In *Proceedings of the 17th Python in Science Conference*, pages 113 – 120.

Peng Qi, Yuhao Zhang, Yuhui Zhang, Jason Bolton, and Christopher D. Manning. 2020. Stanza: A Python natural language processing toolkit for many human languages. In *Proceedings of the 58th Annual Meeting of the Association for Computational Linguistics: System Demonstrations*, pages 101–108. Association for Computational Linguistics.

Amir Zeldes. 2017. The GUM corpus: Creating multilayer resources in the classroom. *Language Resources and Evaluation*, 51(3):581–612.

A Crash Course on Ethics for Natural Language Processing

Annemarie Friedrich[1] **Torsten Zesch**[2]
[1]Bosch Center for Artificial Intelligence, Renningen, Germany
[2]Language Technology Lab, University Duisburg-Essen, Germany
annemarie.friedrich@de.bosch.com
torsten.zesch@uni-due.de

Abstract

It is generally agreed upon in the natural language processing (NLP) community that ethics should be integrated into any curriculum. Being aware of and understanding the relevant core concepts is a prerequisite for following and participating in the discourse on ethical NLP. We here present ready-made teaching material in the form of slides and practical exercises on ethical issues in NLP, which is primarily intended to be integrated into introductory NLP or computational linguistics courses. By making this material freely available, we aim at lowering the threshold to adding ethics to the curriculum. We hope that increased awareness will enable students to identify potentially unethical behavior.

1 Motivation and Overview

The recent sharp rise in the capabilities of natural language processing (NLP) methods has led to a wide application of language technology, influencing many aspects of our daily lives. As a result, NLP technology can have considerable real-world consequences (Vitak et al., 2016; Hovy and Spruit, 2016). While language technology has the aim of supporting humans, mis-use of data or abuse of subjects, mis-representation, or direct harm are some of numerous potentially critical problems. Hence, it is crucial for NLP researchers, developers, and deciders to be aware of the social implications of deploying a particular piece of language technology. They should be able to analyze the degree to which a setup conforms with *ethical* principles, which guide what is considered 'right' or 'wrong' (Deigh, 2010), and be aware of the potentially harmful side even of components developed with the aim of supporting humans.

As a consequence, it is crucial to start early and embed ethics into the NLP curriculum to be taught along with the technological and linguistic material in an interactive manner (Bender et al., 2020). While many teachers are very open to the topic area as demonstrated by the lively participation in events such as the 2020 Workshop on Integrating Ethics into the NLP Curriculum (Bender et al., 2020), ethics for NLP also constitutes a very broad topic area where even teachers might not feel knowledgeable enough. We argue that many more lecturers would include ethics if there existed some freely available **ready-made** teaching material that can be easily integrated in existing courses, or that could serve as a starting point for designing a more in-depth course. In this paper, we describe such a material, which is primarily intended to be integrated into introductory NLP courses.

Our "crash course" does not claim exhaustiveness and aims at breadth rather than depth, intending to give a good overview of the field and highlighting potential issues. The main focus is to enable students to behave ethically in their future research and work careers, and to continue their own research and reading. To be able to participate in the discourse on ethical issues in NLP, the first step is to learn about the important **concepts** and **terminology**. The material also provides numerous suggestions for in-class **discussions** and exercises with the aim of gaining a deeper understanding.

The material consists of **extensively commented slides and suggestions for practical exercises**. The comments and lists of references serve both for teacher preparation and as a script for students. The teaching material is freely available under CC-BY-SA from our website.[1] Finally, both ethics and NLP are dynamic fields which may require updating views, beliefs, opinions, and theories. We therefore welcome continuous feedback regarding and contributions to the teaching material.

Benefit of this Course. The main difference versus existing freely available material is that our crash course is **short**, **self-explanatory** in the con-

[1] https://gscl.org/en/resources/ethics-crash-course

Proceedings of the Fifth Workshop on Teaching NLP, pages 49–51
June 10–11, 2021. ©2021 Association for Computational Linguistics

text of the provided comments such that other lecturers can easily work with it, and contains many **linked exercises**. The Markkula Center for Applied Ethics at Santa Clara University offers a slide set with a crash course on ethics along with materials for discussions focusing of ethics in the general area of technology.[2] Our intention is very similar, but the focus is on NLP-specific issues. We found most existing freely-available courses on ethics in NLP to go into depth and usually span an entire semester.[3] In addition, we are aware of several recent tutorials at ACL venues. Most similar to our materials is the tutorial on socially responsible NLP by Tsvetkov et al. (2018), which is a condensed version of a full-semester class.[4] Our course differs from this tutorial in length and by mostly concentrating on NLP-specific examples. Chang et al. (2019) focus on sub-topics of ethical NLP such as fairness and mitigating bias.[5] Bender et al. (2020) have started a collection of pointers to existing materials, as well as general pointers for teaching ethics for NLP.[6] This collection has been a very valuable starting point for our own research.

Ethical Considerations. Admittedly, a potential issue is that teachers could just "check off" the topic by using our material without deeper engagement, individual reading or reasoning. However, we believe that having a good starting point will actually lead to both teachers and students doing more research on this subject, and our companion material emphasizes the benefit of digging deeper.

2 Course Description

Format. The crash course consists of an interactive lecture accompanied by practical exercises. The slides are available as extensively commented Google slides, which can be easily adapted and exported into a number of common formats. Exercises consist of reading assignments, examples and case studies that serve as the basis for pair or group discussions, or essays if submitting written material is essential, e.g., for grading purposes.

Learning Goals. After the crash course, students will have acquired a basic understanding of the relevant terminology and concepts. They should understand that there are different ethical theories at interplay with the field of NLP which are currently developing best practices for ethical conduct and systems (Prabhumoye et al., 2019). As a result, they should be able to critically reflect the on-going discourse in the community and, last but not least, have acquired the basis for behaving ethically in their own work. It is not our goal to provide 'ultimate' definitions of the concepts and we strongly advise lecturers not to pose exam questions aiming at memorizing definitions. Instead, the learning goals could be tested in the form of group presentations or written essays.

The predominant principle behind the design of our crash course is **activation.** Besides giving clear descriptions of relevant concepts and terminology, we believe that a sensitivity for ethical issues can only be achieved by actively thinking about problems. We hence provide discussion questions for most topics covered in the crash course. We strongly recommend taking the time for short pair- or small-group discussions on these questions before further discussion in the plenum.

Topics Covered. Our course aims at providing a good overview of the field, offering references as starting points for deeper research. We consider our teaching materials to be a 'living document' that will be updated or extended continuously. Topics covered in our first version include, among others, bias, fairness, privacy, and analyzing NLP use cases or methods from different ethical perspectives. For an up-to-date overview of the course content, please refer directly to the material.

3 Discussion

Our stated goal is to inform a broader public about the on-going discourse about ethics in NLP, and educate future NLP researchers, developers and deciders about an ethical approach to NLP research technology. We hope that our materials will be of benefit not only in university classrooms, but also in other settings such as reading groups or industrial meet-ups. We hence publish our resources under the CC-BY-SA 4.0 license,[7] which, under the conditions of stating the source and redistribution under the same license, allows copying, redistributing, adapting and mixing the material in any medium or format.

[2] https://www.scu.edu/ethics-in-technology-practice

[3] See, e.g, http://demo.clab.cs.cmu.edu/ethical_nlp2020/#readings, http://faculty.washington.edu/ebender/2017_575

[4] Materials are also publicly available at https://sites.google.com/view/srnlp/.

[5] http://web.cs.ucla.edu/~kwchang/talks/emnlp19-fairnlp

[6] https://aclweb.org/aclwiki/Notes_on_Teaching_Ethics_in_NLP, https://aclweb.org/aclwiki/Ethics_in_NLP

[7] https://creativecommons.org/licenses/by-sa/4.0/

Acknowledgments

We thank Dirk Hovy for sharing his materials on ethics and for his feedback on this crash course. We also thank Ronja Laarman-Quante, Sophie Henning, Heike Adel, Andrea Horbach, and the anonymous reviewers for their valuable feedback.

References

Emily M. Bender, Dirk Hovy, and Alexandra Schofield. 2020. Integrating ethics into the NLP curriculum. In *Proceedings of the 58th Annual Meeting of the Association for Computational Linguistics: Tutorial Abstracts*, pages 6–9, Online. Association for Computational Linguistics.

Kai-Wei Chang, Vinod Prabhakaran, and Vicente Ordonez. 2019. Bias and fairness in natural language processing. In *Proceedings of the 2019 Conference on Empirical Methods in Natural Language Processing and the 9th International Joint Conference on Natural Language Processing (EMNLP-IJCNLP): Tutorial Abstracts*, Hong Kong, China. Association for Computational Linguistics.

John Deigh. 2010. *An Introduction to Ethics*. Cambridge University Press.

Dirk Hovy and Shannon L. Spruit. 2016. The social impact of natural language processing. In *Proceedings of the 54th Annual Meeting of the Association for Computational Linguistics (Volume 2: Short Papers)*, pages 591–598, Berlin, Germany. Association for Computational Linguistics.

Shrimai Prabhumoye, Elijah Mayfield, and Alan W Black. 2019. Principled Frameworks for Evaluating Ethics in NLP Systems. *arXiv preprint arXiv:1906.06425*.

Yulia Tsvetkov, Vinodkumar Prabhakaran, and Rob Voigt. 2018. Socially responsible NLP. In *Proceedings of the 2018 Conference of the North American Chapter of the Association for Computational Linguistics: Tutorial Abstracts*, pages 24–26, New Orleans, Louisiana. Association for Computational Linguistics.

Jessica Vitak, Katie Shilton, and Zahra Ashktorab. 2016. Beyond the Belmont Principles: Ethical Challenges, Practices, and Beliefs in the Online Data Research Community. In *Proceedings of the 19th ACM Conference on Computer-Supported Cooperative Work & Social Computing*, CSCW '16, page 941–953, New York, NY, USA. Association for Computing Machinery.

A dissemination workshop for introducing young Italian students to NLP

Lucio Messina
Independent Researcher
lucio.messina@autistici.org

Lucia Busso
Aston University
l.busso@aston.ac.uk

Claudia Roberta Combei
University of Bologna
claudiaroberta.combei@unibo.it

Ludovica Pannitto
University of Trento
ludovica.pannitto@unitn.it

Alessio Miaschi
University of Pisa
alessio.miaschi@phd.unipi.it

Gabriele Sarti
University of Trieste
gsarti@sissa.it

Malvina Nissim
University of Groningen
m.nissim@rug.nl

Abstract

We describe and make available the game-based material developed for a laboratory run at several Italian science festivals to popularize NLP among young students.

1 Introduction

The present paper aims at describing in detail the teaching materials developed and used for a series of interactive dissemination workshops on NLP and computational linguistics[1]. These workshops were designed and delivered by the authors on behalf of the Italian Association for Computational Linguistics (AILC, www.ai-lc.it), with the aim of popularizing Natural Language Processing (NLP) among young Italian students (13+) and the general public. The workshops were run in the context of nationwide popular science festivals and open-day events both onsite (at *BergamoScienza*, and Scuola Internazionale Superiore di Studi Avanzati [SISSA], Trieste) and online (at *Festival della Scienza di Genova*, the BRIGHT European Researchers' Night, high school ITS Tullio Buzzi in Prato and the second edition of *Science Web Festival*, engaging over 700 participants in Center and Northern Italy from 2019 to 2021.[2]

The core approach of the workshop remained the same throughout all the events. However, the materials and activities were adapted to a variety of different formats and time-slots, ranging from 30 to 90 minutes. We find that this workshop – thanks to its modular nature – can fit different target audiences and different time slots, depending on the level of interactive engagement required from participants and on the level of granularity of the presentation itself. Other than on the level of engagement expected of participants, time required can also vary depending on the participants' background and metalinguistic awareness.

Our interactive workshops took the form of modular games where participants, guided by trained tutors, acted as if they were computers that had to recognize speech and text, as well as to generate written sentences in a mysterious language they knew nothing about.

The present contribution only describes the teaching materials and provide a general outline of the activities composing the workshop. For a detailed discussion and reflection on the workshop genesis and goals and on how it was received by the participants see (Pannitto et al., 2021).

The teaching support consist in an interactive presentation plus hands-on material, either in hard-copy or digital form. We share a sample presentation[3] and an open-access repository[4] containing both printable materials to download and scripts to reproduce them on different input data.

2 Workshop and materials

The activity contains both more theoretical and hands-on parts, which are cast as games.

[1] In this discussion, and throughout the paper, we conflate the terms Natural Language Processing and Computational Linguistics and use them interchangeably.

[2] Links to events are in the repository's README file.

[3] https://docs.google.com/presentation/d/1ebES_K8o3I2ND_1iMyBlQmrH733eQ6m_K8a0tON8reo/edit?usp=sharing

[4] https://bitbucket.org/melfnt/malvisindi

Proceedings of the Fifth Workshop on Teaching NLP, pages 52–54
June 10–11, 2021. ©2021 Association for Computational Linguistics

Awareness The first part consists of a brief introduction to (computational) linguistics, focusing on some common misconceptions (slides 3-5), and on examples of linguistic questions (slides 6-12). Due to their increasing popularity, we chose vocal assistants as practical examples of NLP technologies accounting for how humans and machines differ in processing speech in particular and language in general (slides 20-39).

Games The core of the activity is inspired by the *word salad* puzzle (Radev and Pustejovsky, 2013) and is organized as a game revolving around a fundamental problem in NLP: given a set of words, participants are asked to determine the most likely ordering for a sentence containing those words. This is a trivial problem when approached in a known language (i.e., consider reordering the tokens *garden, my, is, the, in, dog*), but an apparently impossible task when semantics is not accessible, which is the most common situation for simple NLP algorithms.

To make participants deal with language as a computer would do, we asked them to compose sentences using tokens obtained by transliterating and annotating 60 sentences from the well known fairy tale "Snow White" to a set of symbols. We produced two possible versions of the masked materials: either replacing each word with a random sequence of *DINGs* (e.g. ❄♦➔† for the word *morning*) or replacing them with a corresponding non-word (for example `croto` for the word *morning*). The grammatical structure of each sentence is represented by horizontal lines on top of it representing phrases (such as noun or verb phrases), while the parts of speech are indicated by numbers from 0 to 9 placed as superscripts on each word (Figure 1).

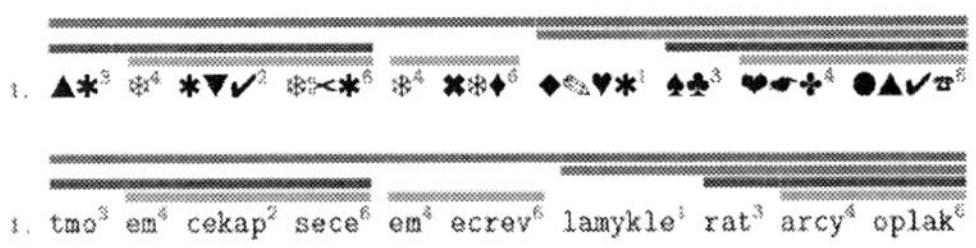

Figure 1: The first sentence of the corpus "`on a snowy day a queen was sewing by her window`" translated using *DINGs* (above) and using non-words (below)

Participants were divided into two teams, one team would be working on masked Italian and the other on masked English. Both teams were given the corpus in A3 format and were told that the texts are written in a fictional language.

Two activities were then run, focusing on two different algorithms for sentence generation. In the first, participants received a deck of cards each equipped with a button loop (Figure 2) and showing a token from the corpus. Participants had to create new valid sentences by rearranging the cards according to the bigrams' distribution in the corpus. Using the *bracelet method* (slides 52-61), they could physically thread tokens into sentences.

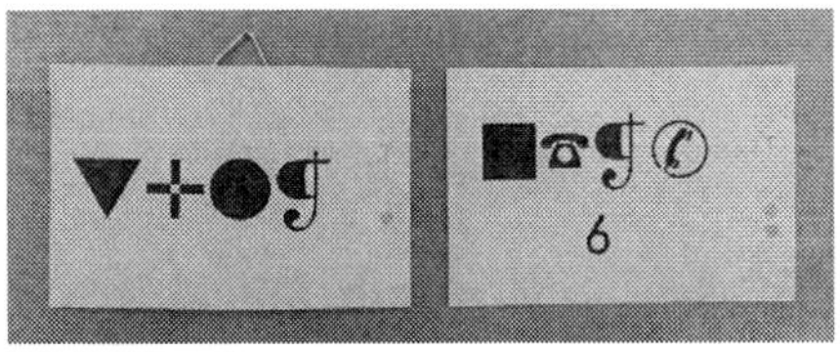

Figure 2: Example cards, both showing a word. Left: a card for the first activity, with a button loop to thread it in a sentence. Right: a card for the second activity, with part of speech (number) at the bottom.

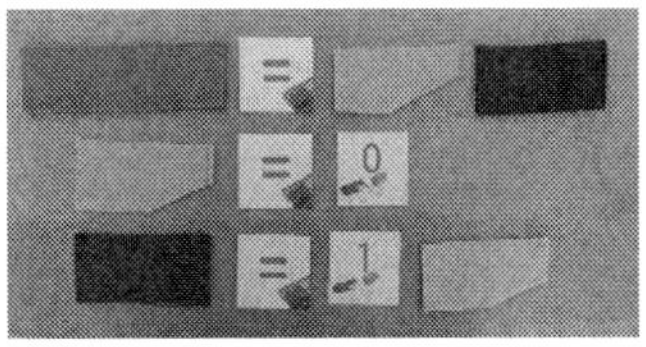

Figure 3: Possible rules extracted from the corpus. Each rule is made of felt strips for phrases, cards with numbers for parts of speech, and "=" cards.

In the second activity (slides 63-92), the participants extracted grammatical rules from the corpus, and used them to generate new sentences. In order to write the grammar, participants were given felt strips reproducing the colors of the annotation, a deck of cards with numbers (identifying parts of speech) and a deck of "=" symbols (Figure 3). With a new deck of words (Figure 2), not all present in the corpus, participants had to generate a sentence using the previously composed rules.

Reflection and Outlook By superimposing a plexiglass frame on the A3 corpus pages (Figure 4), the true nature of the corpora was eventually revealed. The participants could see the original texts (in Italian and English) and translate the sentences they had created previously.

The activity ended with a discussion of recent NLP technologies and their commercial applications (slides 93-96), and of what it takes to become a computational linguist today (slides 97-99).

Figure 4: A session of the workshop: the original language of the corpus has just been revealed by superimposing plexiglass supports on the corpus tables.

3 Activity Preparation

The preparation of the activity consists of several steps: (1) creating and tagging the corpora with morpho-syntactic and syntactic categories as described in the repository; (2) choosing the words to include in the card decks: these must be manually selected but scripts are provided to generate possible sentences based on bigram co-occurrences, and to extract all the possible grammar rules present in the annotation; (3) when the produced sentences and grammar are satisfactory, scripts are provided to generate (i) the printable formats of corpora and decks of cards, (ii) a dictionary to support the translation of sentences in the last part of the workshop, and (iii) clear-text corpora; (4) sentences from the clear-text corpora have to be manually cut and glued on a transparent support that can be superimposed on the printed corpora to reveal the sentences; (5) finally, some manual work is necessary: producing strips of felt or any material with the same colors used in the corpus; cutting threads; attaching a button loop to the relevant cards, etc.

4 Reusability

In the spirit of open science and to encourage the popularization of NLP, the teaching materials and source code are freely available in our repository (see footnotes 2-3 for the links). The print-ready material is released under CC BY-NC; the source code is distributed under the GNU gpl license version 3. All scripts work for Python versions 3.6 or above and the overall process requires `python3`, `lualatex`, `pdftk` and `pdfnup` as detailed in the `README.md` file in the repository, which contains all necessary instructions.

Acknowledgements

We would like to thank the board of the Italian Association for Computational Linguistics (AILC) for the support given to the workshop development and delivery. We are also grateful to BergamoScienza, Festival della Scienza di Genova, Science Web Festival for hosting the activity during the festivals; to ILC-CNR "Antonio Zampolli" and ColingLab (University of Pisa) for hosting us during the European Night of Research; and to the Scuola Internazionale Superiore di Studi Avanzati (SISSA) and ITI Tullio Buzzi for hosting our activities with their students. We also thank Dr. Mirko Lai, who has collaborated on the development of the web interface for the online versions of our activity.

References

Ludovica Pannitto, Lucia Busso, Claudia Roberta Combei, Lucio Messina, Alessio Miaschi, Gabriele Sarti, and Malvina Nissim. 2021. Teaching NLP with bracelets and restaurant menus: An interactive workshop for italian students. In *Proceedings of the Fifth Workshop on Teaching NLP and CL*, Online event. Association for Computational Linguistics.

Dragomir Radev and James Pustejovsky. 2013. *Puzzles in logic, languages and computation: the red book*. Springer.

MiniVQA - A resource to build your tailored VQA competition

Jean-Benoit Delbrouck
Stanford University
jeanbenoit.delbrouck@stanford.edu

Abstract

MiniVQA[1] is a Jupyter notebook to build a tailored VQA competition for your students. The resource creates all the needed resources to create a classroom competition that engages and inspires your students on the free, self-service Kaggle platform. "InClass competitions make machine learning fun!"[2].

1 Task overview

Beyond simply recognizing what objects are present, vision-and-language tasks, such as captioning (Chen et al., 2015) or visual question answering (Antol et al., 2015), challenge systems to understand a wide range of detailed semantics of an image, including objects, attributes, spatial relationships, actions and intentions, and how all these concepts are referred to and grounded in natural language. VQA is therefore viewed as a suitable way to evaluate a system reading comprehension.

"Since questions can be devised to query any aspect of text comprehension, the ability to answer questions is the strongest possible demonstration of understanding" (Lehnert, 1977)

2 To teach NLP

A trained model cannot perform satisfactorily on the Visual Question Answering task without language understanding abilities. A visual-only system (i.e., processing only the image) will not have the visual reasoning skills required to provide correct answers (as it doesn't process the questions as input). Two NLP challenges arise to build a multimodal model:

- The questions must be processed by the system as input. This is the opportunity to teach different features extractions techniques for sentences. The techniques can range from unsupervised methods (bag of words, tf-idf or Word2Vec/Doc2Vec (Mikolov et al., 2013) models) to supervised methods (Recurrent Neural Networks (Hochreiter and Schmidhuber, 1997) or Transformers (Vaswani et al., 2017) neural networks).
- The extracted linguistic features must be incorporated into the visual processing pipeline. This challenge lies at the intersection of vision and language research. Different approaches, such as early and late fusion techniques, can be introduced.

All implemented techniques can be evaluated on the difficult task that is VQA. Because answering questions about a visual context is a hard cognitive task, using different NLP approaches can lead to significant performance differences.

3 Resource overview

The source code is split into several sections, each section containing tunable parameters to modulate the dataset to match your needs. For example, you can choose the number of possible answers, the sample size per answer or the balance of labels between splits.

MiniVQA built upon two datasets, the VQA V2 dataset (Goyal et al., 2017) and the VQA-Med dataset (Ben Abacha et al., 2020). You can choose to create a competition based on natural images or medical images. MiniVQA proposes 443k questions on 82.7k images and 4547 unique answers for the former, and 7.4k unique image-question pairs and 332 answers for the latter [3].

Finally, MiniVQA provides a second Jupyter notebook that trains and evaluates a baseline VQA

[1] https://github.com/jbdel/miniVQA
[2] https://www.kaggle.com/
[3] As of 2021

Proceedings of the Fifth Workshop on Teaching NLP, pages 55–58
June 10–11, 2021. ©2021 Association for Computational Linguistics

model on any dataset you create. You are free to share it or not amongst your class.

4 Resource presentation

The following sections present the features of MiniVQA. We illustrate these features using the VQA v2.0 dataset as a matter of example. The same can be applied to the VQA-Med dataset.

4.1 Automatic download

The resource automatically downloads annotations (questions, image_ids and answer)s from the official datasets websites. Any pre-processing that must be done is carried out. The number of possible questions and unique answers are printed to the user, along with random examples.

4.2 Decide the volume of your dataset

Using MiniVQA, you can choose the size of your dataset according to several settings.

num_answers the number of possible different answers (i.e., how many classes).

sampling_type how to select samples, choose between "top" or "random". Value "top" gets the 'num_answers' most common answers in the dataset.

sampling_exclude_top and **sampling_exclude_bottom** you can choose to exclude the n most popular or least popular answers (the most popular answers is "no" and contains 80.000 examples).

min_samples and **max_samples** if sampling_type is random, you can choose a minimum and maximum number of samples with min_samples and max_samples.

This section outputs a bar graph containing the label distributions and some additional information. Figure 1 shows two examples.

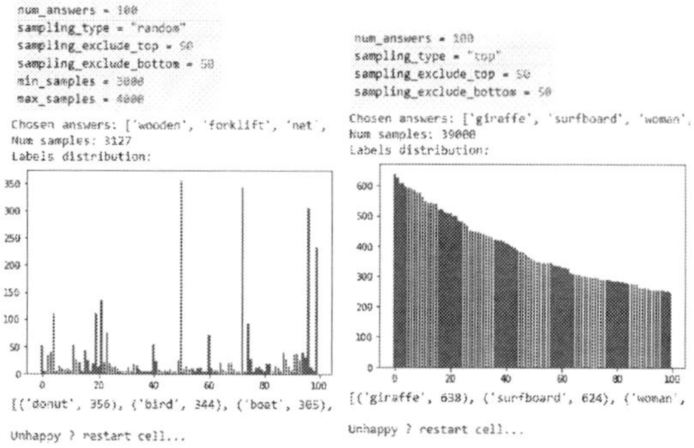

Figure 1: sampling_type random (left) and sampling_type top (right).

4.3 Create dataset files

This section creates the chosen samples a json format. Two more parameters are available.

sample_clipping set to select n maximum samples per answer. This setting is particularly handy if you chose the "top" sampling_type in the previous section.

im_download you can choose to download the images of the selected samples directly through http requests. Though rather slow, this allows the user not to download the images of the full dataset.

resize if im_download is set to True, images are squared-resized to n pixels. For your mini-VQA project, you might want to use lower resolution for your images (faster training). $n = 128$ is a good choice.

4.4 Create splits

As in any competition, participants are provided a train and validation set with ground-truth answers, and a test-set without these answers.

train_size and **valid_size** fraction of the total examples selected to populate the splits. 0.8 and 0.1 are usually good values. The rest (0.1) goes in the test set.

balanced whether or not labels are homogeneously distributed across splits.

Figure 2 shows an example of the balanced setting effect:

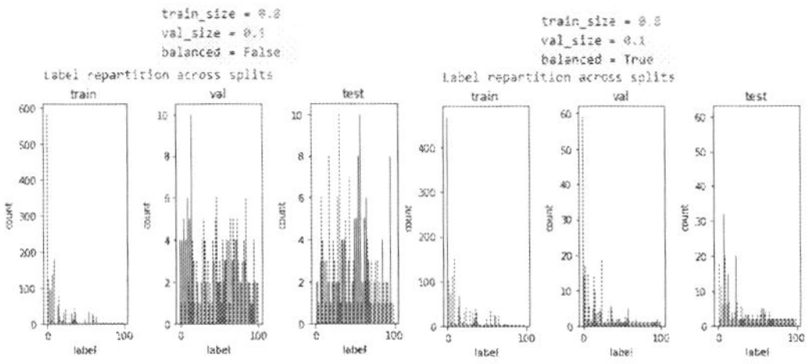

Figure 2: balance set to True (left) and to False (right).

Regardless of the balanced value, at least one sample of each label is put in each split.

4.5 Explore the question embedding space

It is possible to compute questions embedding using pre-trained transformer models. Each representation is then reduced into a two-dimensional point using t-SNE algorithm (van der Maaten and Hinton, 2008). These embeddings can also be used for section 5. MiniVQA plots two projections, one for the 5 most popular question types and one with randomly chosen question types.

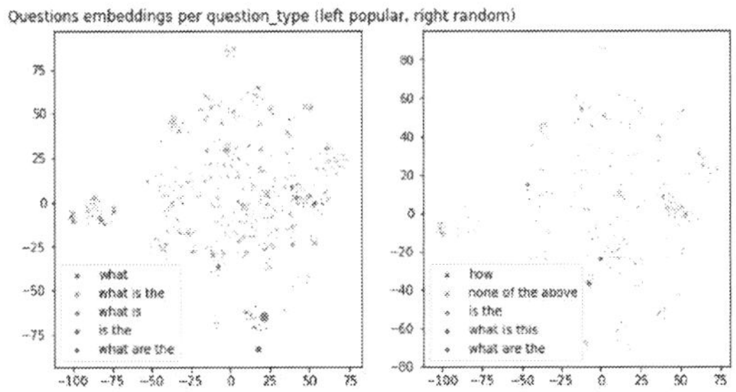

Figure 3: Questions embedding using a pretrained bert-base-nli-mean-tokens model.

4.6 Download files

Finally, you can download the dataset file in json, the splits, and optionally, the images.

{train, val, sample_submission}.csv csv files containing question_id, label.

test.csv must be given to students. They must fill it with their systems predictions formatted like sample_submission.csv which contains random predictions.

answer_key.csv is the ground-truth file that has to be stored on Kaggle (see Appendix A).

answer_list.csv maps the label to the answer in natural language (i.e., label 0 is answer at line 1 in answer_list, etc.).

image_question.json maps an image_id to a list of questions (that concerns image_id). Each question is a tuple (question_id, question).

5 Baseline Model

The provided baseline consists of a dataloader that opens images and resize them to 112×112 pixels and that embeds questions to a feature vector of size 768 from a pre-trained DistilBERT (Sanh et al.).

The network consists a modified Resnet (He et al., 2016) that takes as input an RBG image of size 112×112 and outputs a feature map of size $512 \times 4 \times 4$ that is flattened and then concatenated with the question representation of size 768. Finally, a classification layer projects this representation to probabilities over answers. The network is trained until no improvements is recorded on the validation set (early-stopping).

References

Stanislaw Antol, Aishwarya Agrawal, Jiasen Lu, Margaret Mitchell, Dhruv Batra, C. Lawrence Zitnick, and Devi Parikh. 2015. VQA: Visual Question Answering. In *International Conference on Computer Vision (ICCV)*.

Asma Ben Abacha, Vivek V. Datla, Sadid A. Hasan, Dina Demner-Fushman, and Henning Müller. 2020. Overview of the vqa-med task at imageclef 2020: Visual question answering and generation in the medical domain. In *CLEF 2020 Working Notes*, CEUR Workshop Proceedings, Thessaloniki, Greece. CEUR-WS.org <http://ceur-ws.org>.

Xinlei Chen, Hao Fang, Tsung-Yi Lin, Ramakrishna Vedantam, Saurabh Gupta, Piotr Dollár, and C Lawrence Zitnick. 2015. Microsoft coco captions: Data collection and evaluation server. *arXiv preprint arXiv:1504.00325*.

Yash Goyal, Tejas Khot, Douglas Summers-Stay, Dhruv Batra, and Devi Parikh. 2017. Making the V in VQA matter: Elevating the role of image understanding in Visual Question Answering. In *Conference on Computer Vision and Pattern Recognition (CVPR)*.

Kaiming He, Xiangyu Zhang, Shaoqing Ren, and Jian Sun. 2016. Deep residual learning for image recognition. In *Proceedings of the IEEE Conference on Computer Vision and Pattern Recognition (CVPR)*.

Sepp Hochreiter and Jürgen Schmidhuber. 1997. Long short-term memory. *Neural computation*, 9(8):1735–1780.

Wendy Lehnert. 1977. Human and computational question answering. *Cognitive Science*, 1(1):47–73.

Tomas Mikolov, Ilya Sutskever, Kai Chen, Greg S Corrado, and Jeff Dean. 2013. Distributed representations of words and phrases and their compositionality. In *Advances in Neural Information Processing Systems*, volume 26. Curran Associates, Inc.

Victor Sanh, Lysandre DEBUT, Julien CHAUMOND, Thomas WOLF, and Hugging Face. Distilbert, a distilled version of bert: smaller, faster, cheaper and lighter.

Laurens van der Maaten and Geoffrey Hinton. 2008. Visualizing data using t-SNE. *Journal of Machine Learning Research*, 9:2579–2605.

Ashish Vaswani, Noam Shazeer, Niki Parmar, Jakob Uszkoreit, Llion Jones, Aidan N Gomez, Ł ukasz Kaiser, and Illia Polosukhin. 2017. Attention is all you need. In *Advances in Neural Information Processing Systems*, volume 30. Curran Associates, Inc.

A Create a competition on Kaggle

Navigate to `http://www.kaggle.com/inclass`. Follow the instructions to setup an InClass competition. Upload files train.csv, val.csv, test.csv, answer_key.csv, and sample_submission.csv when prompted.

B image_question.json structure

```
"159987": [
  [
    159987002,
    "What street is the first bus going to?"
  ]
],
"160452": [
  [
    160452000,
    "What word is written on one of the train cars?"
  ],
  [
    160452002,
    "What is on the side of the front train car?"
  ]
],
"160516": [
  [
    160516001,
    "What is she doing?"
  ]
```

Figure 4: Maps an image_id to a list of questions (that concerns image_id). Each question is a tuple (question_id, question).

From back to the roots into the gated woods: Deep learning for NLP

Barbara Plank
IT University of Copenhagen
bplank@gmail.com

Abstract

Deep neural networks have revolutionized many fields, including Natural Language Processing. This paper outlines teaching materials for an introductory lecture on deep learning in Natural Language Processing (NLP). The main submitted material covers a summer school lecture on *encoder-decoder models*. Complementary to this is a set of jupyter notebook slides from earlier teaching, on which parts of the lecture were based on. The main goal of this teaching material is to provide an overview of neural network approaches to natural language processing, while linking modern concepts back to the roots showing traditional essential counterparts. The lecture departs from count-based statistical methods and spans up to gated recurrent networks and attention, which is ubiquitous in today's NLP.

1 Introduction

In 2015, the "deep learning tsunami" hit our field (Manning, 2015). In 2011, neural networks were not really "a thing" yet in NLP; they were even hardly taught. I remember when in 2011 Andrew Ng introduced the free online course on machine learning, which soon after led Daphne Koller and him to start massive online education: "Many scientists think the best way to make progress [..] is through learning algorithms called *neural networks*".[1] Ten years later, it is hard to imagine any NLP education not touching upon neural networks and in particular, representation learning. While neural networks have undoubtedly pushed the field, it has led to a more homogenized field; some lecturers even question whether to include pre neural methods. I believe it is essential to teach statistical foundations besides modern DL, ie., to go back to the roots, to better be equipped for the future.[2]

[1]Accessed March 15, 2021: https://bit.ly/2OZH2MZ

[2]Disclaimer: This submitted teaching material is limited as it spans a single lecture. However, I believe it to be essential to teach traditional methods besides modern neural approaches (e.g. count-based vs prediction-based word representations; statistical n-grams vs neural LMs; naive Bayes and logistic regression vs neural classifiers, to name a few examples).

2 Structure of the summer school lecture

This paper outlines teaching material (Keynote slides, Jupyter notebooks), which I would like to provide to the community for reuse when teaching an introductory course on deep learning for NLP.[3]

The main material outlined in this paper is a Keynote presentation slide deck for a 3-h lecture on encoder-decoder models. An overview of the lecture (in non-temporal form), from foundations, to representations to neural networks (NNs) beyond vanilla NNs is given in Figure 1. Moreover, I provide complementary teaching material in form of Jupyter notebook (convertable to slides). I've used these notebooks (slides and exercises) during earlier teaching and in parts formed the basis of the summer school lecture (see Section 3).

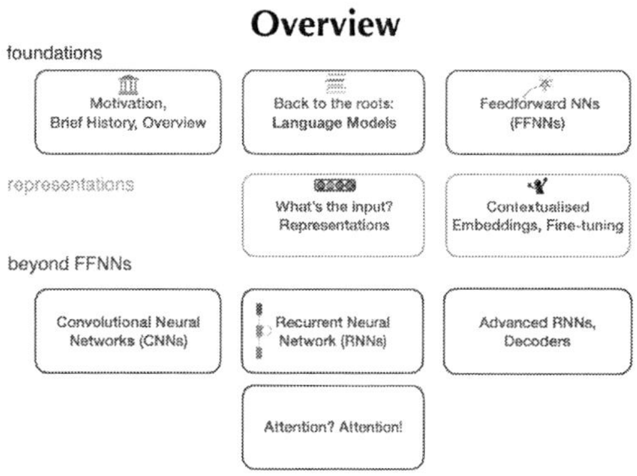

Figure 1: Overview of the core concepts covered.

The lecture covers NLP methods broadly from introduction concepts of more traditional NLP methods to recent deep learning methods. A particular focus is to contrast traditional approaches from the statistical NLP literature (sparse repre-

[3]Available at: https://github.com/bplank/teaching-dl4nlp

Proceedings of the Fifth Workshop on Teaching NLP, pages 59–61
June 10–11, 2021. ©2021 Association for Computational Linguistics

sentations, n-grams) to their deep learning-based counterparts (dense representations, 'soft' ngrams in CNNS and RNN-based encoders). Consequently, the following topics are covered in the lecture:

- Introduction to NLP and DL (deep learning), what makes language so difficult; traditional versus neural approaches
- N-gram Language Models,
- Feedforward Neural Networks (FFNNs)
- What's the input? Sparse traditional vs dense representations; Bag of words (BOW) vs continuous BOW (CBOW)
- Neural Language Models (LMs)
- Convolutional Neural Networks (CNNs) for Text Classification ('soft n-grams')
- Recurrent Neural Networks (RNNs) for Text Processing, RNNs as LMs
- Bidirectional RNNs, stacking, character representations
- Gated RNNs (GRU, LSTMs)
- Deep contextualized embeddings (Embeddings as LMs, Elmo)
- Attention

The lecture was held as 3-h lecture at the first Athens in NLP (AthNLP) summer school in 2019. In the overall schedule of the summer school, this lecture was the 3rd in a row of six. It was scheduled after an introduction to classification (by Ryan McDonald), and a lecture on structured prediction (by Xavier Carreras). The outlined encoder-decoder lecture was then followed by a lecture on machine translation (by Arianna Bisazza; the lecture build upon this lecture here and included the transformer), machine reading (by Sebastian Riedel) and dialogue (by Vivian Chen).[4] Each lecture was enhanced by unified lab exercises.[5]

As key textbook references, I would like to refer the reader to chapters 3-9 of Jurafsky and Martin's 3rd edition (under development) (Jurafsky and Martin, 2020),[6] and Yoav Goldberg's NLP primer (Goldberg, 2015). Besides these textbooks, key papers include (Kim, 2014) for CNNs on texts, attention (Luong et al., 2015) and Elmo (Peters et al., 2018).

3 Complementary notebooks of earlier material

This lecture evolved from a series of lectures given earlier, amongst which a short course given in Malta in 2019, and a MSc-level course I taught at the University of Groningen (Language Technology Project). To complement the Keynote slides of the summer school lecture provided here, earlier Jupyter notebooks can be found at the website. These cover a subset of the material above.

4 Conclusions

This short paper outlines teaching material for an introductory lecture on deep learning for NLP. By releasing this teaching material, I hope to contribute material that fellow researchers find useful when teaching introductory courses on DL for NLP. For comments and suggestions to improve upon this material, please reach out to me.

Acknowledgements

I would like to thank Arianna Bisazza for many fruitful discussions in preparing this summer school lecture, and the AthNLP 2019 organizers for the invitation, with special thanks to Andreas Vlachos, Yannis Konstas and Ion Androutsopoulos. I would like to thank many colleagues who inspired me throughout the years in so many ways, including those who provide excellent teaching material online. Thanks goes to Abigal See, Anders Johannsen, Alexander Koller, Chris Manning, Dan Jurafsky, Dirk Hovy, Graham Neubig, Greg Durrett, Malvina Nissim, Richard Johannson, Ryan McDonald and Philip Koehn. Special thank to those who inspired me in one way or another for teaching the beauty and challenges of computational linguistics, NLP or deep learning (in chronological order): Raffaella Bernardi, Reut Tsarfaty and Khalil Sima'an, Gertjan van Noord, Ryan McDonald and Yoav Goldberg.

[4] Videos of all lectures are available at: `http://athnlp2019.iit.demokritos.gr/schedule/index.html`

[5] Exercises were kindly provided as unified framework by the AthNLP team, and hence are not provided here. They included, lab 1: Part-of-Speech tagging with the perceptron; lab 2: POS tagging with the structured perceptron; lab 3: neural encoding for text classification; lab 4: neural language modeling; lab 5: machine translation; lab 6: question answering

[6] `https://web.stanford.edu/~jurafsky/slp3/`

References

Yoav Goldberg. 2015. A primer on neural network models for natural language processing.

Dan Jurafsky and James H. Martin. 2020. *Speech and language processing : an introduction to natural language processing, computational linguistics, and speech recognition*. Upper Saddle River, N.J.

Yoon Kim. 2014. Convolutional neural networks for sentence classification. In *Proceedings of the 2014 Conference on Empirical Methods in Natural Language Processing (EMNLP)*, pages 1746–1751, Doha, Qatar. Association for Computational Linguistics.

Thang Luong, Hieu Pham, and Christopher D. Manning. 2015. Effective approaches to attention-based neural machine translation. In *Proceedings of the 2015 Conference on Empirical Methods in Natural Language Processing*, pages 1412–1421, Lisbon, Portugal. Association for Computational Linguistics.

Christopher D Manning. 2015. Computational linguistics and deep learning. *Computational Linguistics*, 41(4):701–707.

Matthew Peters, Mark Neumann, Mohit Iyyer, Matt Gardner, Christopher Clark, Kenton Lee, and Luke Zettlemoyer. 2018. Deep contextualized word representations. In *Proceedings of the 2018 Conference of the North American Chapter of the Association for Computational Linguistics: Human Language Technologies, Volume 1 (Long Papers)*, pages 2227–2237, New Orleans, Louisiana. Association for Computational Linguistics.

Learning PyTorch Through A Neural Dependency Parsing Exercise

David Jurgens
School of Information
University of Michigan
jurgens@umich.edu

Abstract

Dependency parsing is increasingly the popular parsing formalism in practice. This assignment provides a practice exercise in implementing the shift-reduce dependency parser of Chen and Manning (2014). This parser is a two-layer feed-forward neural network, which students implement in PyTorch, providing practice in developing deep learning models and exposure to developing parser models.

1 Introduction

Deep learning methods are ubiquitous in nearly all areas of NLP. However, some applications for these models require extensive training or data that make implementing the model in a classroom infeasible without additional computational support. This homework introduces a simple-yet-powerful network for performing dependency parsing using the shift-reduce parser of Chen and Manning (2014). This three-layer network is efficient to train, making it suitable for development by all students, exposes students to dependency parsing, and helps connect how a neural network can be used in practice. Through the assignment, students implement the network, the training procedure, and explore how the parser operates.

2 Design and Learning Goals

This exercise is designed for an advanced undergraduate or graduate-level course in NLP. The material is appropriate for students who have previously covered simple neural networks and are learning about dependency parsing. The exercise contains extensive scaffolding code that simplifies the training process by turning the CoNLL treebank data (Nivre et al., 2007) into training examples for the students and computing the unlabeled attachment score (UAS) for evaluating the model. The technical depth of the material is likely too involved for an Applied NLP or Linguistics-focus setting; the material could be re-purposed for an early exercise in a Machine-learning focused course with the addition of more content on network design. Students typically have three weeks to complete the assignment, with the majority finishing the main tasks within a week. Through doing the exercise, students practice building neural models and understanding how the core training procedure is implemented in PyTorch (Paszke et al., 2019, e.g., what is a loss function and an optimizer), which enables them to design, extend, or modify a variety of PyTorch implementations for later assignments and course projects.

The assignment has the following three broad learning objectives. First, the exercise is an introduction to developing neural models using the PyTorch library. The relatively simple nature of the network reduces the scope of design (e.g., compared with implementing an RNN or LSTM), which allows students to understand how to construct a basic network, use layers, embeddings, and loss functions. Further, because the model can be trained efficiently, this allows students to complete the entire assignment on a laptop that is several years old, which reduces the overhead of needing students to gain access to GPUs or more advanced computing. Through the exercise, students experiment with changing different network hyperparameters and designs and measuring their effect on performance. These simple modifications allow students to build confidence and gain intuition on which kinds of modifications may improve performance—or dramatically slow training time.

Second, students gain familiarity with how to use pre-trained embeddings in downstream applications. The dependency parser makes use of these embeddings for its initial word representations and the assignment provides an optional exercise to have students try embeddings from different sources (e.g., Twitter-based embeddings) or no pre-training at all in order to see how these affect

Proceedings of the Fifth Workshop on Teaching NLP, pages 62–64
June 10–11, 2021. ©2021 Association for Computational Linguistics

performance and convergence time. This learning objective helps bridge the conceptual material to later pre-trained language models like BERT if they have not been introduced earlier.

Third, students should gain a basic familiarity with dependency parsing and how a shift-reduce parser works. Shift-reduce parsing is a classic technique (Aho and Ullman, 1973) and has been widely adopted for multiple parsing tasks beyond syntax, such as semantic parsing (Misra and Artzi, 2016) or discourse parsing (Ji and Eisenstein, 2014). This assignment helps students understand the basic structures for parsing (e.g., the stack and buffer) to see how neural approaches can be used in practice. The concepts in the homework are connected to textbook material in Chapter 14 of *Speech & Language Processing* (Jurafsky and Martin, 2021, 3rd ed.), which provides additional examples and definitions.

3 Homework Description

This homework has students implement two key components of the Chen and Manning (2014) parser in PyTorch, using extensive scaffolding code to handle the parsing preparation. First, students implement the feed-forward neural network, which requires using three common elements of neural networks in NLP: multiple layers, embeddings, and a custom activation function. These elements provide conceptual scaffolding for later implementations on attention and recurrent layers in networks. Second, students implement the main training loop, which requires students to understand how the loss is computed and gradient descent is applied. This second step is found in nearly all code using networks built from scratch (or built upon pre-trained parameters) and enables students to learn this process in a simplified setting for use later. These two components are broken into multiple discrete steps to help students figure out where to start in the code.

The second part of the homework has students explore the parser in two ways. First, students examine the parsing data structures and report the full parse of a sentence of their choice; this exploration has students consider the steps required for a successful parse. As a part of this exploration, students are required to report a parse that is incorrect; this latter task requires students to understand what is a correct dependency parse and diagnose what steps the parser has taken to introduce the error. In some iterations, we have asked the students to report on an error introduced from a non-projective parse of their choice, though some students found it difficult to come up with an example of their own. Second, students are asked to extend the network in some way of their choice (e.g., add a layer or add dropout). This extension helps introduce additional design components and build intuition.

4 Potential Extensions

Prior parts of the course examine word vectors and this parsing exercise includes an optional extension to allow students to see their effect in practice. Here, we provide students with multiple pre-trained vectors from different domains (e.g., Twitter and Wikipedia) and ask them to report on convergence times and accuracy. Students may also optionally freeze these embeddings to test how well their information can generalize. Since training data are known to contain biases that affect downstream performance (e.g., Garimella et al., 2019), one additional extension could be to test how particular embeddings perform better or worse on parsing text from specific groups.

After implementing the model, the assignment has students explore the parsing outputs and intermediate state, which provides some grounding for how shift-reduce works in practice. However, due to the focus on learning PyTorch, the parsing component of the exercise is less in-depth; a more parsing-focus variant of this assignment could have students perform the CoNLL-to-training-data conversion in order to see how dependency trees can be turned into a sequence of shift-reduce operations and how such a process introduces errors for non-projective parses.

5 Reflection on Student Experiences

In two iterations of the homework, students have reported the exercise helped demystify deep learning and make the concepts accessible. Once the model was implemented and working, some students were surprisingly active in trying different model designs; these students reported feeling excited that making these simple extensions could be so easy, which encouraged them to try implementing deep learning models in their course projects.

The initial version of this homework did not include any parsing introspection. Students expressed feeling like the homework was more about building a network than learning about parsing. As a result, the second iteration added more diagnostics for students to see what the parser is doing and the exploration component. This addition was intentionally simple to avoid substantially expanding the scope of the assignment. However, adding more parsing-oriented tasks remains an active area of development for this homework.

References

Alfred V Aho and Jeffrey D Ullman. 1973. *The theory of parsing, translation, and compiling*, volume 1. Prentice-Hall Englewood Cliffs, NJ.

Danqi Chen and Christopher D Manning. 2014. A fast and accurate dependency parser using neural networks. In *Proceedings of the 2014 conference on empirical methods in natural language processing (EMNLP)*, pages 740–750.

Aparna Garimella, Carmen Banea, Dirk Hovy, and Rada Mihalcea. 2019. Women's syntactic resilience and men's grammatical luck: Gender-bias in part-of-speech tagging and dependency parsing. In *Proceedings of the 57th Annual Meeting of the Association for Computational Linguistics*, pages 3493–3498.

Yangfeng Ji and Jacob Eisenstein. 2014. Representation learning for text-level discourse parsing. In *Proceedings of the 52nd annual meeting of the association for computational linguistics (volume 1: Long papers)*, pages 13–24.

Dan Jurafsky and James H. Martin. 2021. *Speech & Language Processing*, 3rd edition. Prentice Hall.

Dipendra Misra and Yoav Artzi. 2016. Neural shift-reduce ccg semantic parsing. In *Proceedings of the 2016 conference on empirical methods in natural language processing*, pages 1775–1786.

Joakim Nivre, Johan Hall, Sandra Kübler, Ryan McDonald, Jens Nilsson, Sebastian Riedel, and Deniz Yuret. 2007. The conll 2007 shared task on dependency parsing. In *Proceedings of the 2007 Joint Conference on Empirical Methods in Natural Language Processing and Computational Natural Language Learning (EMNLP-CoNLL)*, pages 915–932.

Adam Paszke, Sam Gross, Francisco Massa, Adam Lerer, James Bradbury, Gregory Chanan, Trevor Killeen, Zeming Lin, Natalia Gimelshein, Luca Antiga, et al. 2019. Pytorch: An imperative style, high-performance deep learning library. *arXiv preprint arXiv:1912.01703*.

A Balanced and Broadly Targeted Computational Linguistics Curriculum

Emma Manning **Nathan Schneider** **Amir Zeldes**
Georgetown University
{esm76, nathan.schneider, amir.zeldes}@georgetown.edu

Abstract

This paper describes the primarily-graduate computational linguistics and NLP curriculum at Georgetown University, a U.S. research university that has seen significant growth in these areas in recent years. We discuss the principles behind our curriculum choices, including recognizing the various academic backgrounds and goals of our students; teaching a variety of skills with an emphasis on working directly with data; encouraging collaboration and interdisciplinary work; and including languages beyond English. We reflect on challenges we have encountered, such as the difficulty of teaching programming skills alongside NLP fundamentals, and discuss areas for future growth.

1 Introduction

This paper describes the computational linguistics and NLP curriculum at Georgetown University, a private research university whose computational linguistics program has grown significantly over the past 7 years. This curriculum has been developed with a high degree of collaboration between the Linguistics and Computer Science departments, as well as involvement with related programs such as the Master's in Data Science and Analytics. We reflect on several principles that underlie our curriculum, and discuss opportunities for further expansion.

2 Course Offerings

Table 1 summarizes our main graduate-level courses focusing on computational linguistics and NLP.[1] These include:

- A 3-course NLP sequence for novice programmers, which can be shortened to 1 or 2 courses for students proficient in Python (discussed in §3).
- A group of courses targeting methods for computational linguistics research: corpus design and use (§5), statistical analysis with R, and machine learning techniques.
- A selection of application-oriented speech and language technology courses encompassing speech processing, dialogue systems, and machine translation.
- Special topics courses addressing issues such as social factors and ethics in NLP, discourse parsing, grammar formalisms, and meaning representation design and parsing. These tend to be reading- and research-oriented courses, whereas the other courses place more emphasis on implementation and theory learning.

Advanced students of NLP can also take a number of related courses in the CS and Analytics departments on topics like information retrieval and machine learning for general (and not only language-oriented) purposes.[2]

Syllabi for courses taught by Nathan Schneider (instructor S in the table), including detailed schedules with course materials, can be found via http://people.cs.georgetown.edu/nschneid/teaching.html. Recent syllabi for courses taught by Amir Zeldes (instructor Z) can be found at https://corpling.uis.georgetown.edu/amir/pdf/syllabi/.

3 Interdisciplinarity

Our students include many from both the Linguistics and Computer Science departments, as well as some from other programs, such as Data Science & Analytics and language departments. We have developed a sequence of NLP courses designed

[1] All are standard fall or spring semester courses for 3 credits, with 150 minutes of instruction time per week. The total number of 3-credit courses a student takes varies considerably by graduate program: 8–10 for the CS MS; 10 for the CS Ph.D.; 8–12 for the Linguistics MS; and 18 for the Linguistics Ph.D. This includes departmental core requirements and other course options beyond computational linguistics and NLP.

[2] A full list of CL-relevant courses are described at: http://gucl.georgetown.edu/gu-cl-curriculum.pdf

Proceedings of the Fifth Workshop on Teaching NLP, pages 65–69
June 10–11, 2021. ©2021 Association for Computational Linguistics

	Course	Target audience	Frequency	Instructor
NLP	Intro NLP (INLP)	any except CS	Annual	Z
	Advanced Python for CL	Ling+Analytics	Annual	A
	Empirical Methods in NLP (ENLP)	Ling+CS	Annual	S
CL METHODS	Computational Corpus Linguistics	any	Annual	Z
	Analyzing Language Data with R	Ling	2 Years	Z
	Machine Learning for Linguistics	Ling	2 Years	Z
APPLICATIONS	Speech Processing	Ling	2 Years	A
	Dialogue Systems	any	2 Years	A
	Statistical/Neural Machine Translation	any	2 Years	A
SPECIAL TOPICS	Social Factors in CL/AI	any	2 Years	A
	Discourse Modeling	Ling+CS	2 Years	Z
	Grammar Formalisms	Ling	3–4 Years	P
	Meaning Representations	Ling+CS	2 Years	S

Table 1: Courses oriented specifically at computational linguistics or NLP and targeting graduate students (many are also open to undergraduates in their third and fourth years). The first group is the main NLP sequence that includes Python programming and fundamental algorithms, representations, and tasks; fluent Python programmers can start with ENLP. The second group focuses on computational linguistic methods. The third group focuses on application areas and associated tools. The last group consists of special topics. **Instructors**: Courses designated S or Z are taught by dedicated computational linguistics faculty, Nathan **S**chneider and Amir **Z**eldes. Grammar Formalisms is taught by Paul **P**ortner, a Linguistics professor. Other courses, designated A, are taught by **A**djunct professors (different for each course).

to accommodate these various backgrounds. Linguistics students with little or no prior programming experience are introduced to basic Python and NLP foundations in an Introduction to NLP (INLP) course;[3] they can then further develop their programming skills with Computational Linguistics with Advanced Python before taking Empirical Methods in NLP (ENLP). Students who already have strong programming skills, such as Computer Science graduate students, can begin their NLP journey in this same ENLP course, which has projects emphasizing collaboration between students of different backgrounds;[4] as discussed in Fosler-Lussier (2008), cross-disciplinary collaborations are helpful to establish respect between students from different fields and mitigate the challenges of disparate backgrounds. Many other NLP courses, such as those focusing on Dialogue Systems and Machine Translation, are also cross-listed between the Linguistics and CS departments, which, as noted in e.g. Baldridge and Erk (2008), helps these courses reach a wider audience.

Teaching NLP concepts alongside basic programming skills has been a significant challenge. INLP requires no prior programming experience, but students who enter the course with none sometimes struggle to grasp programming concepts at the speed they are taught, and many students rely on significant support from teaching assistants to successfully complete the course's programming assignments. Our experience has taught us that frequent contact and check-ins initiated by teaching assistants are very important for catching students who may fall behind before assignment submissions make problems more obvious. Use of IDEs with syntax validation and auto-complete facilities, which are freely available for academic purposes, are also very useful in this respect, and in recent years students have used PyCharm (`https://www.jetbrains.com/pycharm/`) as their first Python IDE for this purpose.

Previously, linguistics students who completed INLP were encouraged to enroll in ENLP immediately afterward. However, we found that INLP alone did not adequately prepare students for the more advanced programming assignments in ENLP—INLP assignments tend to involve making fairly limited modifications to provided starter code, while ENLP expects independent implementation of more substantial algorithms. Thus, the Advanced Python course was introduced to give

[3] Introducing these together allows linguistics students who are unsure how interested they are in NLP to get a taste of it in just one class, without requiring them to spend time on an non-language-related programming class first.

[4] Depending on class makeup, there are sometimes requirements for the composition project groups to enforce this, e.g. that each group needs to contain at least one linguist.

students more practice implementing algorithms for linguistic tasks as code. This bridges the gap between the introductory and more advanced NLP courses; however, it does mean that linguistics students who enter the program with little or no programming experience may need to take a sequence of 3 courses to gain a thorough understanding of NLP fundamentals, while students with a CS background only need to take one course. ENLP's Assignment 0 is a diagnostic of Python proficiency to help students choose the appropriate course level.[5]

4 Balancing Skills Taught

Along with coming from different academic backgrounds, we acknowledge that students studying NLP have a variety of goals: for example, they may wish to pursue NLP in academia or industry, or they may be interested in using computational methods for linguistics, or other Digital Humanities or Social Science fields. To support these varying goals, we endeavor to teach a balance of different skills and perspectives on NLP. While some courses emphasize algorithms, others focus more on computational representations of language, on creating and using resources such as corpora, or on using existing NLP tools. We are also careful to consider that not all NLP applications are realized in a Big Data context, and we therefore include units targeting low resource settings across our course offerings.

5 Focus on Data

In all courses, we emphasize working directly with language data. This is perhaps best exemplified in the Computational Corpus Linguistics course, which teaches corpus design and construction methods along with analytical Corpus Linguistics methodology and relevant readings on data and its potential pitfalls. As part of its assignment structure, the course integrates a set of five annotation projects in which each student chooses a single document from a selection of genres to annotate throughout the semester with a variety of annotations layers, including structural markup (which teaches XML basics), part-of-speech tagging, dependency treebanking, entity and coreference resolution, and finally discourse parsing. A unit on inter-annotator agreement evaluates and compares the students' own work, underscoring the subjective nature of 'ground-truth' data, the range of linguistic variation across genres, and the importance of consistency and validation. At its end, the course engages students in a 'real-world' research project, which produces valuable linguistically annotated data, which can be released to the research community under an open license as part of the Georgetown University Multilayer (GUM) Corpus (Zeldes, 2017) if students so wish.[6]

Several other courses also include practice annotation of data, including a POS tagging in-class exercise in ENLP, and annotation in three different semantic representations in Meaning Representations. Others include error analysis of NLP systems, such as a comparison of the output from statistical and neural translation systems in Machine Translation. The Discourse Modeling course teaches discourse parsing frameworks and algorithms, including introducing students to topics in annotating Rhetorical Structure Theory (Mann and Thompson, 1988), Segmented Discourse Representation Theory (SDRT, Asher and Lascarides 2003) and the Penn Discourse Treebank framework (PDTB, Prasad et al. 2014).

6 Collaboration

Our coursework emphasizes frequent collaboration among students. This includes in-class group activities, such as practicing part-of-speech tagging in small groups in ENLP, or working together as a class to create a morphological analyzer for a low resource language in INLP (an activity which literally runs in a simultaneous collaborative online code editing format). On a larger scale, students work in groups on final projects in courses such as ENLP, and have collaborated on an entry to a shared task in a our discourse parsing course, with the resulting system winning some shared task categories. For this latter project, students attempted to tackle the same task in small groups, and finally submitted an ensemble system fed by each group's model to the competition.

Some classes use wikis to maintain information about course content, such as annotation guidelines for Computational Corpus Linguistics and some seminars tackling specific topics; this allows students to collaborate not only with their classmates, but with past and future students of the same course, which also increases the sense of relevance

[5] `http://people.cs.georgetown.edu/cosc572/s21/a0/`

[6] `https://corpling.uis.georgetown.edu/gum/`

of course work, as students can see that their work may live on long after they complete the course.

7 Including Languages Beyond English

In response to an unfortunate tendency of NLP teaching and research to focus primarily on English, we try to include data and examples from other languages when possible, while keeping in mind that students cannot be expected to know these languages in detail. In ENLP, for example, each student gives a short presentation on a different language of their choosing to develop awareness of the diversity of the world's languages, and the challenges of NLP on different languages. Other assignments integrating data from other languages include a finite state transducer for Japanese morphology in INLP as well as a unit on a 'surprise' low resource language, work on multilingual discourse treebanks in our discourse parsing course, statistical analysis of non-English data in our stats-centered R course for language data, and analysis of data from other languages in Lexical Functional Grammar (LFG) and Head-driven Phrase Structure Grammar (HPSG) in Grammar Formalisms. In the past we have also offered a dedicated course on parallel and other types of multilingual corpora, which we hope to be able to offer again, based on the availability of resources.

8 Teaching Research Skills

While many of the courses in table 1 cover textbook-style fundamentals, the Special Topics courses expose students to the scientific literature in particular areas. For Ph.D. students in particular, this provides the opportunity to engage with research ideas by reading critically and developing original ideas as term papers or projects. Two courses include a mock reviewing activity simulating an ACL reviewing experience. Final projects in several courses—including Corpus Linguistics, Machine Learning for Linguistics, ENLP, and Meaning Representations—consist of an open-ended research project with an ACL-style writeup for the final report.

9 Directions for Growth

The current curriculum caters primarily to graduate students, though many of the courses are also available to advanced undergraduates, who sometimes continue on into our regular Computational Linguistics MS, or Accelerated MS programs. While we do offer a few undergrad-specific classes, such as 'Algorithms for NLP,' 'Languages and Computers,' and 'Multilingual and Parallel Corpora,' these are taught on an occasional basis; in the future, resources allowing, we would like to develop a more consistent NLP curriculum aimed at undergraduates.

We have recently introduced a course on Social Factors in NLP to address a major gap in our curriculum, which is the lack of material focusing on the impact of real world NLP applications on society, and the ways in which models reflect demographic and other types of bias. While this is a step toward teaching a better understanding of the relationship of NLP to society, we believe it is worthwhile to integrate more content on societal impact and ethical considerations into the core NLP courses as well, and are working to do so for coming years. We would also like to continue to expand our curriculum to address other topics that currently receive little coverage, such as grammar engineering and computational psycholinguistics.

Acknowledgments

We would like to acknowledge the other faculty who teach the courses described in this paper: Matthew Marge, Corey Miller, Elizabeth Merkhofer, Paul Portner, Achim Ruopp, and Shabnam Tafreshi. We thank the anonymous reviewers and members of the NERT lab for feedback on this paper, as well as the organizers of the workshop.

References

Nicholas Asher and Alex Lascarides. 2003. *Logics of Conversation*. Studies in Natural Language Processing. Cambridge University Press, Cambridge.

Jason Baldridge and Katrin Erk. 2008. Teaching computational linguistics to a large, diverse student body: Courses, tools, and interdepartmental interaction. In *Proceedings of the Third Workshop on Issues in Teaching Computational Linguistics*, pages 1–9, Columbus, Ohio. Association for Computational Linguistics.

Eric Fosler-Lussier. 2008. Strategies for teaching "mixed" computational linguistics classes. In *Proceedings of the Third Workshop on Issues in Teaching Computational Linguistics*, pages 36–44, Columbus, Ohio. Association for Computational Linguistics.

William C. Mann and Sandra A. Thompson. 1988. Rhetorical Structure Theory: Toward a functional theory of text organization. *Text*, 8(3):243–281.

Rashmi Prasad, Bonnie Webber, and Aravind Joshi. 2014. Reflections on the Penn Discourse TreeBank, comparable corpora, and complementary annotation. *Computational Linguistics*, 40(4):921–950.

Amir Zeldes. 2017. The GUM corpus: Creating multilayer resources in the classroom. *Language Resources and Evaluation*, 51(3):581–612.

Gaining Experience with Structured Data: Using the Resources of Dialog State Tracking Challenge 2

Ronnie W. Smith
Department of Computer Science
East Carolina University
Greenville, NC 27858 USA
rws@cs.ecu.edu

Abstract

This paper describes a class project for a recently introduced undergraduate NLP course that gives computer science students the opportunity to explore the data of Dialog State Tracking Challenge 2 (DSTC 2). Student background, curriculum choices, and project details are discussed. The paper concludes with some instructor advice and final reflections.

1 Introduction

One of the consequences of the data explosion of the past twenty-five years is the likelihood that a large number of computer scientists and computing professionals will have the opportunity to develop analytical tools for processing large, structured datasets during their careers. This is of course especially true in the domain of NLP. A variety of NLP application domains can serve as an opportunity to provide undergraduate students with a chance to gain experience with the processing of structured data in order to solve an interesting "real world" problem. This paper describes a class project for an undergraduate NLP course that gives students the opportunity to explore the data of Dialog State Tracking Challenge 2 (DSTC 2). Student background, curriculum choices, and project details are discussed. The paper concludes with some advice for instructors who might be interested in incorporating a DSTC 2 based project into their course and final reflections about student feedback.

2 Background

At East Carolina University, a Natural Language Processing course was added to our curriculum during academic year 2015-2016. It is a junior/senior level course for which the prerequisites are data structures and introductory statistics. Significant factors that influenced the decisions about curriculum and pedagogy during the initial offerings of the course (spring semesters 2017 through 2019) include the following.

- While we also have a machine learning course, it is not a prerequisite. Consequently, the NLP instructor cannot assume all students have completed the machine learning course.
- While Python is a rapidly growing programming language of choice, our students have not had significant exposure to the language prior to the NLP course. We use Java and C++ in our introductory and data structures courses.
- Only a small percentage of our students choose graduate study and almost all of those who do only seek a terminal masters degree. Nevertheless, it is important to expose undergraduate computer science majors to the tools of research if for no other reason than to give them an awareness of how research advancements are made.
- It is this author's belief that an undergraduate degree in computer science is merely a "license to learn." It is essential that our students understand the necessity of and gain experience with self-directed learning before they graduate.

Based on these factors, *Natural Language Processing with Python* (Bird et al., 2009) was chosen as the textbook for the course. It had been the basis for a successful independent study course with a Duke University undergraduate during spring 2013. Notable advantages of this choice include the following.

1. Gives students the opportunity to engage in some self-directed learning of a new programming language (Python) and a new API (the Natural Language Toolkit (Bird et al., 2008)).
2. Provides a gentle introduction to machine learning techniques suitable for our students

Proceedings of the Fifth Workshop on Teaching NLP, pages 70–79
June 10–11, 2021. ©2021 Association for Computational Linguistics

who had not yet taken the machine learning course.

3. Offers a low cost to students as it is available free of charge online.

4. Provides a rich collection of exercises by which students can begin to gain proficiency and confidence in working with collections of structured data.

A main disadvantage of this text is its limited discussion of linguistic theory, but that can be addressed by other assigned readings.

With the cooperation of the department chair, the class size was restricted (15 in 2017, 25 in 2018, and 29 in 2019). This enabled the opportunity to provide more individualized learning opportunities. The primary such opportunity was the class project using the DSTC 2 data that was assigned for the spring 2018 and spring 2019 offerings of the course. Discussion of this project will be the focus of the remainder of the paper.

3 DSTC 2 Overview

For DSTC 2 a general discussion of the challenge and challenge results are provided in (Henderson et al., 2014a). The ground rules for the challenge are specified in (Henderson et al., 2013). A summary of the details most relevant to its use for a class project is provided below.

3.1 Problem Domain

The dialog environment was a telephone-based dialog system where the user task was to obtain restaurant information. During data collection each system user was given a dialog scenario to follow. Example scenario descriptions extracted from two of the log files are given below.

- `Task 09825: You want to find a cheap restaurant and it should be in the south part of town. Make sure you get the address and phone number.`

- `Task 11937: You want to find an expensive restaurant and it should serve portuguese food. If there is no such venue how about north american type of food. You want to know the phone number and postcode of the venue.`

The basic structure of the dialogs has the following pattern.

1. Acquire from the user a set of constraints about the type of restaurant desired. Users may supply constraint information about area, food, name, and price range. This phase may require multiple iterations as user goals change (such as from portuguese food to north american food for task 11937).

2. Once the constraints have been acquired, provide information about one or more restaurants that satisfy the constraints. Users may request that additional attributes about a restaurant be provided (such as address and phone number).

An example transcript of an actual dialog for completing task 11937 is provided in appendix A.

As described in the challenge handbook (Henderson et al., 2013), during each call, the dialog system logged detailed information that provides the needed input for a separate module for handling dialog state tracking. Further details about the data collection process are described next.

3.2 Data Collection Process

There were two different speech recognition (SR) models and 3 different dialog management models for a total of six different dialog systems that were used in the data collection process. Approximately 500 dialogs were collected using each of the six systems. There were a total of 184 unique users that were recruited using Amazon Mechanical Turk. Data using two of the dialog managers across both SR models (i.e., four of the six dialog systems) were used for training and development while data collected using the third dialog manager (1117 dialogs) was used as the test set for evaluation.[1]

4 Possible Activities with the DSTC 2 Data

For a group of students with sufficient technical background with Python and/or machine learning, a class project that allows students to develop their own dialog state tracking system is certainly feasible. Students could start from scratch and enhance

[1]The total number of dialogs was 3235. They were subdivided by the challenge organizers into a training set of 1612 dialogs, a dev set of 506 dialogs and then the test set of 1117 dialogs.

one of the rule-based baseline trackers that are provided in the DSTC 2 dataset or else develop or enhance a machine learning approach for tracking (e.g. (Williams, 2014), (Henderson et al., 2014b))[2]. In either case students should base their approach on a data-driven analysis of the nature of the dialogs.

However, this is not the only possible use of the data. In a circumstance where students do not have the necessary background to develop their own tracker, they can still engage with the data by developing their own analysis tools to glean information useful for studying other aspects of dialog processing such as miscommunication handling. Given the instructor's personal research interests and the students' background, this seemed to be the best way to proceed with a project as described next.

5 In-class Project Activities

About midway through the semester after completing the first five chapters of *Natural Language Processing with Python*, a week of class is taken to introduce students to dialog state tracking and the project. The goals for that week of class include the following.

- Introduce students to the natural language dialog problem. Resources used include a video of the Circuit Fix-it Shoppe dialog system (Hipp and Smith, 1993) and an introductory paper on natural language interfaces (Smith, 2005).

- Introduce students to the dialog state tracking problem using selected information from the first four sections of the DSTC 2 handbook (Henderson et al., 2013).

- Introduce students to the project requirements (see section 6).

- Provide a brief introduction to the structure of the raw data used in the project. The data is represented using JavaScript Object Notation (JSON). This introduction includes a template Python program that can be used as the basis for the software development activities of the students. Detailed study of appendix A in the challenge handbook is essential for successful completion of the project. This template program can access all dialogs based on a list of dialog ID's that are specified in a file whose name is specified as a command line argument. For each accessed dialog the template program extracts and displays the dialog acts of the system and speaker.

- Introduce students to other data resources available for the project. Besides the raw data, a supplemental resource that is provided are annotated transcripts of the dialogs. To keep students from being overwhelmed, each student is assigned the dialogs of a specific speaker. Several of the speakers interacted with all six of the dialog systems. Each student is assigned a different speaker.[3] The total number of dialogs in each set is between 15 and 20 dialogs per speaker. Besides the transcribed system output and Automatic Speech Recognition (ASR) input, other information provided in the annotated transcript includes the following.[4]

  1. The formal dialog act of the system utterance.
  2. The list of hypotheses provided by the Spoken Language Understanding (SLU) module including scoring.
  3. The actual transcription of what was spoken by the user.
  4. The chosen hypothesis of the SLU along with a comparison of that hypothesis to what was actually spoken.
  5. The current state of the dialog tracking process with respect to the informable attributes (area, food, name, and pricerange) for which information has been provided at some point in the dialog. Note that as in the case of the sample dialog for task 11937, the information for a specific goal can change (such as the food preference changing from "portuguese" to "north american".).

There are a few other in-class activities that relate more specifically to the project requirements.

[2]There are also several other papers related to DSTC 2 in the SIGDIAL 2014 proceedings (Georgila et al., 2014). The two specifically cited discuss the two best performing trackers in the original challenge.

[3]Besides acting as a limit on the amount of data a student had to consider, another reason for this was to generate data that could be used to study if speakers behaved differently with the different dialog systems.

[4]Details about the formal notation are provided in (Henderson et al., 2013).

They will be mentioned in the following section that discusses the project requirements.

6 Project Requirements

Students are required to submit a separate Python program for carrying out each of the following tasks.

1. Basic performance analysis of the speech quality.
2. Automatic annotation of dialog state change.
3. Automatic generation of dialog feature information for miscommunication detection.

More detailed discussion about each of these activities will follow.

6.1 Basic performance analysis of the speech quality

The intent of this requirement was to give students a gentle introduction to modifying the Python template program to access other elements in the raw dialog data. Their program was required to produce the following information for each user utterance.

- Number of words actually spoken by the human speaker.
- Number of words in the highest scored live speech recognition hypothesis.
- Total number of unique words found in the union of all the live speech recognition hypotheses.
- A label describing whether or not the utterance was understood.[5]

6.2 Automatic annotation of dialog state change

Dialog state change occurs when the user either supplies constraint information for possible restaurant recommendations (area, food, name, or price range) or else requests that additional attributes about a restaurant be provided (such as address and phone number). In this task students must implement a program that tracks the changes in these supplied values as the dialog proceeds. The algorithm for carrying out this task was discussed as part of the in-class activities. For each user utterance, the program had to specify the set of attributes for which (1) a new value had been supplied; (2) a modified value has been supplied; and (3) a value has been removed.

6.3 Automatic generation of dialog feature information for miscommunication detection

This part of the project gave students a chance to conduct their own analysis and offer their own insight into what readily computable features of the dialogs might be helpful to a dialog manager in determining that miscommunication occurred. Each student was required to propose three possibilities for feature detection, and in a one-on-one meeting, we would discuss the options and settle on a particular choice.[6] Details about chosen features and the results are presented in section 9.3.

This particular project requirement was used spring semester 2018 but not spring semester 2019. The reason for this was not due to any problem with the requirement other than the amount of time required by the instructor to meet with the students and then evaluate the work. Unfortunately for spring semester 2019 due to workload constraints the instructor did not have sufficient time to oversee and evaluate that requirement. Instead a standardized third requirement was used that asked students to conduct a performance analysis for the SLU module that looked at its performance as a function of the presence or absence of a "high-scoring" NULL semantic hypothesis where the definition of "high-scoring" was specified as a run-time parameter.

6.4 Project Report Requirements

Detailed requirements are provided in appendix B. The intent of the report requirement was to give students a chance to reflect on the dialog state tracking problem and its relationship to detection of dialog miscommunication. In earlier course assignments, students had been asked to reflect and write about the domain problem at hand. One such assignment was from the second chapter of the *Natural Language Processing with Python* textbook where students were asked to calculate word frequencies for words of their choice for five different genres in the Brown corpus. Students were asked to come up with words whose presence or

[5]This required using a function call to an instructor-provided Python module.

[6]Students were required to submit their proposal for advance review. Meetings were scheduled at 10 minute intervals.

absence might be typical for that genre. In their reflection, students were asked to explain their rationale for the genres they chose and to discuss the sequence of insights/lessons learned as different sets of words were tested. Students were specifically challenged to provide evidence of thoughtful inquiry—demonstrate a sequence of cycling through hypothesis, test, result, and refinement. It was hoped that prior experience with this mode of activity would be helpful while working on the project.

7 Project Assessment

7.1 Weightings

The three parts of the project were weighted as follows.

1. Speech quality performance (30%).
2. Dialog state change annotation (40%).
3. Generation of dialog feature information (2018)/SLU performance (2019) (30%).

For each part, code correctness/quality was weighted at 70% while report quality was weighted at 30%.

7.2 Evaluating code correctness/quality

For the first two parts of the project as well as the 2019 part 3 requirement to analyze SLU performance, it is certainly possible to base code correctness on automated testing. Unfortunately, that is likely to penalize excessively logic errors of a minor nature that could lead to large discrepancies in output results. Given the limited scope of each program, a checklist of features can be manually inspected reasonably quickly. A time estimate would be 20 to 30 minutes per student. As would be expected, correct solutions do not take as long to check.

Checking correctness of the 2018 part 3 requirement where students implemented their own feature generation algorithm is not as straightforward. While it was possible to steer the students towards a total of about five different dialog features rather than more than 20 different programs, it was still not a simple task.

7.3 Evaluating report quality

Two main questions were examined.

1. Did the student address each of the report requirements?
2. Does the report exhibit evidence that the student seriously looked at the results of running the software and base their observations on that.

As might be expected, there was a wide disparity in the quality of the efforts. Some excerpts from the reports are the following.

- "Part 3 of this assignment seems to work when it wants to."
- "... much of our language is fluff."

In contrast, some students wrote multiple paragraphs analyzing details and making tangible proposals for how to use the results to help with handling dialog miscommunication. One student who was concurrently enrolled in an information retrieval course and had learned about Naive Bayes classifiers chose to explore using the data produced from part 1 (speech quality), and implement a classifier to see how it would perform (unsurprisingly, not well).

Fortunately in general, many students engaged in meaningful self-discovery of principles for effective human-computer dialog interaction such as the usefulness of careful design in the phrasing of questions to the user. Several students also noted that excessive user terseness is not always helpful.

8 Classroom reinforcement of their research efforts

Given the challenging nature of this project to our students, it would have been unwise to have spent the final weeks of the semester with excessive presentation of new material. To reinforce the goal of student exposure to the process of research and to connect their work to the research community, two 50 minute class periods were used looking at four papers from the 2014 SIGDial conference where the work from DSTC 2 was presented. Class time was spent watching the videos of the original conference presentations of these papers ((Henderson et al., 2014a), (Smith, 2014), (Williams, 2014), and (Henderson et al., 2014b)). These are available at `https://www.superlectures.com/sigdial2014/`. This classroom activity was conducted two weeks prior to the end of the semester. The final week was spent being available for additional consultation about projects as well as spending class time on answering questions about NLP that were posed by students at the beginning of the semester. This was a chance to help them see what they had learned during the semester, and to understand better what remains an unsolved problem.

9 Student Outcomes

9.1 Part 1: Speech quality performance

This requirement served its purpose beautifully. One problem that exists in undergraduate computer science study is the pervasive belief that almost any programming question is answerable by an Internet search—you just have to submit the magic words to get the answer to appear. To meet this requirement and do the rest of the project, students really had to study the handbook and apply the information it contained to the provided template program. This was mentioned several times in student project reports in response to the "what was your biggest challenge and how did you overcome it?" question.

9.2 Part 2: Dialog state change annotation

The algorithm presentation in class did not go into the details of how to access the needed data. Again, students had to apply the lessons learned from part 1 as well as further investigate the handbook to understand how to access needed data. Between the data access and the required data structures needed in their implementation, students because much more capable of identifying the differences in use between Python lists and dictionaries. This part of the project tended to be the most challenging for the students.

9.3 Part 3: Generation of dialog feature information (2018)

Besides setting a flag to indicate repetition of a system response, the primary choice of students was to drill deeper into the ASR and SLU data. The most common approaches are given below.

- Counting the occurrences of an <attribute,value> pair (e.g. <food,italian>) in the different SLU hypotheses.
- Calculating cumulative confidence in an <attribute,value> pair over the various SLU hypotheses.
- Combining SLU score with utterance length in some fashion.
- Detecting the presence or absence of the NULL (no interpretation) hypothesis for the SLU.
- Detecting the presence or absence of <attribute,value> information in the SLU that appeared in the ASR.

Given the technical challenges required, the final item was only attempted by a few students.

A key misconception that arose in several students initial proposals for feature generation was a confusion over what is available at the time the dialog is occurring. Several students tried to propose using information only available after the dialogs had completed (i.e. using the correctness annotations for what was actually spoken and what the correct SLU hypothesis updated dialog state tracking values should be). While this information can be helpful in reassessing the performance of dialog system modules, it cannot be directly used in detecting miscommunication during an ongoing dialog. I believe that their work on part 2: dialog state change annotation led to this confusion since they were using the post-dialog annotations to complete that task. An extra 15 minutes of class time addressing this issue prior to student proposals should have cleared up this misconception.

9.4 Part 3: SLU performance (2019)

Most students implemented this correctly. This was one place where it might have been helpful to have the students also run their solution on the entire DSTC 2 dataset as well as the dialogs of their assigned speaker to see if the SLU performance on their speaker was representative of overall performance.

10 Advice for Instructors

Besides in an introductory undergraduate NLP class for computer science majors with limited background in machine learning and Python, I believe a project based on the DSTC 2 data can be used in a variety of contexts.

- In an advanced NLP class where students already have a machine learning background.
- In an advanced undergraduate data structures class. The project could be a means to get students interested in NLP based on a common

activity—having a conversation with someone else.

- In an accelerated summer camp environment for talented undergraduates.

If interested in using the DSTC 2 data for a class project, I would suggest the following steps.

1. Go to `https://github.com/matthen/dstc` and download the following files at a minimum.
    - `handbook.pdf`
    - `dstc2_traindev.tar.gz` - Train and development datasets for DSTC 2.
    - `dstc2_test.tar.gz` - Test dataset for DSTC 2.
    - `dstc2_scripts.tar.gz` - Evaluation scripts, baseline tracker and other tools.
    - `HWU_baseline.zip` - Alternative baseline tracker, provided by Zhuoran Wang.
2. Install the downloaded files and make sure you can run one of the supplied trackers on the entire dataset.
3. Streamline the baseline tracker code and/or scoring code to access and process a subset of the features from the datasets. Alternatively, you may wish to consult the teaching materials web site for this workshop to access the demo scripts that should be made available.
4. Explore the `/scripts/config` subdirectory within the installation to understand the use of the `flist` files for listing the specific dialogs to be processed during the execution of a script.

Once you've successfully completed these tasks, you should be well on your way to developing your own project with this data. Feel free to consult the author of this paper as needed.

11 Lessons Learned

Student feedback was largely anecdotal and quite favorable. While it is certainly the case that in response to the "What would you change to improve the course?", the most common answer was to have more time spent on classifiers/machine learning, students did enjoy working on the project. The most interesting piece of feedback that was acquired was from a student who originally submitted an incomplete project during the first offering of the assignment (spring 2018). The student was allowed an extra couple of weeks to complete the project. At some point during fall semester 2018 the student took the time to communicate with me to let me know that the student had used the project as part of a job interview when asked to give a technical presentation about a previous project the student had completed. The student said, "...the final project in your NLP class was by far the most interesting one that I've been assigned in college ...".

While this was gratifying feedback, the more important outcome is the belief that the course and project did achieve the goals of giving students experience with self-directed learning and engagement with the tools of research. We are fortunate in NLP to have a wide variety of interesting problems available to us that will naturally intrigue our students regardless of their original interest in NLP. If one wishes to use dialog processing as the interesting problem, the DSTC 2 data is a valuable resource for use in the classroom. Regardless, I would encourage instructors to pick a task that excites them. Our teaching is much stronger when we are demonstrating the need for self-directed learning ourselves. Our research provides such a means.

12 Acknowledgements

I would like to thank my computer science department chair, Dr. Venkat Gudivada, for allowing me to teach the initial offerings of the course with a restricted enrollment. This enabled me to offer more individualized exploratory research opportunities with our undergraduates.

None of this would have been possible without the existence of the DSTC 2 challenge. A special thanks goes to the DSTC 2 organizers, Matthew Henderson, Blaise Thomson, and Jason Williams as well as to the University of Cambridge, Microsoft Research, and SIGDIAL (Special Interest Group on Discourse and Dialogue) for their sponsorship and support of the challenge.

A final thanks goes to the anonymous reviewers who helped me better understand what would be of most value to the readers of this paper.

References

Steven Bird, Ewan Klein, and Edward Loper. 2009. *Natural Language Processing with Python: Analyzing Text with the Natural Language Toolkit*. O'Reilly, Beijing. Current version of the book is available at http://www.nltk.org/book/.

Steven Bird, Ewan Klein, Edward Loper, and Jason Baldridge. 2008. Multidisciplinary instruction with the natural language toolkit. In *Proceedings of the Third Workshop on Issues in Teaching Computational Linguistics*, pages 62–70, Columbus, Ohio. Association for Computational Linguistics.

Kallirroi Georgila, Matthew Stone, Helen Hastie, and Ani Nenkova, editors. 2014. *Proceedings of the 15th Annual Meeting of the Special Interest Group on Discourse and Dialogue (SIGDIAL)*. Association for Computational Linguistics, Philadelphia, PA, U.S.A.

M. Henderson, B. Thomson, and J. Williams. 2013. *Dialog State Tracking Challenge 2 & 3*. `https://github.com/matthen/dstc/blob/master/handbook.pdf`.

M. Henderson, B. Thomson, and J. Williams. 2014a. The second dialog state tracking challenge. In *Proceedings of the SIGdial 2014 Conference*, pages 263–272, Philadelphia, U.S.A. Association for Computational Linguistics.

Matthew Henderson, Blaise Thomson, and Steve Young. 2014b. Word-based dialog state tracking with recurrent neural networks. In *Proceedings of the 15th Annual Meeting of the Special Interest Group on Discourse and Dialogue (SIGDIAL)*, pages 292–299, Philadelphia, PA, U.S.A. Association for Computational Linguistics.

D. R. Hipp and R. W. Smith. 1993. A demonstration of the "circuit fix-it shoppe". In *Video Proceedings of the AAAI Conference*.

Ronnie Smith. 2014. Comparative error analysis of dialog state tracking. In *Proceedings of the 15th Annual Meeting of the Special Interest Group on Discourse and Dialogue (SIGDIAL)*, pages 300–309, Philadelphia, PA, U.S.A. Association for Computational Linguistics.

R.W. Smith. 2005. Natural language interfaces. In *Encyclopedia of Language and Linguistics*, 2 edition, pages 496–503. Elsevier Limited, Oxford.

Jason D. Williams. 2014. Web-style ranking and SLU combination for dialog state tracking. In *Proceedings of the 15th Annual Meeting of the Special Interest Group on Discourse and Dialogue (SIGDIAL)*, pages 282–291, Philadelphia, PA, U.S.A. Association for Computational Linguistics.

A Sample Dialog Transcript

Figure 1 is the transcript of an actual dialog for completing Task 11937 (description listed in section 3.1). SYS denotes utterances by the computer system and ASR is the speech returned by the speech recognizer. This sample dialog was used during class presentation about DSTC 2. It was used in order to make clear to the students that what ASR returns is not always what was actually said, but it is close enough in this example so that the intent is still understood. A more detailed transcript including what was actually said is also made available to the students.

B Sample Project Report Requirements

This information comes from the second offering of the dialog state tracking project during spring semester 2019. The report requirements for the previous year (where part three of the project allowed students to choose a dialog miscommunication feature to extract) is identical except the final paragraph was omitted.

B.1 Report Organization

Your report should have three sections, one section for each required investigation.

Section 1: Basic performance analysis of the speech quality

Section 2: Automatic annotation of dialog state change

Section 3: Basic performance analysis of the SLU module

Each section should contain the following.

- A list of any known deficiencies in the software. If you have no known deficiencies, explicitly say so.

- A description of the biggest challenge you faced in successfully completing the software for the given investigation. Did you overcome the challenge and if so, how?

- A discussion of your most interesting observation based on the data produced by the software. A quality discussion will not only present the results, but also present some thoughtful analysis that relates to the challenge of dialog state tracking. Possible contexts in which to frame the discussion include the following.

1. An observation based on differences as a function of the dialog system being used (recall that each `S[0-2]A[0-1]` combination represents a different dialog system).
2. An observation based on differences as a function of dialog type (goal change vs. non-goal change).
3. An observation that provides insight about one or more areas of exploration that could lead to improved performance by dialog state trackers, especially in regards to detecting possible miscommunication.

NOTE: You are not required to use the same context (or any of these contexts for that matter) for each section. Use whatever seems appropriate based on your observations as it relates to the specific topic.

IMPORTANT: A quality discussion of your most interesting observation for Section 3 should also include a proposal for either extending the program you wrote, or proposing a completely new software tool (i.e. program) for deeper investigation of the relevant issues you have identified for improving performance in dialog state tracking.

```
Session: data/Mar13_S2A0/voip-72e50baa85-20130326_053416

Turn 0
SYS  > Hello , welcome to the Cambridge restaurant system. You can ask for
restaurants by area , price range or food type . How may I help you?
ASR  > i don't mind an expensive restaurant that serves portuguese food

Turn 1
SYS  > I'm sorry but there is no restaurant serving expensive portuguese food
ASR  > what about north american food

Turn 2
SYS  > I'm sorry but there is no restaurant serving expensive portuguese food
ASR  > north american food

Turn 3
SYS  > Could you please repeat that?
ASR  > what about north american food

Turn 4
SYS  > gourmet burger kitchen serves north american food in the expensive
price range
ASR  > what is the phone number

Turn 5
SYS  > The phone number of gourmet burger kitchen is 01223 312598 .
ASR  > what is the post code

Turn 6
SYS  > The post code of gourmet burger kitchen is C.B 2, 1 A.B
ASR  > bad

Turn 7
SYS  > I am sorry but there is no other north american restaurant in the
expensive price range
ASR  > thank you been bad

Turn 8
SYS  > gourmet burger kitchen serves north american food in the expensive
price range
ASR  > can you get back

Turn 9
SYS  > Can I help you with anything else?
ASR  > thank you good bye
```

Figure 1: Sample dialog for completing Task 11937

The Flipped Classroom model for teaching Conditional Random Fields in an NLP course

Manex Agirrezabal
Centre for Language Technology (CST) - Department of Nordic Studies and Linguistics
University of Copenhagen / Københavns Universitet
Emil Holms Kanal 2
2300 Copenhagen (Denmark)
manex.aguirrezabal@hum.ku.dk

Abstract

In this article, we show and discuss our experience in applying the flipped classroom method for teaching Conditional Random Fields in a Natural Language Processing course. We present the activities that we developed together with their relationship to a cognitive complexity model (Bloom's taxonomy). After this, we provide our own reflections and expectations of the model itself. Based on the evaluation got from students, it seems that students learn about the topic and also that the method is rewarding for some students. Additionally, we discuss some shortcomings and we propose possible solutions to them. We conclude the paper with some possible future work.

1 Introduction

In this article we would like to provide experience on developing a flipped classroom environment in a Natural Language Processing course. The most common approach of teaching involves a teacher "pouring" knowledge to its students, as if students were plants and knowledge was water. There is a tendency, though, to make classes more active and interactive, in which communication does not only happen from the teacher to the students, but also from student to student.

Bloom's taxonomy[1] (Bloom et al., 1956; Anderson et al., 2001) is a model that describes the cognitive load of different types of work or activities. On the one hand, some activities, such as remembering or understanding specific characteristics of, for instance, a model of any kind, would be considered to require a low cognitive load. On the other hand, evaluating which model is best by considering the characteristics of each, could be considered to be in a higher level of complexity in Bloom's taxonomy.

If we want our students to be more knowledgeable and reflective, we need to go beyond the lower levels in Bloom's taxonomy. The traditional approach of introducing topics in a lecture would make students remember and understand the covered topics. We believe, though, that with these teaching practices there is a time limitation to go beyond the first two levels of Bloom's taxonomy.

A more efficient approach could be to ask students to work on a set of topics beforehand, get prepared, and then, work on activities that involve a higher cognitive load. These activities could involve applying and analyzing the acquired knowledge to other aspects. In this article, we present our experience in teaching Conditional Random Fields as a Flipped Classroom. We teach this in a course at the Master level about Natural Language Processing (NLP).

The article is structured as follows. First we introduce the flipped classroom method and some challenges. After that, we present the program, course and lecture in which the new teaching method will be used. Then, we discuss the characteristics of the implied student and also the evaluation method that we use. Later, we describe the lectures structure and the different activities and we classify them according to Bloom's taxonomy. We then include some discussion, based on the experience. Finally, we conclude the work and suggest some possible future directions.

2 Flipped Classroom: Are we going to turn around the desks?

Flipped Classroom (Lage et al., 2000; Brame, 2013) is a teaching approach in which students get first exposure to the material of a lecture outside of class, and the in-class activities involve applying the learned content. Provision of lecture material can be done in a number of ways, such as reading material, video lectures as slideshows, podcasts, and so on.

[1] https://www.flickr.com/photos/vandycft/29428436431

Proceedings of the Fifth Workshop on Teaching NLP, pages 80–86
June 10–11, 2021. ©2021 Association for Computational Linguistics

Students are expected to do the homework, and the majority of the in-class activities fully depend on that. Because of that, the teacher should make sure that students do their homework, because even though we name it in various ways, watching lectures or reading articles is still homework (Nielsen, 2012), and the challenge of making students accomplish with that is still there. A possible idea for making sure that students do the reading homework could be to ask them to do a quiz or reward them somehow.

Apart from challenges regarding students, we may not forget that all the activities, homework, readings, and so on have to be retrieved, selected or produced. Furthermore, as the content covered in class is more complex, the teacher will have to be more prepared. All this results in a larger working load in the preparation of the class and its activities.

3 Background about program, course and lecture

In this section, we briefly introduce the M. Sc. program, the course and the specific lecture in which we will be focusing on.

The IT & Cognition program

The IT & Cognition program at the University of Copenhagen is an international and interdisciplinary program[2] that accepts a small group of students every year. The program covers three main areas: Natural Language Processing, Image Processing and Cognitive Science.

In the first semester, the students acquire the required basic skills for their further development in the specialization area in which they are interested. Scientific Programming, Language Processing I, Cognitive Science I and Vision and Image Processing are mandatory subjects that cover these basic skills.

In the second semester students continue learning about Language Processing and Cognitive Science in further specialized courses, and they also get an introduction to Data Science. Besides, they start their specialization process with an elective course.

The third and forth semesters are devoted to a third course about Cognitive Science and three different electives and after that, students work on their thesis project.

Language Processing 1 and 2 (LP1 and LP2)

These courses are taught during a whole academic year (two semesters). There is one lecture per week which lasts for two hours. Each course, LP1 and LP2, goes through fourteen weeks in the fall and spring semesters, respectively.

The Intended Learning Outcomes (ILOs) of both courses are quite similar. The main differences are in the degree of depth in which topics are covered. On the one hand, the first course offers basic knowledge about different tasks relevant to Natural Language Processing and their relationship to current society. On the other hand, the second course is more geared towards the development of more advanced algorithms and their application in more specific tasks.

Assessment method

We assess students by asking them to work on a predefined topic. The common procedure is to perform experiments for a relevant NLP task and afterwards, they should write a scientific article reporting on these experiments.

Lecture: Conditional Random Fields

One of the topics covered in the second Language Processing course covers knowledge about sequence tagging. We cover Hidden Markov Models, Maximum Entropy Markov Models and Conditional Random Fields, as sequential tagging models. This last model will be covered in one and a half sessions. In the first session (2 hours) we will cover theoretical questions and students are expected to understand them. In the following week, there will be one hour, and students will get hands-on practice about Conditional Random Fields.

The lecture itself has the goal of providing the students an understanding of how Maximum Entropy Markov Models (MEMMs) (McCallum et al., 2000) and Conditional Random Fields (CRFs) (Lafferty et al., 2001) make predictions compared to hard classification methods. Additionally, they should understand a common problem of MEMMs (Label Bias problem (Bottou, 1991; Lafferty et al., 2001)) and how CRFs solve such limitation. Finally, students should also be able to use CRFs for their own research after the lectures.

4 The implied student

The background of our student group is very heterogeneous. Some people may have a Computer

[2] `https://studies.ku.dk/masters/it-and-cognition/`

Science related background, and therefore, sufficient experience in programming. Other students do not have the same background, but they are strong in other aspects, such as linguistics, neuroscience or psychology. Besides, at the time that our analyzed lecture happens, students have already received lectures about programming (first semester), so therefore, this level gap should be significantly smaller.

5 Evaluation method

In recent years, the usual teaching practice in the Language Processing series has been lectures. As the goal of this experiment is to check whether the flipped classroom can support students in their learning or not, we will implement this teaching method for the section about Conditional Random Fields, and analyze how students feel about it.

We evaluate this teaching practice by asking students to fill in a survey. In the survey we ask students about their general knowledge about some topics (MEMMs, CRFs, Label Bias problem) but also about whether they would be able to use CRFs for their own work. Please find below the questions that we asked in the questionnaire:

1. Do you know what a MEMM is (Maximum Entropy Markov Model)?
2. Do you know what a CRF is (Conditional Random Field)?
3. Do you know what the Label Bias problem is?
4. Do you feel capable of using a CRF for your own problems, such as developing a Named Entity Recognition system?
5. Do you feel that this structure (teaching style) is more rewarding?
6. Do you feel that this structure is more demanding (mentally)?

The response to these questions could be either "Yes", "Roughly" or "No". Finally, there are two questions related to the specific teaching method, in which we ask students whether the teaching practice is more demanding (mentally) and also whether it is more rewarding, compared to the lecturing approach. The survey was made one week before the lecture day and after the lecture was done.

6 Activities

In this section we describe the activities that we made for students before the lectures, during the lectures and after the lectures. The activities will be made public, hoping that they will be useful for other NLP teachers and/or researchers.

6.1 Before lecture

Before the lecture, students were asked to watch two video lectures. The two videos were available at the university learning platform and they were made by ourselves. The first video covers Maximum Entropy Markov Models and we introduce them by showing the relationship to Logistic Regression and Hidden Markov Models. These last models (HMMs) were introduced two weeks before in this same course. We use Maximum Entropy Markov Models as a middle step in order to understand Conditional Random Fields, which are discussed in the second video. We talk about the Label Bias problem and show how this is solved by using global normalization in Conditional Random Fields.

Students should also read the paper that introduces Conditional Random Fields (Lafferty et al., 2001)[3].

6.2 In classroom (online)

As mentioned before, CRFs will be covered in one and a half lecture sessions. These sessions are held online because of the current situation, following our health authorities requirements.

Before we start the lecture, students are asked whether there are questions regarding the reading and watching activities. We will briefly recapitulate some aspects, such as where could sequential models like HMM, MEMM or CRFs be useful: Part-of-Speech (POS) tagging, Named Entity Recognition (NER), and besides, any other task that requires the production of tags for a given sequence of elements.

Then, the goal of the remaining time in the session is threefold: (1) to revise and get an understanding of why sequential models such as HMMs, MEMMs or CRFs are more powerful than hard classification models, e.g. Maximum Entropy, Support Vector Machines (SVM), and so on; (2) to make it clear what the Label Bias problem is; and (3) to show how CRFs solve the Label Bias problem by using global normalization. After this session, there will be time to show CRFs working in practice, so that students get hands-on experience.

We describe below four different exercises that students will have to do in small groups (3-4 people). These exercises have an increasing level of

[3]We believe that including an additional article about Maximum Entropy Markov Models (McCallum et al., 2000) is relevant and very helpful for students. Unfortunately, we did not include it this year.

t	0	1	2	3	4
WORDS	My	smartphone	worked	very	well
POS tags	PRP	N	VP	MOD	RB
Features	`1,2,0`	`0,10,0`	`0,6,1`	`0,4,0`	`0,4,0`

complexity, as it will be seen.

Exercise 1

Understand how prediction is made in a Maximum Entropy POS tagger. Students are given one sentence and the POS tags for each word in that sentence. They are told that the model is trained using three very simple features: `isUpperCase`, `length_chars`, `endsInEd`), and they have to simulate by hand how predictions are made for each word. We also provide a list of 10 possible POS tags. In order to make sure that the concepts about the weight matrix are understood, we ask some checkpoint questions, such as the shape of the weight matrix, provided that the input matrix has a size of `1x3` and the output matrix has a size of `1x10`.

Each group of students should provide two outputs to the teacher. Given an input and a weight matrix,[4] they should be able to see which POS tag would be returned by the model. We also ask them to describe, in one sentence with their own words, how the model produces the output for each word.

Considering Bloom's taxonomy (Bloom et al., 1956), this exercise could be considered an exercise to remember, understand and apply concepts, and thus, in the three lower levels.

6.2.1 Exercise 2

In this exercise, students are given the same exact sentence as before. The difference is that the POS tagger with which the students will work is a Maximum Entropy Markov Model (MEMM), and therefore, there is no independent predictions.

Students already learned about the Viterbi algorithm for Hidden Markov Models (HMM). The goal of this exercise is to remember how this algorithm works and also to try to be aware which is the difference between HMMs and MEMMs, i.e. the use of an extended set of features besides single words and tags.

In order to raise that awareness, the exercise is to go through the pseudo-code of the Viterbi algorithm for HMMs (Jurafsky and Martin, 2008, p. 220), understand it and find out which are the specific elements that have to be changed, so that this works with MEMMs. As a hint in order to guess what should be put there, we provide students a trellis of the example above. We highlight one node in that trellis and discuss what its outgoing arcs represent: A probability distribution $P_{S'}(S|0) = [P_1, P_2, ..., P_k]$. The value of k depends on the number of states, i.e. output classes.

This exercise requires understanding the Viterbi algorithm for HMMs and understanding what should be modified to make it work with MEMMs. As students have to draw connections between these two models, we consider that the cognitive load, based on Bloom's taxonomy, is higher than in exercise 1.

Exercise 3

In the previous exercise, when we mention the probability distribution $P_{S'}(S|O)$, we mention that some of those probabilities could be zero. Because of that, in this exercise we ask students to reflect on what would happen if we have a node with many zero probabilities. For example, what happens if a node has 2 non-zero probabilities? What if it has 10 non-zero probabilities? We ask them this question to think about those probabilities and make them aware of the Label Bias problem.

In Bloom's taxonomy this exercise could be seen as evaluating and/or analyzing, as students should be able to find out the problem by themselves. We do not ask them to apply what they know, but to think about how having more or less arcs could affect the probabilities of nodes, and thus, the final sequence probabilities.

Exercise 4

As they already identified the problem, the last exercise is to suggest a solution for that problem. They should analyze the trellis given in exercise 2 and think about a possible solution. Students are given 5-10 minutes to discuss the topic. Afterwards, we discuss their possible solutions and if nobody reaches the actual solution, we introduce global normalization (per observation sequence), which is used in Conditional Random Fields.

In this case, the students would be in a similar scenario as the researchers that found out the Label

[4] we also provide the dot product output to save time

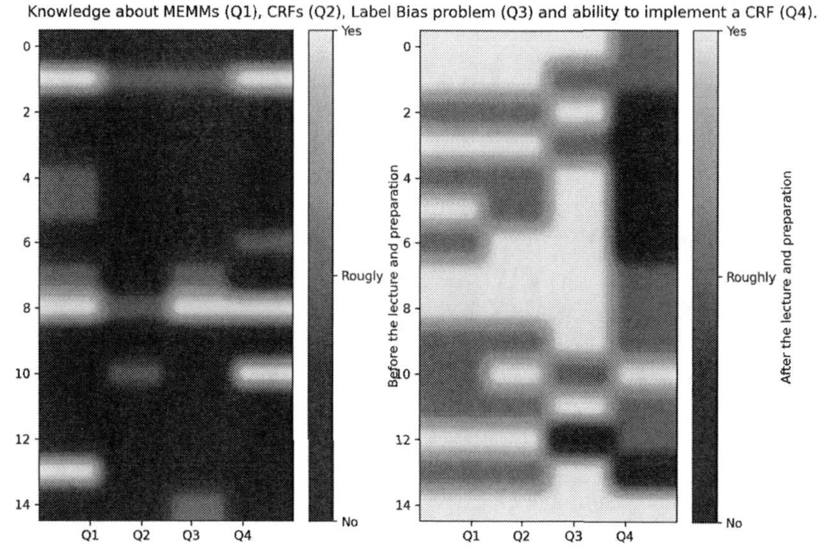

Figure 1: The left plot shows the responses to the survey that we did one week before the flipped classroom session started. The one on the right shows the responses to the same questions, but after the session was over. Based on the responses, we can say that students felt that they understood these four relevant aspects. It looks like, though, that in the future we should emphasize in the practical aspect of the taught models (Look at the right column in the second figure).

Bias problem. As such, we consider that this is at the highest level of Bloom's taxonomy, in which students discuss and conjecture about a possible solution for the problem.

Practical applications

After covering the previous exercises, in the next session, we cover Conditional Random Fields from a practical perspective, for which we show students how to process text to use it with Conditional Random Fields. We also discuss how to extract relevant features.

6.3 After classroom (exam project)

With regards to the final project, there will be a practical session in which different methods, including CRFs, will be shown. The students will be then able to apply the obtained knowledge.

7 Discussion and evaluation

Our expectation is that students will learn more, in a better way with a similar effort (from their side). We think that the reward (for students) of this teaching method is high, on the one hand. On the other hand, the required time for preparation (for teachers) is higher.

The preparation time increase is directly related with the fact that the topics that are covered are expected to be more complex. As students already got lecturing as homework, then the in-class activities become more complicated, and it is because of this that the teacher must have a deeper understanding of the topic in question. Besides, in our specific case the video lectures were made by us. We could save time by using the available resources in online learning platforms, but we decided to make them ourselves, making the preparation more time-consuming.

The evaluation, based on a survey that students had to answer, seems positive, although there are issues. Considering how much students learned, we can say that the learning goals were satisfied, as it can be seen in Figure 1. Each column in the plots represents the answers of our students to a question regarding knowledge on different concepts. They had to answer either Yes, Roughly or No. As we can see, students did not have much expertise on the topic before the lecture and preparation. Afterwards, the responses show that students got the required understanding.

Besides, we also asked whether this teaching method is more rewarding. 7 out of 15 answered yes. There was one that answered no. Finally, there were other 7 out of 15 people that did not take any stance, as they responded "I don't know". From these results we cannot strongly confirm that the method, in the way that we implemented it, is rewarding. It seems quite rewarding, though.

Together with these answers, we gave the students the option of writing further comments. There were some positive comments, and some others were possible issues with suggestions for improvements. One mentions that it is hard not to be able to ask questions when you watch the lecture, and that it is hard to remember the context of the question in class. A possible solution to this issue could be to include a discussion forum for each video lecture, so that students could post the question immediately in the forum. Another student pointed out that homework distribution was far from being optimal, as all homework was given in the first week and in the second week there was nothing. This should definitely be thought in a way that the homework load is more balanced. On the bright side, it seemed positive to have the chance of watching again the lecture videos. Also, some felt that group work was better and that it was nice to have more time to understand code and exercises.

8 Conclusion and Future directions

In this paper, we presented a possible class structure for teaching Conditional Random Fields in almost two lectures. This class is formulated as a Flipped classroom, in which there is a strong workload in the students' preparation and this allows students to get a further understanding of the topic, compared to traditional lecturing.

We contemplate the Flipped Classroom as a relevant teaching method for teaching complex topics. We believe that by asking students to do part of the work beforehand has allowed us to go one step beyond in the understanding of CRFs. Furthermore, the exercise types that we covered were in the highest orders in Bloom's taxonomy, showing the efficiency of the method.

The feedback that we got from students seems to show that, in general, they learn about the topic in question. It further seems that the method is rewarding for some students. We believe that the methodology has advantages, e.g. students get a deeper understanding of the topic, and disadvantages, for instance a higher preparation time. Considering both aspects, a possibility could be to find a balance between flipping only a portion of the whole lecture and having the other portion as a more traditional lecture.

In our prepared lectures, we decided to emphasize on a problem that Conditional Random Fields fix, the Label Bias problem. In the future, it would be interesting to include a discussion about the observation bias (Klein and Manning, 2002), which happens when the prediction is made by totally ignoring the labels.

As students have a very varied background, we could already observe differences in the time of execution of the exercises. A possible solution to this is to apply differentiated teaching (Rock et al., 2008), where the teaching content is adjusted to some groups of students, making the activities more tailored to those student clusters.

Acknowledgements

First of all, I would like to acknowledge the whole Teaching and Learning in Higher Education (TLHE) program taught at the University of Copenhagen, especially to my pedagogical and academic supervisors, Lis Lak Risager (TEACH centre) and Patrizia Paggio (Centre for Language Technology), respectively. I would like to thank also the students at Language Processing 2 (Spring semester, course 2020/2021, IT & Cognition program) for being so helpful in the development of this model. Last, but not least, I thank the anonymous reviewers for their valuable comments and revisions. These reviews are not only useful for this article, but also for the development of the whole course of Language Processing.

References

L.W. Anderson, B.S. Bloom, D.R. Krathwohl, P. Airasian, K. Cruikshank, R. Mayer, P. Pintrich, J. Raths, and M. Wittrock. 2001. *A Taxonomy for Learning, Teaching, and Assessing: A Revision of Bloom's Taxonomy of Educational Objectives*. Longman.

Benjamin S Bloom et al. 1956. Taxonomy of educational objectives. vol. 1: Cognitive domain. *New York: McKay*, 20:24.

Léon Bottou. 1991. *Une Approche théorique de l'Apprentissage Connexionniste: Applications à la Reconnaissance de la Parole*. Ph.D. thesis, Université de Paris XI, Orsay, France.

Cynthia Brame. 2013. Flipping the classroom (retrieved last 2021-03-15).

Daniel Jurafsky and James H Martin. 2008. Speech and language processing: An introduction to speech recognition, computational linguistics and natural language processing. *Upper Saddle River, NJ: Prentice Hall.*

Dan Klein and Christopher D Manning. 2002. Conditional structure versus conditional estimation in nlp models. In *Proceedings of the 2002 Conference on Empirical Methods in Natural Language Processing (EMNLP 2002)*, pages 9–16.

John Lafferty, Andrew McCallum, and Fernando CN Pereira. 2001. Conditional random fields: Probabilistic models for segmenting and labeling sequence data.

Maureen J Lage, Glenn J Platt, and Michael Treglia. 2000. Inverting the classroom: A gateway to creating an inclusive learning environment. *The journal of economic education*, 31(1):30–43.

Andrew McCallum, Dayne Freitag, and Fernando CN Pereira. 2000. Maximum entropy markov models for information extraction and segmentation. In *Icml*, volume 17, pages 591–598.

Lisa Nielsen. 2012. Five reasons i'm not flipping over the flipped classroom. *Technology & Learning*, 32(10):46–46.

Marcia L Rock, Madeleine Gregg, Edwin Ellis, and Robert A Gable. 2008. REACH: A framework for differentiating classroom instruction. *Preventing School Failure: Alternative Education for Children and Youth*, 52(2):31–47.

Flamingos and Hedgehogs in the Croquet-Ground: Teaching Evaluation of NLP Systems for Undergraduate Students

Brielen Madureira
Computational Linguistics
Department of Linguistics
University of Potsdam
madureiralasota@uni-potsdam.de

Abstract

This report describes the course *Evaluation of NLP Systems*, taught for Computational Linguistics undergraduate students during the winter semester 20/21 at the University of Potsdam, Germany. It was a discussion-based seminar that covered different aspects of evaluation in NLP, namely paradigms, common procedures, data annotation, metrics and measurements, statistical significance testing, best practices and common approaches in specific NLP tasks and applications.

1 Motivation

"Alice soon came to the conclusion that it was a very difficult game indeed." [1]

When the Queen of Hearts invited Alice to her croquet-ground, Alice had no idea how to play that strange game with flamingos and hedgehogs. NLP newcomers may be as puzzled as her when they enter the Wonderland of NLP and encounter a myriad of strange new concepts: Baseline, F1 score, glass box, ablation, diagnostic, extrinsic and intrinsic, performance, annotation, metrics, human-based, test suite, shared task...

Although experienced researchers and practitioners may easily relate them to the evaluation of NLP models and systems, for newcomers like undergraduate students it is not simply a matter of looking up their definition. It is necessary to show them the big picture of what and how we play in the croquet-ground of evaluation in NLP.

The NLP community clearly cares for doing proper evaluation. From earlier works like the book by Karen Spärck Jones and Julia R. Galliers (1995) to the winner of ACL 2020 best paper award (Ribeiro et al., 2020) and recent dedicated workshops, *e.g.* Eger et al. (2020), the formulation of evaluation methodologies has been a prominent topic in the field.

Despite its importance, evaluation is usually covered very briefly in NLP courses due to a tight schedule. Teachers barely have time to discuss dataset splits, simple metrics like accuracy, precision, recall and F1 Score, and some techniques like cross validation. As a result, students end up learning about evaluation on-the-fly as they begin their careers in NLP. The lack of structured knowledge may cause them to be unacquainted with the multifaceted metrics and procedures, which can render them partially unable to evaluate models critically and responsibly. The leap from that one lecture to what is expected in good NLP papers and software should not be underestimated.

The course *Evaluation of NLP Systems*, which I taught for undergraduate Computational Linguistics students in the winter semester of 20/21 at the University of Potsdam, Germany, was a reading and discussion-based learning approach with three main goals: i) helping participants become aware of the importance of evaluation in NLP; ii) discussing different evaluation methods, metrics and techniques; and iii) showing how evaluation is being done for different NLP tasks.

The following sections provide an overview of the course content and structure. With some adaptation, this course can also be suitable for more advanced students.

[1] Alice in Wonderland by Lewis Carroll, public domain. Illustration by John Tenniel, public domain, via Wikimedia Commons.

Proceedings of the Fifth Workshop on Teaching NLP, pages 87–91
June 10–11, 2021. ©2021 Association for Computational Linguistics

Topic	Content
Paradigms	Kinds of evaluation and main steps, *e.g.* intrinsic and extrinsic, manual and automatic, black box and glass box.
Common Procedures	Overview about the use of measurements, baselines, dataset splits, cross validation, error analysis, ablation, human evaluation and comparisons.
Annotation	How to annotate linguistic data, evaluate the annotation and how the annotation scheme can affect the evaluation of a system's performance.
Metrics and Measurements	Outline of the different metrics commonly used in NLP, what they aim to quantify and how to interpret them.
Statistical Significance Testing	Hypothesis testing for comparing the performance of two systems in the same dataset.
Best Practices	The linguistic aspect of NLP, reproducibility and the social impact of NLP.
NLP Case Studies	Group presentations about specific approaches in four NLP tasks/applications (machine translation, natural language generation, dialogue and speech synthesis) and related themes (the history of evaluation, shared tasks, ethics and ACL's code of conduct and replication crisis).

Table 1: Overview of the course content.

2 Course Content and Format

Table 1 presents an overview of the topics discussed in the course. Details about the weekly reading lists are available at the course's website.[2]

The course happened 100% online due to the pandemic. It was divided into two parts. In the first half of the semester, students learned about the evaluation methods used in general in NLP and, to some extent, machine learning. After each meeting, I posted a pre-recorded short lecture, slides and a reading list about the next week's content. The participants had thus one week to work through the material anytime before the next meeting slot. I provided diverse sources like papers, blogposts, tutorials, slides and videos.

I started the online meetings with a wrap-up and feedback about the previous week's content. Then, I randomly split them into groups of 3 or 4 participants in breakout sessions so that they could discuss a worksheet together for about 45 minutes. I encouraged them to use this occasion to profit from the interaction and brainstorming with their peers and exchange arguments and thoughts. After the meeting, they had one week to write down their solutions individually and submit it.

In the second half of the semester, they divided into 4 groups to analyze how evaluation is being done in specific NLP tasks. For larger groups, other NLP tasks can be added. They prepared group presentations and discussion topics according to general guidelines and an initial bibliography that they could expand. Students provided anonymous feedback about each other's presentations for me and I then shared it with the presenters, to have the chance to filter abusive or offensive comments.

The last lecture was a tutorial about useful metrics available in *scikit-learn* and *nltk* Python libraries using Jupyter Notebook (Kluyver et al., 2016).

Finally, they had six weeks to work on a final project. Students could select one of the following three options: i) a critical essay on the development and current state of evaluation in NLP, discussing the positive and negative aspects and where to go from here; ii) a hands-on detailed evaluation of an NLP system of their choice, which could be,

[2]https://briemadu.github.io/evalNLP/schedule

for example, an algorithm they implemented for another course; or iii) a summary of the course in the format of a small newspaper.

3 Participants

Seventeen bachelor students of Computational Linguistics attended the course. At the University of Potsdam, this seminar falls into the category of a module called *Methods of Computational Linguistics*, which is intended for students in the 5th semester of their bachelor course. Still, one student in the 3rd and many students in higher semesters also took part.

By the 5th semester, students are expected to have completed introductory courses on linguistics (phonetic and phonology, syntax, morphology, semantics and psycho- and neurolinguistics), computational linguistics techniques, computer science and programming (finite state automata, advanced Python and other courses of their choice), introduction to statistics and empirical methods and foundations of mathematics and logic, as well as varying seminars related to computational linguistics.

Although there were no formal requirements for taking this course, students should preferably be familiar some common tasks and practices in NLP and the basics of statistics.

4 Outcomes

I believe this course successfully introduced students to several fundamental principles of evaluation in NLP. The quality of their submissions, especially the final project, was, in general, very high. By knowing how to properly manage flamingos and hedgehogs, they will hopefully be spared the sentence "*off with their head!*" as they continue their careers in NLP. The game is not very difficult when one learns the rules.

Students gave very positive feedback at the end of the semester about the content, the literature and the format. They particularly enjoyed the opportunity to discuss with each other, saying it was good to exchange what they recalled from the reading. They also stated that what they learned contributed to their understanding in other courses and improved their ability to document and evaluate models they implement. The course was also useful for them to start reading more scientific literature.

In terms of improvements, they mentioned that the weekly workload could be reduced. They also reported that the reading for the week when we covered statistical significance testing was too advanced. Still, they could do the worksheet since it did not dive deep into the theory.

The syllabus, slides and suggested readings are available on the course's website.[3] The references here list the papers and books used to put together the course and has no ambition of being exhaustive. In case this course is replicated, the references should be updated with the most recent papers. I can share the worksheets and guidelines for the group presentation and the project upon request. Feedback from readers is very welcome.

Acknowledgments

In this course, I was inspired and used material available online by many people, to whom I am thankful. I also thank the students who were very engaged during the semester and made it a rewarding experience for me. Moreover, I am grateful for the anonymous reviewers for their detailed and encouraging feedback.

References

Valerie Barr and Judith L. Klavans. 2001. Verification and validation of language processing systems: Is it evaluation? In *Proceedings of the ACL 2001 Workshop on Evaluation Methodologies for Language and Dialogue Systems*.

Yonatan Belinkov and James Glass. 2019. Analysis methods in neural language processing: A survey. *Transactions of the Association for Computational Linguistics*, 7:49–72.

Anja Belz. 2009. That's nice… what can you do with it? *Computational Linguistics*, 35(1):111–118.

Emily M. Bender and Batya Friedman. 2018. Data statements for natural language processing: Toward mitigating system bias and enabling better science. *Transactions of the Association for Computational Linguistics*, 6:587–604.

Taylor Berg-Kirkpatrick, David Burkett, and Dan Klein. 2012. An empirical investigation of statistical significance in NLP. In *Proceedings of the 2012 Joint Conference on Empirical Methods in Natural Language Processing and Computational Natural Language Learning*, pages 995–1005, Jeju Island, Korea. Association for Computational Linguistics.

Chris Callison-Burch, Cameron Fordyce, Philipp Koehn, Christof Monz, and Josh Schroeder. 2007.

[3] https://briemadu.github.io/evalNLP/

(meta-) evaluation of machine translation. In *Proceedings of the Second Workshop on Statistical Machine Translation*, pages 136–158, Prague, Czech Republic. Association for Computational Linguistics.

Asli Celikyilmaz, Elizabeth Clark, and Jianfeng Gao. 2020. Evaluation of text generation: A survey. *arXiv preprint arXiv:2006.14799*.

Eirini Chatzikoumi. 2020. How to evaluate machine translation: A review of automated and human metrics. *Natural Language Engineering*, 26(2):137–161.

Jan Deriu, Alvaro Rodrigo, Arantxa Otegi, Guillermo Echegoyen, Sophie Rosset, Eneko Agirre, and Mark Cieliebak. 2021. Survey on evaluation methods for dialogue systems. *Artificial Intelligence Review*, 54(1):755–810.

Rotem Dror, Gili Baumer, Marina Bogomolov, and Roi Reichart. 2017. Replicability analysis for natural language processing: Testing significance with multiple datasets. *Transactions of the Association for Computational Linguistics*, 5:471–486.

Rotem Dror, Gili Baumer, Segev Shlomov, and Roi Reichart. 2018. The hitchhiker's guide to testing statistical significance in natural language processing. In *Proceedings of the 56th Annual Meeting of the Association for Computational Linguistics (Volume 1: Long Papers)*, pages 1383–1392, Melbourne, Australia. Association for Computational Linguistics.

Rotem Dror, Lotem Peled-Cohen, Segev Shlomov, and Roi Reichart. 2020. Statistical significance testing for natural language processing. *Synthesis Lectures on Human Language Technologies*, 13(2):1–116.

Steffen Eger, Yang Gao, Maxime Peyrard, Wei Zhao, and Eduard Hovy, editors. 2020. *Proceedings of the First Workshop on Evaluation and Comparison of NLP Systems*. Association for Computational Linguistics, Online.

Karën Fort, Gilles Adda, and K. Bretonnel Cohen. 2011. Last words: Amazon Mechanical Turk: Gold mine or coal mine? *Computational Linguistics*, 37(2):413–420.

J.R. Galliers, K.S. Jones, and University of Cambridge. Computer Laboratory. 1993. *Evaluating Natural Language Processing Systems*. Computer Laboratory Cambridge: Technical report. University of Cambridge, Computer Laboratory.

Albert Gatt and Emiel Krahmer. 2018. Survey of the state of the art in natural language generation: Core tasks, applications and evaluation. *Journal of Artificial Intelligence Research*, 61:65–170.

Kyle Gorman and Steven Bedrick. 2019. We need to talk about standard splits. In *Proceedings of the 57th Annual Meeting of the Association for Computational Linguistics*, pages 2786–2791, Florence, Italy. Association for Computational Linguistics.

Lynette Hirschman and Henry S. Thompson. 1997. *Overview of Evaluation in Speech and Natural Language Processing*, page 409–414. Cambridge University Press, USA.

Dirk Hovy and Shannon L. Spruit. 2016. The social impact of natural language processing. In *Proceedings of the 54th Annual Meeting of the Association for Computational Linguistics (Volume 2: Short Papers)*, pages 591–598, Berlin, Germany. Association for Computational Linguistics.

David M. Howcroft, Anya Belz, Miruna-Adriana Clinciu, Dimitra Gkatzia, Sadid A. Hasan, Saad Mahamood, Simon Mille, Emiel van Miltenburg, Sashank Santhanam, and Verena Rieser. 2020. Twenty years of confusion in human evaluation: NLG needs evaluation sheets and standardised definitions. In *Proceedings of the 13th International Conference on Natural Language Generation*, pages 169–182, Dublin, Ireland. Association for Computational Linguistics.

Karen Sparck Jones and Julia R Galliers. 1995. *Evaluating natural language processing systems: An analysis and review*, volume 1083 of *Lecture Notes in Artificial Intelligence*. Springer-Verlag Berlin Heidelberg.

Margaret King. 1996. Evaluating natural language processing systems. *Communications of the ACM*, 39(1):73–79.

Thomas Kluyver, Benjamin Ragan-Kelley, Fernando Pérez, Brian Granger, Matthias Bussonnier, Jonathan Frederic, Kyle Kelley, Jessica Hamrick, Jason Grout, Sylvain Corlay, Paul Ivanov, Damián Avila, Safia Abdalla, and Carol Willing. 2016. Jupyter notebooks – a publishing format for reproducible computational workflows. In *Positioning and Power in Academic Publishing: Players, Agents and Agendas*, pages 87 – 90. IOS Press.

Zachary C. Lipton and Jacob Steinhardt. 2019. Troubling trends in machine learning scholarship: Some ml papers suffer from flaws that could mislead the public and stymie future research. *Queue*, 17(1):45–77.

Chia-Wei Liu, Ryan Lowe, Iulian Serban, Mike Noseworthy, Laurent Charlin, and Joelle Pineau. 2016. How NOT to evaluate your dialogue system: An empirical study of unsupervised evaluation metrics for dialogue response generation. In *Proceedings of the 2016 Conference on Empirical Methods in Natural Language Processing*, pages 2122–2132, Austin, Texas. Association for Computational Linguistics.

Jekaterina Novikova, Ondřej Dušek, Amanda Cercas Curry, and Verena Rieser. 2017. Why we need new evaluation metrics for NLG. In *Proceedings of the 2017 Conference on Empirical Methods in Natural Language Processing*, pages 2241–2252, Copenhagen, Denmark. Association for Computational Linguistics.

Patrick Paroubek, Stéphane Chaudiron, and Lynette Hirschman. 2007. Principles of evaluation in natural language processing. *Traitement Automatique des Langues*, 48(1):7–31.

Carla Parra Escartín, Wessel Reijers, Teresa Lynn, Joss Moorkens, Andy Way, and Chao-Hong Liu. 2017. Ethical considerations in NLP shared tasks. In *Proceedings of the First ACL Workshop on Ethics in Natural Language Processing*, pages 66–73, Valencia, Spain. Association for Computational Linguistics.

Ehud Reiter and Anja Belz. 2009. An investigation into the validity of some metrics for automatically evaluating natural language generation systems. *Computational Linguistics*, 35(4):529–558.

Philip Resnik and Jimmy Lin. 2010. Evaluation of NLP systems. *The handbook of computational linguistics and natural language processing. Chapter 11.*, 57.

Marco Tulio Ribeiro, Tongshuang Wu, Carlos Guestrin, and Sameer Singh. 2020. Beyond accuracy: Behavioral testing of NLP models with CheckList. In *Proceedings of the 58th Annual Meeting of the Association for Computational Linguistics*, pages 4902–4912, Online. Association for Computational Linguistics.

Stefan Riezler and John T. Maxwell. 2005. On some pitfalls in automatic evaluation and significance testing for MT. In *Proceedings of the ACL Workshop on Intrinsic and Extrinsic Evaluation Measures for Machine Translation and/or Summarization*, pages 57–64, Ann Arbor, Michigan. Association for Computational Linguistics.

Nathan Schneider. 2015. What I've learned about annotating informal text (and why you shouldn't take my word for it). In *Proceedings of The 9th Linguistic Annotation Workshop*, pages 152–157, Denver, Colorado, USA. Association for Computational Linguistics.

Noah A Smith. 2011. Linguistic structure prediction. *Synthesis lectures on human language technologies*, 4(2):1–274.

Anders Søgaard, Anders Johannsen, Barbara Plank, Dirk Hovy, and Hector Martínez Alonso. 2014. What's in a p-value in NLP? In *Proceedings of the Eighteenth Conference on Computational Natural Language Learning*, pages 1–10, Ann Arbor, Michigan. Association for Computational Linguistics.

Karen Sparck Jones. 1994. Towards better NLP system evaluation. In *Human Language Technology: Proceedings of a Workshop held at Plainsboro, New Jersey, March 8-11, 1994.*

Chris van der Lee, Albert Gatt, Emiel van Miltenburg, Sander Wubben, and Emiel Krahmer. 2019. Best practices for the human evaluation of automatically generated text. In *Proceedings of the 12th International Conference on Natural Language Generation*, pages 355–368, Tokyo, Japan. Association for Computational Linguistics.

Petra Wagner, Jonas Beskow, Simon Betz, Jens Edlund, Joakim Gustafson, Gustav Eje Henter, Sébastien Le Maguer, Zofia Malisz, Éva Székely, Christina Tånnander, et al. 2019. Speech synthesis evaluation—state-of-the-art assessment and suggestion for a novel research program. In *Proceedings of the 10th Speech Synthesis Workshop (SSW10)*.

An Immersive Computational Text Analysis Course for Non-Computer Science Students at Barnard College

Adam Poliak **Jalisha Jenifer**
Barnard College, Columbia University
{apoliak,jjenifer}@barnard.edu

Abstract

We provide an overview of a new Computational Text Analysis course that will be taught at Barnard College over a six week period in May and June 2021. The course is targeted to non Computer Science at a U.S. Liberal Arts college that wish to incorporate fundamental Natural Language Processing tools in their research and studies. During the course, students will complete daily programming tutorials, read and review contemporary research papers, and propose and develop independent research projects.

1 Introduction

As computing has become foundational to 21st century literacy (Guzdial, 2019), students across many disciplines are increasingly interested in gaining computing literacy and skills. Barnard College is meeting this increased demand through its *Thinking Quantitatively and Empirically* and *Thinking Technologically and Digitally* requirements that respectively aim for students "to develop basic competence in the use of one or more mathematical, statistical, or deductive methods" and "foster students' abilities to use advanced technologies for creative productions, scholarly projects, scientific analysis or experimentation."[1]

This new 3-credit Computational Text Analysis course will enable roughly 25 students to leverage advanced NLP technologies in their work.[2] The goal of the course is to introduce students to the tools and quantitative methods to discover, measure, and infer phenomena from large amounts of text. Unlike a traditional Natural Language Processing class, students will not implement key algorithms from scratch. Rather, students will learn how to use existing python libraries like nltk (Loper and Bird, 2002), gensim (Rehurek and Sojka, 2011), spacy (Honnibal et al., 2020), and sklearn (Pedregosa et al., 2011) to analyze large amounts of textual data. Students will also gain famillarity with webscraping tools and APIs often used to collect textual data.

Week	Topic
1	Bash, Python, & Math bootcamp
2	Words, Words, Words
3	Topic Modeling
4	Data Collection
5	Machine Learning
6	Advanced Topics & Final Projects

Table 1: Theme for each of the six weeks.

2 Course Design

Due to COVID-19 schedule changes, the course will meet remotely for 95 minutes four days a week over 6 weeks. Each week will revolve around a class of methods used in computational text analysis, shown in Table 1. Course meetings will begin with a 30 minute lecture motivating and explaining a specific concept or method. Corresponding readings introducing these methods will be provided before class. In the subsequent 30 minute interval, we will collaboratively work through a Jupyter-Notebook demonstrating the day's concept using real-world textual data.[3] Both the lecture and collaborative demo will be recorded and available to students after class. Students can use the remaining 35 minutes to begin and complete daily homework tutorials where they will further experiment with applying methods to provided real-world text.

[1] http://catalog.barnard.edu/barnard-college/curriculum/requirements-liberal-arts-degree/foundations/

[2] https://coms2710.barnard.edu/

[3] We will continue this practice from a previous online Introductory Data Science class (https://coms1016.barnard.edu/) where students found live coding demos to be helpful.

Proceedings of the Fifth Workshop on Teaching NLP, pages 92–95
June 10–11, 2021. ©2021 Association for Computational Linguistics

Assignment	Grade Percent
Daily Tutorials	20
Weekly Homework	30
Paper Reviews	15
Final Project	35

Table 2: Assignments and corresponding grade weights.

2.1 Assignments

Students will complete four types of assignments during the six week course to gain familiarity, comfort, and confidence applying computational textual analysis methods to large corpora (Table 2). With an emphasis on learning by doing, completing **daily tutorials** independently will help students solidify their understanding of the day's material while working through examples where these methods have been successfully deployed. Daily tutorials will primarily be graded using an autograder. Many of the daily tutorials are adaptions of notebooks from similar courses, e.g. Jonathan Reeve's *Computational Literary Analysis* course[4] at Columbia University, Matthew Wilkens's and David Mimno's *Text Mining for History and Literature* course[5] at Cornell, and Christopher Hench's and Claudia von Vacano's *Rediscovering Text as Data* course[6] at Berkeley.

Each week, students will be given a corpus and a research question and will be tasked with using the previous week's methods to try answering the specific research question. These **weekly homeworks** will give students freedom to experiment with different methods and see how different design choices can have significant impacts. Table 3 outlines the theme and corpora for each weekly homework. Students will be allowed to work on these assignments in pairs. Completed notebooks containing students' code, figures, and a brief write-up will be graded manually. To help prepare students for final projects, feedback will include questions and comments related to both the technical methods used and presentation.[7]

[4]`https://icla2020b.jonreeve.com/`

[5]`https://github.com/wilkens-teaching/info3350-f20`

[6]`https://github.com/henchc/Rediscovering-Text-as-Data`

[7]Daily tutorials and weekly homeworks will be publicly available at `https://github.com/BC-COMS-2710/summer21-material`. Solutions and autograders will be available to other instructors wishing to adopt this course.

Theme	Corpus
Readability	U.S Presidential Inaugural Addresses
Document Similarity	NYTimes Obituaries
Web Scraping	Columbia Course Reviews
Machine Learning	Political Tweets

Table 3: Themes and corresponding corpus for the four week-long homeworks different assignments.

Students will complete five brief **paper reviews** during the course. Each week, students will choose from a set of research papers and write a brief review of the paper. Each review will include a short summary and a few sentences reflecting on their opinion on the paper's methods and findings. This will help students appreciate the wide-ranging applicability of these methods and see more examples where researchers in other fields have successfully leveraged computational text analysis methods.

For their **final projects**, students will develop their own research question based on a corpus that they will collect. Students will apply at least two methods covered in the course to answer their research question. By the end of the fourth week, students will propose their research question and will begin to collect a corpus to study. Students will present a brief progress update to the rest of the class during the last scheduled course meeting (Monday June 14th) and provide feedback to each other. Students will use the official finals period to incorporate feedback and submit a final write up describing their research.

2.2 Computational Infrastructure

All assignments will be completed using JupyterLabs hosted on a JupyterHub server maintained by Columbia University IT at no cost to students. This enables equal access for students who might not have resources to store and process large amounts of text. Additionally, this will ensure students use the same library and tools versions.

2.3 Prerequisites

We strongly recommend students to have taken at least one prior programming course. While we make no assumptions about students prior programming experience and we cover bash and python basics, we believe having one prior programming course will help students hit the ground running. Furthermore, this allows us to cover more advanced topics in depth. In future versions of the course taking place during a traditional 13-week semester, we

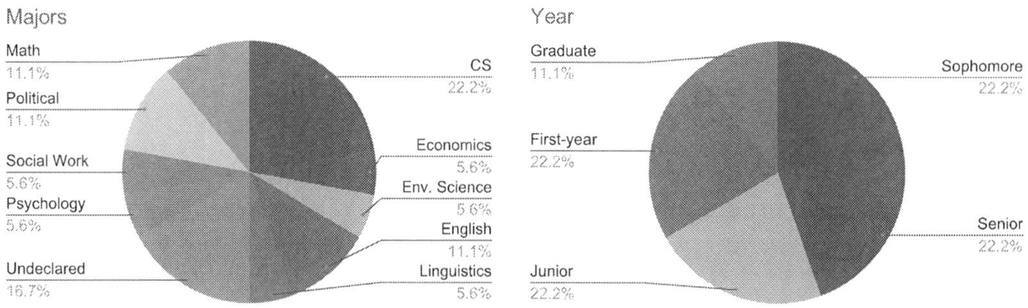

Figure 1: Statistics from 18 registered students who completed a pre-course interest form. Breakdown of students by major (left) and year (right).

will consider removing this recommendation.

2.4 Textbooks

We will primarily use the recent *Text Analysis in Python for Social Scientists: Discovery and Exploration* textbook (Hovy, 2021) because of its assertion that "using off-the-shelf libraries . . . strips away some of the complexity of the task, which makes it a lot more approachable" thus enabling "programming novices to use efficient code to try out a research idea." We will use select readings from the NLTK book (Bird et al., 2009), the most recent edition of *Speech and Language Processing* (Jurafsky and Martin, 2000),[8], An Introduction to Text Mining: Research Design, Data Collection, and Analysis (Ignatow and Mihalcea, 2017), and Melanie Walsh's online *Cultural Analytics & Python* textbook.[9]

3 Prospective Students

With summer course registration underway, 25 students are currently registered for the course. Since the course is under active development and students come from a range of academic backgrounds, we have asked students to complete a brief survey to help us prepare and tailor the class as much as possible. Figure 1 shows results from the 12 students who have completed the survey so far. While we see interest from Computer Science students, most of the students are programming novices – half of the survey participants indicated they have no prior programming experience outside of one or two programming courses.[10] Many students indicated they have corpora in mind that they are interested in studying or that they plan on using these methods to enhance their undergraduate theses in other fields.

4 Measuring STEM-Related Attitudes & Beliefs

The beliefs and attitudes students possess about learning play a significant role in their academic performance (Elliot and Dweck, 2013). Given the fact that our course is targeting non-computer science majors, we are interested in seeing how the academic attitudes held by participating students relate to and change throughout their participation in the course. We are particularly interested in measuring students' beliefs about the malleability of their own intelligence, as these beliefs have been shown to predict student motivation, engagement, and performance in academic courses (De Castella and Byrne, 2015). To measure the effect such beliefs on students in this course, we will administer the self-theory implicit theories of intelligence scale (De Castella and Byrne, 2015). We will also measure students' motivation for computer science using an adapted version of the Science Motivation Questionnaire (Glynn et al., 2007). We will have students complete these surveys at the beginning and end of the course, which will enable us to a) measure whether students' initial attitudes significantly relate to their performance in the course, and b) measure whether participation in the course leads to changes in student attitudes over time.

5 Conclusion

We described a new Computational Text Analysis course that will be taught at Barnard College in

[8]Specifically Chapters 4 and 5 for Machine Learning.

[9]`https://melaniewalsh.github.io/Intro-Cultural-Analytics/welcome.html`

[10]The larger number of interested computer science students might be due to the course being offered by the Computer Science department.

May-June 2021. The broad goal of the course is for students to gain technical skills allowing them to successfully incorporate Natural Language Processing methods into their respective fields and research. We will rely on proven methods to measure the effect the course has on students' perception of their abilities and skills. All material developed for the course (slides, assignments, autograders) will be available for instructors to adopt at their institutions. An updated version of this paper will be available on the first author's webpage with reflections and lessons learned once the course is completed.

Acknowledgements

We thank Maya Bickel for providing feedback and debugging assignments. Additionally, we thank Michael Weisner and his team at Columbia University Information Technology for helping maintain the computational infrastructure for the course.

References

Steven Bird, Ewan Klein, and Edward Loper. 2009. *Natural language processing with Python: analyzing text with the natural language toolkit.* " O'Reilly Media, Inc.".

Krista De Castella and Donald Byrne. 2015. My intelligence may be more malleable than yours: The revised implicit theories of intelligence (self-theory) scale is a better predictor of achievement, motivation, and student disengagement. *European Journal of Psychology of Education*, 30(3):245–267.

Andrew J Elliot and Carol S Dweck. 2013. *Handbook of competence and motivation.* Guilford Publications.

Shawn M Glynn, Gita Taasoobshirazi, and Peggy Brickman. 2007. Nonscience majors learning science: A theoretical model of motivation. *Journal of Research in Science Teaching: The Official Journal of the National Association for Research in Science Teaching*, 44(8):1088–1107.

Mark Guzdial. 2019. Computing education as a foundation for 21st century literacy. In *Proceedings of the 50th ACM Technical Symposium on Computer Science Education*, pages 502–503.

Matthew Honnibal, Ines Montani, Sofie Van Landeghem, and Adriane Boyd. 2020. spaCy: Industrial-strength Natural Language Processing in Python.

Dirk Hovy. 2021. *Text Analysis in Python for Social Scientists: Discovery and Exploration.* Elements in Quantitative and Computational Methods for the Social Sciences. Cambridge University Press.

Gabe Ignatow and Rada Mihalcea. 2017. *An introduction to text mining: Research design, data collection, and analysis.* Sage Publications.

Daniel Jurafsky and James H Martin. 2000. Speech and language processing: An introduction to natural language processing, computational linguistics, and speech recognition.

Edward Loper and Steven Bird. 2002. Nltk: The natural language toolkit. In *In Proceedings of the ACL Workshop on Effective Tools and Methodologies for Teaching Natural Language Processing and Computational Linguistics. Philadelphia: Association for Computational Linguistics.*

F. Pedregosa, G. Varoquaux, A. Gramfort, V. Michel, B. Thirion, O. Grisel, M. Blondel, P. Prettenhofer, R. Weiss, V. Dubourg, J. Vanderplas, A. Passos, D. Cournapeau, M. Brucher, M. Perrot, and E. Duchesnay. 2011. Scikit-learn: Machine learning in Python. *Journal of Machine Learning Research*, 12:2825–2830.

Radim Rehurek and Petr Sojka. 2011. Gensim–python framework for vector space modelling. *NLP Centre, Faculty of Informatics, Masaryk University, Brno, Czech Republic*, 3(2).

Introducing Information Retrieval for Biomedical Informatics Students

Sanya B. Taneja **Richard D. Boyce** **William T. Reynolds** **Denis Newman-Griffis**
University of Pittsburgh
Pittsburgh, PA, USA
{sbt12, rdb20, wtr8, dnewmangriffis}@pitt.edu

Abstract

Introducing biomedical informatics (BMI) students to natural language processing (NLP) requires balancing technical depth with practical know-how to address application-focused needs. We developed a set of three activities introducing introductory BMI students to information retrieval with NLP, covering document representation strategies and language models from TF-IDF to BERT. These activities provide students with hands-on experience targeted towards common use cases, and introduce fundamental components of NLP workflows for a wide variety of applications.

1 Introduction

Natural language processing (NLP) technologies have become a fundamental tool for biomedical informatics (BMI) research, with uses ranging from mining new protein-protein interactions from scientific literature to recommending medications in clinical care. In most cases, however, the research question at hand is a biological or clinical one, and NLP tools are used off-the-shelf or lightly adapted rather than being the focus of research and development. When introducing BMI students to NLP, instructors must therefore navigate a balance between the computational and linguistic insights behind why NLP technologies work the way they do, and practical know-how for the application-focused settings where most students will go on to use NLP.

We developed a set of three activities designed to expose introductory BMI students to the fundamentals of NLP and provide hands-on experience with NLP techniques. These activities were designed for use in the Foundations of Biomedical Informatics I course at the University of Pittsburgh, a survey course which introduces students to core methods and topics in biomedical informatics. The course is required for all students in the Biomedical Informatics Training Program; students have a range of experience in computer science, and no background in artificial intelligence or NLP is required. The sequence of activities, implemented as Jupyter notebooks, comprise a single assignment focused on information retrieval, a common use case for NLP in all areas of BMI research. The assignment followed lectures focused on information retrieval, word embeddings, and language models (presented online in Fall 2020). §2 gives an overview of the three activities, and we note directions for further refinement of the activities in §3.

2 Assignment Details

Our set of three activities was designed with two primary learning goals in mind:

- Expose introductory BMI students to fundamental strategies for text representation and language models, geared towards information retrieval in biomedical contexts; and
- Provide students with hands-on experience creating NLP workflows using pre-built tools.

Our Jupyter notebooks provide a sequence of code samples to analyze and execute, combined with background questions to assess understanding of the computational and linguistic insights behind the NLP technologies students are using.

Notebook 1: Fundamentals of document analysis. In this notebook, students were first introduced to basic preprocessing tasks in NLP workflows such as tokenization, stemming, casing, and stop-word removal. Using a corpus from the Natural Language Toolkit (NLTK) (Bird et al., 2009), the notebook demonstrated two indexing techniques - inverted indexing and creation of a weighted document-term matrix using term frequency-inverse document frequency (TF-IDF). Students then implemented a synthetic information retrieval task involving a collection of 12 documents mapped to 20 queries as a reference set. The students evaluated the information retrieval system

Proceedings of the Fifth Workshop on Teaching NLP, pages 96–98
June 10–11, 2021. ©2021 Association for Computational Linguistics

with synthetic results for two queries comprising numeric values for each document in the query. Students measured system performance using TREC evaluation measures including recall, precision, interpolated precision-recall average, and mean average precision. The evaluation measures were implemented using the pytrec_eval library (Van Gysel and de Rijke, 2018).

Notebook 2: Introduction to word embeddings. In this notebook, students were introduced to word embeddings as a text representation tool for NLP. The students first created embeddings using singular value decomposition (SVD) of a co-occurrence matrix using the corpus from Notebook 1. This established the idea of capturing semantic similarity in texts as opposed to a tradition bag-of-words model. The notebook then used pretrained word2vec embeddings (Mikolov et al., 2013) to demonstrate a more refined approach of SVD. The students were able to visualize both the embedding approaches in the notebook. This was particularly important as most students did not have prior experience with embeddings and plotting the word embeddings can lead to greater insight into the variable semantic similarity that embedding representations provide over lexical features.

Notebook 3: Introduction to BERT and clinicalBERT. As all the activities are designed for introductory students, YouTube tutorials were used to provide background on neural networks and design decisions in language models for students with minimal background in NLP. Students were introduced to NLP workflows and language models using the Transformers library. Transformers is an open-source library developed by Hugging Face that provides a collection of pretrained models and general-purpose architectures for natural language processing (Wolf et al., 2020), based on the Transformer architecture (Vaswani et al., 2017). This includes BERT (Devlin et al., 2019) and clinicalBERT (Alsentzer et al., 2019), which are used in this notebook to implement Named Entity Recognition and Medical Language Inference tasks.

The notebook guided the students through a Medical Language Inference task to infer knowledge from clinical texts. Language inference in medicine is an important application of NLP as clinical notes such as those containing past medical history of a patient contain vital information that is utilized by clinicians to draw useful inferences (Romanov and Shivade, 2018). The task also introduced BMI students to challenges unique to applying NLP on clinical texts such as domain-specific vocabulary, diversity in abbreviations, content structure, and named entity recognition with clinical jargon. The students used the MedNLI (Romanov and Shivade, 2018) dataset created from MIMIC III (Johnson et al., 2016) clinical notes for this task. Building on knowledge from the previous notebooks, they implemented workflows to compare the performance of BERT and clinicalBERT models for prediction of labels in clinical texts. The students were encouraged to understand the importance of domain representation in pretraining data and the process of fine-tuning NLP models for domain-specific language.

3 Discussion

We designed three activities to demonstrate fundamental concepts and workflows for application of NLP to introductory BMI students. While the scope of NLP in the biomedical field is much larger than one assignment, we developed the activities to provide students with a modular workflow of components that are applicable to other NLP applications besides information retrieval; i.e., text preprocessing, indexing, execution, and evaluation.

One practical challenge for clinically-focused exercises is the limited availability of benchmark datasets. Most clinical datasets require Data Use Agreements and individual training requirements that are cumbersome for a classroom setting.Thus, the first two notebooks use the NLTK corpus which is a popular dataset for introducing NLP concepts without the challenges present in clinical datasets. While MIMIC (Johnson et al., 2016) is a valuable, relatively accessible source for clinical text, available annotations for it are limited. Students can thus be introduced to fine-tuning of language models for the specifics of medical language, but instructors must anticipate challenges in providing train/test splits for supervised machine learning.

We further take advantage of popular pre-built libraries (like Transformers) so that students can focus on the application rather than constructing neural networks. In an application-focused setting, technical knowledge of neural NLP systems is less necessary, but users of those systems still need to understand what kinds of regularities they rely on and when they may be unreliable. The activities are thus designed to reflect the perspective of the practical challenges that students will face when working in biomedical NLP.

Finally, one important area we are investigating as we refine and extend these teaching materials is the ethical considerations of biomedical AI technologies. The intersection of medical and AI ethics poses several challenging questions for designing, training, and applying AI technologies in the biomedical setting (Char et al., 2018; Keskinbora, 2019), and sensitive information often described in medical text presents further ethical questions for NLP systems (Lehman et al., 2021). Thus, determining what BMI students have a responsibility to understand about the NLP tools they use, and how we most effectively teach that information in limited course time, is key to broadening the responsible use of NLP in BMI research.

All materials presented in this paper are available from `https://github.com/dbmi-pitt/bioinf_teachingNLP`.

Acknowledgments

This work was supported in part by the National Library of Medicine of the National Institutes of Health under award number T15 LM007059.

References

Emily Alsentzer, John Murphy, William Boag, Wei-Hung Weng, Di Jin, Tristan Naumann, and Matthew McDermott. 2019. Publicly available clinical BERT embeddings. In *Proceedings of the 2nd Clinical Natural Language Processing Workshop*, pages 72–78, Minneapolis, Minnesota, USA. Association for Computational Linguistics.

Steven Bird, Ewan Klein, and Edward Loper. 2009. *Natural language processing with Python: analyzing text with the natural language toolkit*. " O'Reilly Media, Inc.".

Danton S Char, Nigam H Shah, and David Magnus. 2018. Implementing Machine Learning in Health Care - Addressing Ethical Challenges. *The New England journal of medicine*, 378(11):981–983.

Jacob Devlin, Ming-Wei Chang, Kenton Lee, and Kristina Toutanova. 2019. BERT: Pre-training of Deep Bidirectional Transformers for Language Understanding. In *Proceedings of the 2019 Conference of the North {A}merican Chapter of the Association for Computational Linguistics: Human Language Technologies, Volume 1 (Long and Short Papers)*, pages 4171–4186, Minneapolis, Minnesota. Association for Computational Linguistics.

Alistair EW Johnson, Tom J Pollard, Lu Shen, H Lehman Li-Wei, Mengling Feng, Mohammad Ghassemi, Benjamin Moody, Peter Szolovits, Leo Anthony Celi, and Roger G Mark. 2016. Mimic-iii, a freely accessible critical care database. *Scientific data*, 3(1):1–9.

Kadircan H Keskinbora. 2019. Medical ethics considerations on artificial intelligence. *Journal of Clinical Neuroscience*, 64:277–282.

Eric Lehman, Sarthak Jain, Karl Pichotta, Yoav Goldberg, and Byron C. Wallace. 2021. Does bert pretrained on clinical notes reveal sensitive data? *arXiv preprint arXiv:2104.07762*.

Tomas Mikolov, Ilya Sutskever, Kai Chen, Greg Corrado, and Jeffrey Dean. 2013. Distributed representations of words and phrases and their compositionality. *arXiv preprint arXiv:1310.4546*.

Alexey Romanov and Chaitanya Shivade. 2018. Lessons from natural language inference in the clinical domain. In *Proceedings of the 2018 Conference on Empirical Methods in Natural Language Processing*, pages 1586–1596, Brussels, Belgium. Association for Computational Linguistics.

Christophe Van Gysel and Maarten de Rijke. 2018. Pytrec_eval: An extremely fast python interface to trec_eval. In *SIGIR*. ACM.

Ashish Vaswani, Noam Shazeer, Niki Parmar, Jakob Uszkoreit, Llion Jones, Aidan N Gomez, Łukasz Kaiser, and Illia Polosukhin. 2017. Attention is All you Need. In I Guyon, U V Luxburg, S Bengio, H Wallach, R Fergus, S Vishwanathan, and R Garnett, editors, *Advances in Neural Information Processing Systems 30*, pages 5998–6008. Curran Associates, Inc.

Thomas Wolf, Lysandre Debut, Victor Sanh, Julien Chaumond, Clement Delangue, Anthony Moi, Pierric Cistac, Tim Rault, Rémi Louf, Morgan Funtowicz, Joe Davison, Sam Shleifer, Patrick von Platen, Clara Ma, Yacine Jernite, Julien Plu, Canwen Xu, Teven Le Scao, Sylvain Gugger, Mariama Drame, Quentin Lhoest, and Alexander M. Rush. 2020. Transformers: State-of-the-art natural language processing. In *Proceedings of the 2020 Conference on Empirical Methods in Natural Language Processing: System Demonstrations*, pages 38–45, Online. Association for Computational Linguistics.

Contemporary NLP Modeling in Six Comprehensive Programming Assignments

Greg Durrett* **Jifan Chen** **Shrey Desai** **Tanya Goyal**
Lucas Kabela **Yasumasa Onoe** **Jiacheng Xu**
Department of Computer Science
The University of Texas at Austin
gdurrett@cs.utexas.edu

Abstract

We present a series of programming assignments, adaptable to a range of experience levels from advanced undergraduate to PhD, to teach students design and implementation of modern NLP systems. These assignments build from the ground up and emphasize full-stack understanding of machine learning models: initially, students implement inference and gradient computation by hand, then use PyTorch to build nearly state-of-the-art neural networks using current best practices. Topics are chosen to cover a wide range of modeling and inference techniques that one might encounter, ranging from linear models suitable for industry applications to state-of-the-art deep learning models used in NLP research. The assignments are customizable, with constrained options to guide less experienced students or open-ended options giving advanced students freedom to explore. All of them can be deployed in a fully autogradable fashion, and have collectively been tested on over 300 students across several semesters.[1]

1 Introduction

This paper presents a series of assignments designed to give a survey of modern NLP through the lens of system-building. These assignments provide hands-on experience with concepts and implementation practices that we consider critical for students to master, ranging from linear feature-based models to cutting-edge deep learning approaches. The assignments are as follows:

A1. Sentiment analysis with linear models (Pang et al., 2002) on the Stanford Sentiment Treebank (Socher et al., 2013).

A2. Sentiment analysis with feedforward "deep averaging" networks (Iyyer et al., 2015) using GloVe embeddings (Pennington et al., 2014).

A3. Hidden Markov Models and linear-chain conditional random fields (CRFs) for named entity recognition (NER) (Tjong Kim Sang and De Meulder, 2003), using features similar to those from Zhang and Johnson (2003).

A4. Character-level RNN language modeling (Mikolov et al., 2010).

A5. Semantic parsing with seq2seq models (Jia and Liang, 2016) on the GeoQuery dataset (Zelle and Mooney, 1996).

A6. Reading comprehension on SQuAD (Rajpurkar et al., 2016) using a simplified version of the DrQA model (Chen et al., 2017), similar to BiDAF (Seo et al., 2016).

A1-A5 come with autograders. These train each student's model from scratch and evaluate performance on the development set of each task, verifying whether their code behaves as intended. The autograders are bundled to be deployable on Gradescope using their Docker framework.[2] These coding assignments can also be supplemented with conceptual questions for hybrid assignments, though we do not distribute those as part of this release.

Other Courses and Materials Several other widely-publicized courses like Stanford CS224N and CMU CS 11-747 are much more "neural-first" views of NLP: their assignments delve more heavily into word embeddings and low-level neural implementation like backpropagation. By contrast, this course is designed to be a survey that

*Corresponding author. Subsequent authors listed alphabetically.

[1]See https://cs.utexas.edu/~gdurrett for past offerings and static versions of these assignments; contact Greg Durrett for access to the repository with instructor solutions.

[2]For the CRF and seq2seq modeling assignments, a custom framework must be used, as Gradescope autograders cannot handle these. We grade these in a batch fashion on a single instructional machine, which poses some logistical challenges.

Proceedings of the Fifth Workshop on Teaching NLP, pages 99–103
June 10–11, 2021. ©2021 Association for Computational Linguistics

Assignment	Main Concepts	Output	Components				
			Linear	FFNN	Enc	Dec	Attn
A1: Sentiment (Linear)	Classification, SGD, bag-of-words	Binary	■				
A2: Sentiment (FFNNs)	PyTorch, word embeddings	Binary	■	■			
A3: HMMs and CRFs for NER	Structured prediction, dyn. prog.	Tags	■				
A4: Language Modeling	Neural sequence modeling	Token seq	■	▒	■	▒	
A5: Seq2seq Semantic Parsing	Encoder-decoder, attention	Token seq	■	▒	▒	■	■
A6: Reading Comprehension	QA, domain adaptation	Span	▒	▒	▒		▒

Table 1: Breakdown of assignments. The concepts and model components in each are designed to build on one another. A gray square indicates partial engagement with a concept, typically when students are already given the needed component or it isn't a focus of the assignment.

also covers topics like linear classification, generative modeling (HMMs), and structured inference. Other hands-on courses discussed in prior Teaching NLP papers (Klein, 2005; Madnani and Dorr, 2008; Baldridge and Erk, 2008) make some similar choices about how to blend linguistics and CS concepts, but our desire to integrate deep learning as a primary (but not the sole) focus area guides us towards a different set of assignment topics.

2 Design Principles

This set of assignments was designed after we asked ourselves, *what should a student taking NLP know how to build?* NLP draws on principles from machine learning, statistics, linguistics, algorithms, and more, and we set out to expose students to a range of ideas from these disciplines through the lens of implementation. This choice follows the "text processing first" (Bird, 2008) or "core tools" (Klein, 2005) views of the field, with the idea that students can study undertake additional study of particular topic areas and quickly get up to speed on modeling approaches given the building blocks presented here.

2.1 Covering Model Types

There are far too many NLP tasks and models to cover in a single course. Rather than focus on exposing students to the most important applications, we instead designed these assignments to feature a range of models along the following typological dimensions.

Output space The prediction spaces of models considered here include binary/multiclass (A1, A2), structured (sequence in A3, span in A6), and natural language (sequence of words in A4, executable query in A5). While structured models have fallen out of favor with the advent of neural networks, we view tagging and parsing as fundamental pedagogical tools for getting students to think about linguistic structure and ambiguity, and these are emphasized in our courses.

Modeling framework We cover generative models with categorical distributions (A3), linear feature-based models including logistic regression (A1) and CRFs (A3), and neural networks (A2, A4, A5, A6). These particularly highlight differences in training, optimization, and inference required for these different techniques.

Neural architectures We cover feedforward networks (A2), recurrent neural encoders (A4, A5, A6), seq2seq models (A5), and attention (A5, A6). From these, Transformers (Vaswani et al., 2017) naturally emerge even though they are not explicitly implemented in an assignment.

2.2 Other Desiderata

A major consideration in designing these assignments was to **enable understanding without large-scale computational resources.** Maintaining simplicity and tractability is the major reason we do not feature more exploration of pre-trained models (Devlin et al., 2019). These factors are also why we choose character-level language modeling (rather than word-level) and seq2seq semantic parsing (rather than translation): training large autoregressive models to perform well when output vocabularies are in the tens of thousands requires significant engineering expertise. While we teach students skills like debugging and testing models on simplified settings, we still found it less painful to build our projects around these more tractable tasks where students can iterate quickly.

Another core goal was to allow students to **build systems from the ground-up using simple, understandable code.** We build on PyTorch primitives (Paszke et al., 2019), but otherwise avoid using frameworks like Keras, Huggingface, or AllenNLP. The code is also somewhat "underengineered:" we avoid an overly heavy reliance on Pythonic constructs like list comprehensions or generators as not all students come in with a high level of familiarity with Python.

What's missing **Parsing** is notably absent from these assignments; we judged that both chart parsers and transition-based parsers involved too many engineering details specific to these settings. All of our classes do cover parsing and in some cases have other hands-on components that engage with parsing, but students do not actually build a parser. Instead, sequence models are taken as an example of structured inference, and other classification tasks are used instead of transition systems.

From a system-building perspective, the biggest omissions are **pre-training and Transformers**. These can be explored in the context of final projects, as we describe in the next section.

Finally, our courses integrate additional discussion around **ethics**, with specific discussions surrounding bias in word embeddings (Bolukbasi et al., 2016; Gonen and Goldberg, 2019) and ethical considerations of pre-trained models (Bender et al., 2021), as well as an open-ended discussion surrounding social impact and ethical considerations of NLP, deep learning, and machine learning. These are not formally assessed at present, but we are considering this for future iterations of the course given these topics' importance.

3 Deployment

These assignments have been used in four different versions of an NLP survey course: an upper-level undergraduate course, a masters level course (delivered online), and two PhD-level courses. In the online MS course, these constitute the only assessment. **For courses delivered in a traditional classroom format, we recommend choosing a subset of the assignments and supplementing with additional written assignments testing conceptual understanding.**

Our undergrad courses use A1, A2, A4, and a final project based on A6. We use additional written assignments covering word embedding techniques, syntactic parsing, machine translation, and pre-trained models. Our PhD-level courses use A1, A2, A3, A5, and an independent final project. The assignments also support further "extension" options: for example, in A3, beam search is presented as optional and students can also explore parallel decoding for the CRF or features for NER to work better on German. For the seq2seq model, they could experiment with Transformers or implement constrained decoding to always produce valid logical forms.

Assignment	Eisenstein	Jurafsky + Martin
A1	2, 4	4, 5
A2	3	7
A3	7	8
A4	6	7, 9
A5	12, 18	11, 15
A6	17.5	23.2

Table 2: Book chapters associated with each assignment; gray indicates an imperfect match. Our courses use a combination of Eisenstein, ad hoc lecture notes on certain topics, and academic papers.

We believe that A1 and A2 could be adapted to use in a wide range of courses, but A3-A6 are most appropriate for advanced undergraduates or graduate students.

Syllabus Table 2 pairs these assignments with readings in texts by Jurafsky and Martin (2021) and Eisenstein (2019). See Greg Durrett's course pages for complete sets of readings.

Logistics We typically provide students around 2 weeks per assignment. Their submission either consists of just the code or a code with a brief report, depending on the course format. Students collaborate on assignments through a discussion board on Piazza as well as in person. We have relatively low incidence of students copying code, assessed using Moss over several semesters.

Pain Points Especially on A3, A4, and A5, we come across students who find **debugging** to be a major challenge. In the assignments, we suggest strategies to verify parts of inference code independently of training, as well as simplified tasks to test models on, but some students find it challenging or are unwilling to pursue these avenues. On a similar note, students often **do not have a prior on what the system should do.** It might not raise a red flag that their code takes an hour per epoch, or gets 3% accuracy on the development set, and they end up getting stuck as a result. Understanding what these failures mean is something we emphasize. Finally, students sometimes have (real or perceived) **lack of background** on either coding or the mathematical fundamentals of the course; however, many such students end up doing well in these courses as their first ML/NLP courses.

Acknowledgments

We would like to acknowledge the additional graduate and undergraduate TAs for various offerings of these courses: Christopher Crabtree, Uday Kusupati, Shivangi Mahto, Abhilash Potluri, Shivang Singh, Xi Ye, and Didi Zhou. Our thanks also go out to all of the students who have taken these courses, whose comments and experiences have helped make them stronger. Thanks as well to the anonymous reviewers for their helpful comments.

In the development of these materials, we consulted courses and teaching materials by Emily Bender, Sam Bowman, Chris Dyer, Mohit Iyyer, Vivek Srikumar, and many others. We would also like to thank Jacob Eisenstein, Dan Jurafsky, James H. Martin, and Yoav Goldberg for their helpful textbooks.

References

Jason Baldridge and Katrin Erk. 2008. Teaching computational linguistics to a large, diverse student body: Courses, tools, and interdepartmental interaction. In *Proceedings of the Third Workshop on Issues in Teaching Computational Linguistics*, pages 1–9, Columbus, Ohio. Association for Computational Linguistics.

Emily M. Bender, Timnit Gebru, Angelina McMillan-Major, and Shmargaret Shmitchell. 2021. On the Dangers of Stochastic Parrots: Can Language Models Be Too Big? In *Proceedings of the 2021 ACM Conference on Fairness, Accountability, and Transparency*, FAccT '21, page 610–623, New York, NY, USA. Association for Computing Machinery.

Steven Bird. 2008. Defining a core body of knowledge for the introductory computational linguistics curriculum. In *Proceedings of the Third Workshop on Issues in Teaching Computational Linguistics*, pages 27–35, Columbus, Ohio. Association for Computational Linguistics.

Tolga Bolukbasi, Kai-Wei Chang, James Zou, Venkatesh Saligrama, and Adam Kalai. 2016. Man is to Computer Programmer as Woman is to Homemaker? Debiasing Word Embeddings. In *Proceedings of the 30th International Conference on Neural Information Processing Systems*, NIPS'16, page 4356–4364, Red Hook, NY, USA. Curran Associates Inc.

Danqi Chen, Adam Fisch, Jason Weston, and Antoine Bordes. 2017. Reading Wikipedia to Answer Open-Domain Questions. In *Proceedings of the 55th Annual Meeting of the Association for Computational Linguistics (Volume 1: Long Papers)*, pages 1870–1879, Vancouver, Canada. Association for Computational Linguistics.

Jacob Devlin, Ming-Wei Chang, Kenton Lee, and Kristina Toutanova. 2019. BERT: Pre-training of deep bidirectional transformers for language understanding. In *Proceedings of the 2019 Conference of the North American Chapter of the Association for Computational Linguistics: Human Language Technologies, Volume 1 (Long and Short Papers)*, pages 4171–4186, Minneapolis, Minnesota. Association for Computational Linguistics.

Jacob Eisenstein. 2019. *Introduction to Natural Language Processing*. MIT Press.

Hila Gonen and Yoav Goldberg. 2019. Lipstick on a pig: Debiasing methods cover up systematic gender biases in word embeddings but do not remove them. In *Proceedings of the 2019 Conference of the North American Chapter of the Association for Computational Linguistics: Human Language Technologies, Volume 1 (Long and Short Papers)*, pages 609–614, Minneapolis, Minnesota. Association for Computational Linguistics.

Mohit Iyyer, Varun Manjunatha, Jordan Boyd-Graber, and Hal Daumé III. 2015. Deep Unordered Composition Rivals Syntactic Methods for Text Classification. In *Proceedings of the 53rd Annual Meeting of the Association for Computational Linguistics and the 7th International Joint Conference on Natural Language Processing (Volume 1: Long Papers)*, pages 1681–1691, Beijing, China. Association for Computational Linguistics.

Robin Jia and Percy Liang. 2016. Data Recombination for Neural Semantic Parsing. In *Proceedings of the 54th Annual Meeting of the Association for Computational Linguistics (Volume 1: Long Papers)*, pages 12–22, Berlin, Germany. Association for Computational Linguistics.

Dan Jurafsky and James H. Martin. 2021. *Speech and Language Processing, 3rd Ed.* Online.

Dan Klein. 2005. A core-tools statistical NLP course. In *Proceedings of the Second ACL Workshop on Effective Tools and Methodologies for Teaching NLP and CL*, pages 23–27, Ann Arbor, Michigan. Association for Computational Linguistics.

Nitin Madnani and Bonnie J. Dorr. 2008. Combining open-source with research to re-engineer a hands-on introductory NLP course. In *Proceedings of the Third Workshop on Issues in Teaching Computational Linguistics*, pages 71–79, Columbus, Ohio. Association for Computational Linguistics.

Tomas Mikolov, M. Karafiát, L. Burget, J. Černocký, and S. Khudanpur. 2010. Recurrent neural network based language model. In *Interspeech*.

Bo Pang, Lillian Lee, and Shivakumar Vaithyanathan. 2002. Thumbs up? Sentiment Classification using Machine Learning Techniques. In *Proceedings of the 2002 Conference on Empirical Methods in Natural Language Processing (EMNLP 2002)*, pages 79–86. Association for Computational Linguistics.

Adam Paszke, Sam Gross, Francisco Massa, Adam Lerer, James Bradbury, Gregory Chanan, Trevor Killeen, Zeming Lin, Natalia Gimelshein, Luca Antiga, Alban Desmaison, Andreas Köpf, Edward Yang, Zach DeVito, Martin Raison, Alykhan Tejani, Sasank Chilamkurthy, Benoit Steiner, Lu Fang, Junjie Bai, and Soumith Chintala. 2019. PyTorch: An Imperative Style, High-Performance Deep Learning Library. *arXiv cs.CL 1912.01703.*

Jeffrey Pennington, Richard Socher, and Christopher Manning. 2014. GloVe: Global Vectors for Word Representation. In *Proceedings of the 2014 Conference on Empirical Methods in Natural Language Processing (EMNLP)*, pages 1532–1543, Doha, Qatar. Association for Computational Linguistics.

Pranav Rajpurkar, Jian Zhang, Konstantin Lopyrev, and Percy Liang. 2016. SQuAD: 100,000+ Questions for Machine Comprehension of Text. In *Proceedings of the 2016 Conference on Empirical Methods in Natural Language Processing*, pages 2383–2392, Austin, Texas. Association for Computational Linguistics.

Minjoon Seo, Aniruddha Kembhavi, Ali Farhadi, and Hannaneh Hajishirzi. 2016. Bidirectional attention flow for machine comprehension. *arXiv cs.CL 1611.01603.*

Richard Socher, Alex Perelygin, Jean Wu, Jason Chuang, Christopher D. Manning, Andrew Ng, and Christopher Potts. 2013. Recursive Deep Models for Semantic Compositionality Over a Sentiment Treebank. In *Proceedings of the 2013 Conference on Empirical Methods in Natural Language Processing*, pages 1631–1642, Seattle, Washington, USA. Association for Computational Linguistics.

Erik F. Tjong Kim Sang and Fien De Meulder. 2003. Introduction to the CoNLL-2003 Shared Task: Language-Independent Named Entity Recognition. In *Proceedings of the Seventh Conference on Natural Language Learning at HLT-NAACL 2003*, pages 142–147.

Ashish Vaswani, Noam Shazeer, Niki Parmar, Jakob Uszkoreit, Llion Jones, Aidan N. Gomez, Lukasz Kaiser, and Illia Polosukhin. 2017. Attention is All you Need. In *Advances in Neural Information Processing Systems (NeurIPS)*.

John M. Zelle and Raymond J. Mooney. 1996. Learning to Parse Database Queries Using Inductive Logic Programming. In *Proceedings of the Thirteenth National Conference on Artificial Intelligence - Volume 2 (AAAI)*.

Tong Zhang and David Johnson. 2003. A Robust Risk Minimization based Named Entity Recognition System. In *Proceedings of the Seventh Conference on Natural Language Learning at HLT-NAACL 2003*, pages 204–207.

Interactive Assignments for Teaching Structured Neural NLP

David Gaddy, Daniel Fried, Nikita Kitaev, Mitchell Stern, Rodolfo Corona,
John DeNero and **Dan Klein**
University of California, Berkeley
{dgaddy,denero,klein}@berkeley.edu

Abstract

We present a set of assignments for a graduate-level NLP course. Assignments are designed to be interactive, easily gradable, and to give students hands-on experience with several key types of structure (sequences, tags, parse trees, and logical forms), modern neural architectures (LSTMs and Transformers), inference algorithms (dynamic programs and approximate search) and training methods (full and weak supervision). We designed assignments to build incrementally both within each assignment and across assignments, with the goal of enabling students to undertake graduate-level research in NLP by the end of the course.

1 Overview

Our course contains five implementation projects focusing on neural methods for structured prediction tasks in NLP. Over a range of tasks from language modeling to machine translation to syntactic and semantic parsing, the projects cover methods such as LSTMs and Transformers, dynamic programming, beam search, and weak supervision (learning from denotations). Our aim was to let students incrementally and interactively develop models and see their effectiveness on real NLP datasets. Section 2 describes the tasks and objectives of the projects in more detail. Links to assignments are available at `https://sites.google.com/view/nlp-assignments`.

1.1 Target Audience

Our course is designed for early-stage graduate students in computer science. We expect students to have a good background in machine learning, including prior experience with implementing neural networks. Many of our students will go on to conduct research in NLP or related machine learning disciplines. Some advanced undergraduates may also join the course if they have sufficient background and an interest in NLP research.

1.2 Course Structure

Our course is 14 weeks long. The projects fill nearly the entire semester, with roughly 2 weeks given to complete each project. We used lectures to cover the projects' problems and methods at a high level; however, the projects require students to be relatively skilled at independent implementation.

1.3 Design Strategy

The content of our projects was chosen to cover key topics along three primary dimensions: application tasks, neural components, and inference mechanisms. Our projects introduce students to some of the core tasks in NLP, including language modeling, machine translation, syntactic parsing, and semantic parsing. Key neural network models for NLP are also introduced, covering recurrent networks, attention mechanisms, and the Transformer architecture (Vaswani et al., 2017). Finally, the projects cover inference mechanisms for NLP, including beam search and dynamic programming methods like CKY.

All projects are implemented as interactive Python notebooks designed for use on Google's Colab infrastructure.[1] This setup allows students to use GPUs for free and with minimal setup. The notebooks consist of instructions interleaved with code blocks for students to fill in. We provide scaffolding code with less pedagogically-central components like data loading already filled in, so that students can focus on the learning objectives for the projects. Students implement neural network components using the PyTorch framework (Paszke et al., 2019).

Each project is broken down into a series of modules that can be verified for correctness before moving on. For example, when implementing a neural machine translation system, the students first implement and verify a basic sequence-

[1] `colab.research.google.com`

Proceedings of the Fifth Workshop on Teaching NLP, pages 104–107
June 10–11, 2021. ©2021 Association for Computational Linguistics

to-sequence model, then attention, and finally beam search. This setup allows students to debug each component individually and allows instructors to give partial credit for each module. The modules are designed to validate student code without waiting for long training runs, with a total model training time of less than one hour per project.

Our projects are graded primarily with scripted autograders hosted on Gradescope,[2] allowing a class of hundreds of students to be administered by a small course staff. Grades are generally based on accuracy on a held-out test set, where students are given inputs for this set and submit their model's predictions to the grader. While students cannot see their results on the held-out set until after the due date, the assignments include specific targets for validation set accuracies that can be used by students to verify the correctness of their solutions.

Each project concludes with an open-ended section where the students experiment with modifications or ablations to the models implemented and submit a 1-page report describing the motivation behind their contribution and an analysis of their results. This section gives students more of a chance to explore their own ideas and can also help distinguish students who are putting in extra effort on the projects.

2 Assignments

2.1 Project 0: Intro to PyTorch Mini-Project

This project serves primarily as an introduction to the project infrastructure and to the PyTorch framework. Students implement a classifier to predict the most common part-of-speech tag for English word types from the words' characters. Students first implement a simple neural model based on pooling character embeddings, then a slightly more complex model with character n-gram representations. This project provides much more detailed instructions than later projects to help students who are less familiar with deep learning implementation, walking them through each step of the training and modeling code.

2.2 Project 1: Language Modeling

This project introduces students to sequential output prediction, using classical statistical methods and auto-regressive neural modeling. Students implement a series of language models of increasing complexity and train them on English text. First they implement a basic n-gram model, then add backoff and Kneser-Ney smoothing (Ney et al., 1994). Next, they implement a feed-forward neural n-gram model, and an LSTM language model (Hochreiter and Schmidhuber, 1997). The last section of this project is an open-ended exploration where students can try any method to further improve results, either from a list of ideas we provided or an idea of their own.

2.3 Project 2: Neural Machine Translation

This project covers conditional language modeling, using neural sequence-to-sequence models with attention. Students incrementally implement a neural machine translation model to translate from German to English on the Multi30K dataset (Elliott et al., 2016). This dataset is simpler than standard translation benchmarks and affords training and evaluating an effective model in a matter of minutes rather than days, allowing students to interactively develop and debug models. Students first implement a baseline LSTM-based sequence-to-sequence model (Sutskever et al., 2014) without attention, view the model's predictions, and evaluate performance using greedy decoding. Then, students incrementally add an attention mechanism (Bahdanau et al., 2015) and beam search decoding. Finally, students visualize the model's attention distributions.

2.4 Project 3: Constituency Parsing and Transformers

This project covers constituency parsing, the Transformer neural network architecture (Vaswani et al., 2017), and structured decoding via dynamic programming. Students first implement a Transformer encoder and validate it using a part-of-speech tagging task on the English Penn Treebank (Marcus et al., 1993). Then, students incrementally build a Transformer-based parser by first constructing a model that makes constituency and labeling decisions for each span in a sentence, then implementing CKY decoding (Cocke, 1970; Kasami, 1966; Younger, 1967) to ensure the resulting output is a tree. The resulting model, which is a small version of the parser of Kitaev and Klein (2018), achieves reasonable performance on the English Penn Treebank in under half an hour of training.

2.5 Project 4: Semantic Parsing

This project introduces students to predicting executable logical forms and to training with weak

[2] `www.gradescope.com`

supervision. Students implement a neural semantic parser for the GeoQA geographical question answering dataset of Krishnamurthy and Kollar (2013). This dataset contains English questions about simple relational databases. To familiarize themselves with the syntax and semantics of the dataset, students first implement a simple execution method which evaluates a logical form on a database to produce an answer. To produce logical forms from questions, students then implement a sequence-to-sequence architecture with a constrained decoder and a copy mechanism (Jia and Liang, 2016). Students verify their model by training first in a supervised setting with known logical forms, then finally train it only from question-answer pairs by searching over latent logical forms.

3 Findings in Initial Course Offerings

An initial iteration of the course was taught to 60 students, and an offering for over 100 students is in progress. Overall, we have found the projects to be a great success.

In the first iteration of the course, 81% of students completed the course and submitted all five projects. From a mid-semester survey, students reported taking 19.88 hours on average to complete Project 1. We observed that students with no prior experience programming with deep learning frameworks took significantly longer on the projects and required more assistance. In future semesters, we intend to strengthen the deep learning prerequisites required for the course to ensure adequate background for success.

The online project infrastructure worked with minimal issues. While the Colab platform does have the downside of timeouts due to inactivity, we believe the use of free GPU resources outweighed this cost. By encouraging students to download checkpoints after training runs, they were able to avoid re-training after each timeout. A handful of students who spent very long stretches of time on the projects in a single day reported having temporary limits placed on GPU usage (e.g. after 8+ hours of continuous use), but these limits could be circumvented by logging in with a separate account.

Most students were able to successfully complete the majority of each assignment, but there remained some point spread to distinguish performance for grading (mean 94%, standard deviation 12%). Due to the use of autograding, instructor code grading effort totaled less than several hours per project. One aspect of grading that we are continuing to improve is the open-ended exploration report, and we plan to better define and communicate expectations in future semesters by introducing a clear rubric for the report section.

Overall, these projects proved a valuable resource for the success of our course and for preparing students for NLP research. At the end of last year's course, one student submitted an extension of their exploration work on one project to EMNLP and presented at the conference.

References

Dzmitry Bahdanau, Kyung Hyun Cho, and Yoshua Bengio. 2015. Neural machine translation by jointly learning to align and translate. In *3rd International Conference on Learning Representations, ICLR 2015*.

John Cocke. 1970. Programming languages and their compilers: Preliminary notes.

Desmond Elliott, Stella Frank, Khalil Sima'an, and Lucia Specia. 2016. Multi30K: Multilingual English-German image descriptions. In *Proceedings of the 5th Workshop on Vision and Language*, pages 70–74, Berlin, Germany. Association for Computational Linguistics.

Sepp Hochreiter and Jürgen Schmidhuber. 1997. Long short-term memory. *Neural computation*, 9(8):1735–1780.

Robin Jia and Percy Liang. 2016. Data recombination for neural semantic parsing. In *Proceedings of the 54th Annual Meeting of the Association for Computational Linguistics (Volume 1: Long Papers)*, pages 12–22, Berlin, Germany. Association for Computational Linguistics.

Tadao Kasami. 1966. An efficient recognition and syntax-analysis algorithm for context-free languages. *Coordinated Science Laboratory Report no. R-257*.

Nikita Kitaev and Dan Klein. 2018. Constituency parsing with a self-attentive encoder. In *Proceedings of the 56th Annual Meeting of the Association for Computational Linguistics (Volume 1: Long Papers)*, pages 2676–2686.

Jayant Krishnamurthy and Thomas Kollar. 2013. Jointly learning to parse and perceive: Connecting natural language to the physical world. *Transactions of the Association for Computational Linguistics*, 1:193–206.

Mitch Marcus, Beatrice Santorini, and Mary Ann Marcinkiewicz. 1993. Building a large annotated corpus of English: The Penn Treebank. *Computational Linguistics*, 19(2):313–330.

Hermann Ney, Ute Essen, and Reinhard Kneser. 1994. On structuring probabilistic dependences in stochastic language modelling. *Computer Speech & Language*, 8(1):1–38.

Adam Paszke, Sam Gross, Francisco Massa, Adam Lerer, James Bradbury, Gregory Chanan, Trevor Killeen, Zeming Lin, Natalia Gimelshein, Luca Antiga, et al. 2019. PyTorch: An imperative style, high-performance deep learning library. *Advances in Neural Information Processing Systems*, 32:8026–8037.

Ilya Sutskever, Oriol Vinyals, and Quoc V Le. 2014. Sequence to sequence learning with neural networks. *Advances in Neural Information Processing Systems*, 27:3104–3112.

Ashish Vaswani, Noam Shazeer, Niki Parmar, Jakob Uszkoreit, Llion Jones, Aidan N Gomez, Łukasz Kaiser, and Illia Polosukhin. 2017. Attention is all you need. *Advances in Neural Information Processing Systems*, 30:5998–6008.

Daniel H. Younger. 1967. Recognition and parsing of context-free languages in time n^3. *Information and control*, 10(2):189–208.

Learning about Word Vector Representations and Deep Learning through Implementing Word2vec

David Jurgens
School of Information
University of Michigan
`jurgens@umich.edu`

Abstract

Word vector representations are an essential part of an NLP curriculum. Here, we describe a homework that has students implement a popular method for learning word vectors, word2vec. Students implement the core parts of the method, including text preprocessing, negative sampling, and gradient descent. Starter code provides guidance and handles basic operations, which allows students to focus on the conceptually challenging aspects. After generating their vectors, students evaluate them using qualitative and quantitative tests.

1 Introduction

NLP curricula typically include content on word semantics, how semantics can be learned computationally through word vectors, and what are the vectors' uses. This document describes an assignment for having students implement word2vec (Mikolov et al., 2013a,b), a popular method that relies on a single-layer neural network. This homework is designed to introduce students to word vectors and simple neural networks by having them implement the network from scratch, without the use of deep-learning libraries. The assignment is appropriate for upper-division undergraduates or graduate students who are familiar with python programming, have some experience with the `numpy` library (Harris et al., 2020), and have been exposed to concepts around gradients and neural networks. Through implementing major portions of the word2vec software and using the learned vectors, students will gain a deeper understanding of how networks are trained, how to learn word vectors, and their uses in downstream tasks.

2 Design and Learning Goals

This homework is designed to take place just before the middle stretch of the class, after lexical semantics and machine learning concepts have been introduced. The content is designed at the level of an NLP student who (1) has some technical background and at least one advanced course in statistics and (2) will implement or adapt new NLP methods. This level is deeper than what is needed for a purely Applied NLP setting but too shallow for a more Machine Learning focused NLP class, which would likely benefit from additional derivations and proofs around the gradient descent to solidify understanding. The homework has typically been assigned over a three to four week period; many students complete the homework in the course of a week, but the longer time frame enables students with less background or programming experience to work through the steps. The material prepares students for advanced NLP concepts around deep learning and pre-trained language models, as well as provides intuition for what steps modern deep learning libraries perform.

The homework has three broad learning goals. First, the training portion of the homework helps deepen students' understanding of machine learning concepts, gradient descent, and develop complex NLP software. Central to this design is having students turn the equations in the homework and formal descriptions of word2vec into software operations. This step helps students understand how to ground equations found in some papers into the more-familiar language of programming, while also building a more intuition for how gradient descent and backpropagation work in practice.

Second, the process of software development aids students in developing larger NLP software methods that involve end-to-end development. This goal includes seeing how different algorithmic software designs work and are implemented. The speed of training requires that students be moderately efficient in how they implement their software. For example, the use of for loops instead of vectorized `numpy` operations will lead to a significant slow down in performance. In class instruction and

Proceedings of the Fifth Workshop on Teaching NLP, pages 108–111
June 10–11, 2021. ©2021 Association for Computational Linguistics

tutorials detail how to write the relevant efficient numerical operations, which help guide students to identify where and how to selectively optimize. However, slow code will still finish correctly allowing students to debug for their initial implementations for correctness. This need for performant code creates opportunities for students to practice their performance optimizing skills.

Third, the lexical semantics portion of the homework exposes students to the uses and limitations of word vectors. Through training the vectors, students understand how statistical regularities in co-occurrence can be used to learn meaning. Qualitative and quantitative evaluations show students what their model has learned (e.g., using vector analogies) and introduce them to concepts of polysemy, fostering a larger discussion on what can be captured in a vector representation.

3 Homework Description

The homework has students implement two core aspects of the word2vec algorithm using `numpy` for the numeric portions, and then evaluate with two downstream tasks. The first aspect has students perform the commonly-used text preprocessing steps that turn a raw text corpus into self-supervised training examples. This step includes removing low-frequency tokens and subsampling tokens based on their frequency. The second aspect focuses on the core training procedure, including (i) negative sampling for generating negative examples of context words, (ii) performing gradient descent to update the two word vector matrices, and (iii) computing the negative log-likelihood. These tasks are broken into eight discrete steps that guide students in how to do each aspect. The assignment document includes links to more in-depth descriptions of the method including the extensive description of Rong (2014) and the recent chapter of Jurafsky and Martin (2021, ch. 6) to help students understand the math behind the training procedure.

In the second part of the homework, students evaluate the learned vectors in two downstream tasks. The first task has students load these vectors using the Gensim package (Rehurek and Sojka, 2010) and perform vector arithmetic operations to find word-pair analogies and examine the nearest-neighbors of words; this qualitative evaluation exposes students to what is or is not learned by the model. The second task is quantitative evaluation that has students generate word-pair similarity scores for the subset of the SimLex-999 (Hill et al., 2015) present in their training corpus, which is uploaded to Kaggle InClass[1] to see how their vectors compare with others; this leaderboard helps students identify a bug in their code (via a low-scoring submission) and occasionally prompts students to think about how to improve/extend their code to attain a higher score.

Potential Extensions The word2vec method has been extended in numerous ways in NLP to improve its vectors (e.g., Ling et al., 2015; Yu and Dredze, 2014; Tissier et al., 2017). This assignment includes descriptions of other possible extensions that students can explore, such as implementing dropout, adding learning rate decay, or making use of external knowledge during training. Typically, a single extension to word2vec is included as a part of the homework to help ground the concept in code but without increasing the difficulty of the assignment. Students who are interested in deepening their understanding can use these as starting points to see how to develop their own NLP methods as a part of a course project.

This assignment also provides multiple possibilities for examining the latent biases learned in word vectors. Prior work has established that pretrained vectors often encode gender and racial biases based on the corpora they are trained on (e.g., Caliskan et al., 2017; Manzini et al., 2019). In a future extension, this assignment could be adapted to use Wikipedia biographies as a base corpus and have students identify how occupations become more associated with gendered words during training (Garg et al., 2018). Once this bias is discovered, students can discuss various methods for mitigating it (e.g., Bolukbasi et al., 2016; Zhao et al., 2017) and how their method might be adapted to avoid other forms of bias. This extension can help students critically think about what is and is not being captured in pretrained vectors and models.

4 Reflection on Student Experiences

Student experiences on this homework have been very positive, with multiple students expressing a strong sense of satisfaction at completing the homework and being able to understand the algorithm and software backing word2vec. Several students reported feeling like completing this assignment was a great confidence boost and that they were

[1] `https://www.kaggle.com/c/about/inclass`

now more confident in their ability to understand NLP papers and connect algorithms, equations, and code. The majority of student difficulties happen in two sources. First, the vast majority of bugs happen when implementing the gradient descent and calculating the negative log-likelihood (NLL). While only a few lines of code in total, this step requires translating the loss function for word2vec (in the negative sampling case) into `numpy` code. This translation task appeared daunting at first for many students, though they found creating the eventual solution rewarding for being able to ground similar equations in NLP papers. Two key components for mitigating early frustration were (1) including built-in periodic reports of the NLL, which help students quickly spot whether there are numeric errors that lead to infinity or `NaN` values and (2) adding early-stopping and printing nearest neighbors of instructor-provided words (e.g., "January") which should be thematically coherent after only a few minutes of training. These components help students quickly identify the presence of a bug in the gradient descent.

The second student difficulty comes from the text preprocessing steps. The removal of low-frequency words and frequency-based subsampling steps require students to have a solid distinction of type versus token in practice in order to subsample tokens (versus types). I suspect that because many of these routine preprocessing steps are done for the student by common libraries (e.g., the `CountVectorizer` of Scikit Learn (Pedregosa et al., 2011)), these steps feel unfamiliar. Common errors in this theme were subsampling types or producing a sequence of word types (rather than tokens) to use for training.

References

Tolga Bolukbasi, Kai-Wei Chang, James Zou, Venkatesh Saligrama, and Adam Kalai. 2016. Man is to computer programmer as woman is to homemaker? debiasing word embeddings. In *Proceedings of the 30th Conference on Neural Information Processing Systems (NeurIPS)*.

Aylin Caliskan, Joanna J Bryson, and Arvind Narayanan. 2017. Semantics derived automatically from language corpora contain human-like biases. *Science*, 356(6334):183–186.

Nikhil Garg, Londa Schiebinger, Dan Jurafsky, and James Zou. 2018. Word embeddings quantify 100 years of gender and ethnic stereotypes. *Proceedings of the National Academy of Sciences*, 115(16):E3635–E3644.

Charles R Harris, K Jarrod Millman, Stéfan J van der Walt, Ralf Gommers, Pauli Virtanen, David Cournapeau, Eric Wieser, Julian Taylor, Sebastian Berg, Nathaniel J Smith, et al. 2020. Array programming with numpy. *Nature*, 585(7825):357–362.

Felix Hill, Roi Reichart, and Anna Korhonen. 2015. Simlex-999: Evaluating semantic models with (genuine) similarity estimation. *Computational Linguistics*, 41(4):665–695.

Dan Jurafsky and James H. Martin. 2021. *Speech & Language Processing*, 3rd edition. Prentice Hall.

Wang Ling, Chris Dyer, Alan W Black, and Isabel Trancoso. 2015. Two/too simple adaptations of word2vec for syntax problems. In *Proceedings of the 2015 Conference of the North American Chapter of the Association for Computational Linguistics: Human Language Technologies*, pages 1299–1304.

Thomas Manzini, Lim Yao Chong, Alan W Black, and Yulia Tsvetkov. 2019. Black is to criminal as caucasian is to police: Detecting and removing multiclass bias in word embeddings. In *Proceedings of the 2019 Conference of the North American Chapter of the Association for Computational Linguistics: Human Language Technologies, Volume 1 (Long and Short Papers)*, pages 615–621.

Tomas Mikolov, Kai Chen, Greg Corrado, and Jeffrey Dean. 2013a. Efficient estimation of word representations in vector space. *arXiv preprint arXiv:1301.3781*.

Tomas Mikolov, Ilya Sutskever, Kai Chen, Greg Corrado, and Jeffrey Dean. 2013b. Distributed representations of words and phrases and their compositionality. *arXiv preprint arXiv:1310.4546*.

Fabian Pedregosa, Gaël Varoquaux, Alexandre Gramfort, Vincent Michel, Bertrand Thirion, Olivier Grisel, Mathieu Blondel, Peter Prettenhofer, Ron Weiss, Vincent Dubourg, et al. 2011. Scikit-learn: Machine learning in python. *the Journal of machine Learning research*, 12:2825–2830.

Radim Rehurek and Petr Sojka. 2010. Software framework for topic modelling with large corpora. In *In Proceedings of the LREC 2010 workshop on new challenges for NLP frameworks*. Citeseer.

Xin Rong. 2014. word2vec parameter learning explained. *arXiv preprint arXiv:1411.2738*.

Julien Tissier, Christophe Gravier, and Amaury Habrard. 2017. Dict2vec: Learning word embeddings using lexical dictionaries. In *Proceedings of the 2017 Conference on Empirical Methods in Natural Language Processing*, pages 254–263.

Mo Yu and Mark Dredze. 2014. Improving lexical embeddings with semantic knowledge. In *Proceedings of the 52nd Annual Meeting of the Association for Computational Linguistics (Volume 2: Short Papers)*, pages 545–550.

Jieyu Zhao, Tianlu Wang, Mark Yatskar, Vicente Ordonez, and Kai-Wei Chang. 2017. Men also like shopping: Reducing gender bias amplification using corpus-level constraints. In *Proceedings of the 2017 Conference on Empirical Methods in Natural Language Processing*, pages 2979–2989.

Naive Bayes versus BERT: Jupyter notebook assignments for an introductory NLP course

Jennifer Foster and Joachim Wagner
School of Computing
Dublin City University
`jfoster|jwagner@dcu.ie`

Abstract

We describe two Jupyter notebooks that form the basis of two assignments in an introductory Natural Language Processing (NLP) module taught to final year undergraduate students at Dublin City University. The notebooks show the students how to train a bag-of-words polarity classifier using multinomial Naive Bayes, and how to fine-tune a polarity classifier using BERT. The students take the code as a starting point for their own experiments.

1 Introduction

We describe two Jupyter[1] notebooks that form the basis of two assignments in a new introductory Natural Language Processing (NLP) module taught to final year students on the B.Sc. in Data Science programme at Dublin City University. As part of a prior module on this programme, the students have some experience with the NLP problem of quality estimation for machine translation. They have also studied machine learning and are competent Python programmers. Since this is the first Data Science cohort, there are only seven students. Four graduate students are also taking the module.

The course textbook is the draft 3rd edition of (Jurafsky and Martin, 2009).[2] It is impossible to teach the entire book in a twelve week module and so we concentrate on the first ten chapters. The following topics are covered:

1. Pre-processing
2. N-gram Language Modelling
3. Text Classification using Naive Bayes and Logistic Regression
4. Sequence Labelling using Hidden Markov Models and Conditional Random Fields
5. Word Vectors
6. Neural Net Architectures (feed-forward, recurrent, transformer)
7. Ethical Issues in NLP

The course is fully online for the 2020/2021 academic year. Lectures are pre-recorded and there are weekly live sessions where students anonymously answer comprehension questions via zoom polls and spend 20-30 minutes in breakout rooms working on exercises. These involve working out toy examples, or using online tools such as the AllenNLP online demo[3] (Gardner et al., 2018) to examine the behaviour of neural NLP systems.

Assessment takes the form of an online end-of-semester open-book exam worth 60% and three assignments worth 40%. The first assignment is worth 10% and involves coding a bigram language model from scratch. The second and third assignments are worth 15% each and involve experimentation, using Google Colab[4] as a platform. For both assignments, a Jupyter notebook is provided to the students which they are invited to use as a basis for their experiments. We describe both of these in turn.

2 Notebooks

We describe the assignment objectives, the notebooks we provide to the students[5] and the experiments they carried out.

2.1 Notebook One: Sentiment Polarity with Naive Bayes

The assignment The aim of this assignment is to help students feel comfortable carrying out text classification experiments using *scikit-learn* (Pedregosa et al., 2011). Sentiment analysis of movie reviews is chosen as the application since it is a

[1] `https://jupyter.org/`

[2] `https://web.stanford.edu/~jurafsky/slp3/`

[3] `https://demo.allennlp.org/`

[4] `https://colab.research.google.com`

[5] An updated version of the notebooks will be made available in the materials repository of the Teaching-NLP 2021 workshop.

Proceedings of the Fifth Workshop on Teaching NLP, pages 112–114
June 10–11, 2021. ©2021 Association for Computational Linguistics

familiar and easily understood task and domain, requiring little linguistic expertise. We use the dataset of Pang and Lee (2004) because its relatively small size (2,000 documents) makes it quicker to train on. The documents are provided in tokenised form and have been split into ten cross-validation folds. We provide a Jupyter notebook implementing a baseline bag-of-words Naive Bayes classifier which assigns a label *positive* or *negative* to a review. The students are asked to experiment with this baseline model and to attempt to improve its accuracy by experimenting with

1. different learning algorithms, e.g. logistic regression, decision trees, support vector machines, etc.
2. different feature sets, such as handling negation, including bigrams and trigrams, using sentiment lexicons and performing linguistic analysis of the input

They are asked to use the same cross-validation set-up as the baseline system. Marks are awarded for the breadth of experimentation, the experiment descriptions, code clarity, average 10-fold cross-validation accuracy and accuracy on a 'hidden' test set (also movie reviews).

The notebook We implement document-level sentiment polarity prediction for movie reviews with multinomial Naive Bayes and bag-of-words features. We first build and test the functionality to load the dataset into a nested list of documents, sentences and tokens, each document annotated with its polarity label. Then we show code to collect the training data vocabulary and assign a unique ID to each entry. Documents are then encoded as bag-of-word feature vectors in NumPy (Harris et al., 2020), optionally clipped at frequency one to produce binary vectors. Finally, we show how to train a multinomial Naive Bayes model with scikit-learn, obtain a confusion matrix, measure accuracy and report cross-validation results. The functionality is demonstrated using a series of increasingly specific Python classes.

What the students did Most students carried out an extensive range of experiments, for the most part following the suggestions we provided at the assignment briefing and the strategies outlined in the lectures. The baseline accuracy of 83% was improved in most projects by about 3-5 points. The algorithm which gave the best results was logistic regression, whose default hyper-parameters worked well. The students who reported the highest accuracy scores used a combination of token unigrams, bigrams and trigrams, whereas most students directly compared each n-gram order. The students were free to change the code structure, and indeed some of them took the opportunity to refactor the code to a style that better suited them.

2.2 Notebook Two: Sentiment Polarity with BERT

The assignment The aim of this second assignment is to help students feel comfortable using BERT (Devlin et al., 2019). We provide a sample notebook which shows how to fine-tune BERT on the same task and dataset as in the previous assignment. The students are asked to do one of three things:

1. Perform a comparative error analysis of the output of the BERT system(s) and the systems from the previous assignment. The aim here is to get the students thinking about interpreting system output.
2. Using the code in this notebook and online resources as examples, fine-tune BERT on a different task. The aim here is to 1) allow the students to experiment with something other than movie review polarity classification and explore their own interests, and 2) test their research and problem-solving skills.
3. Attempt to improve the BERT-based system provided in the notebook by experimenting with different ways of overcoming the input length restriction.

The notebook We exemplify how to fine-tune BERT on the (Pang and Lee, 2004) dataset, using Hugging Face Transformers (Wolf et al., 2020) and PyTorch Lightning (Falcon, 2019). We introduce the concept of subword units, showing BERT's token IDs for sample text input, the matching vocabulary entries, the mapping to the original input tokens and BERT's special `[CLS]` and `[SEP]` tokens. Then, we show the length distribution of documents in the data set and sketch strategies to address the limited sequence length of BERT. We implement taking 1) a slice from the start or 2) the end of each document, or 3) combining a slice from the start with a slice from the end of each document. In doing so, we show the students how a dataset can be read from a custom file format into the data loader objects expected by the framework.

What the students did Of the ten students who completed the assignment, three chose the first option of analysing system output and seven chose the second option of fine-tuning BERT on a task of their choosing. These included detection of hate speech in tweets, sentence-level acceptability judgements, document-level human rights violation detection, and sentiment polarity classification applied to tweets instead of movie reviews. No student opted for the third option of examining ways to overcome the input length limit in BERT for the (Pang and Lee, 2004) dataset.

3 Future Improvements

We surveyed the students to see what they thought of the assignments. On the positive side, they found them challenging and interesting, and they appreciated the flexibility provided in the third assignment. On the negative side, they felt that they involved more effort than the marks warranted, and they found the code in the notebooks to be unnecessarily complicated. The object-oriented nature of the code was also highlighted as a negative by some. For next year, we plan to 1) streamline the code, hiding some of the messy details, 2) reduce the scope of the assignments, and 3) provide more BERT fine-tuning example notebooks.

Acknowledgements

The second author's contribution to this work was funded by Science Foundation Ireland through the SFI Frontiers for the Future programme (19/FFP/6942). We thank the reviewers for their helpful suggestions, and the DCU CA4023 students for their hard work and patience!

References

Jacob Devlin, Ming-Wei Chang, Kenton Lee, and Kristina Toutanova. 2019. BERT: Pre-training of deep bidirectional transformers for language understanding. In *Proceedings of the 2019 Conference of the North American Chapter of the Association for Computational Linguistics: Human Language Technologies, Volume 1 (Long and Short Papers)*, pages 4171–4186, Minneapolis, Minnesota. Association for Computational Linguistics.

WA et al. Falcon. 2019. Pytorch lightning. GitHub repository.

Matt Gardner, Joel Grus, Mark Neumann, Oyvind Tafjord, Pradeep Dasigi, Nelson F. Liu, Matthew Peters, Michael Schmitz, and Luke Zettlemoyer. 2018. AllenNLP: A deep semantic natural language processing platform. In *Proceedings of Workshop for NLP Open Source Software (NLP-OSS)*, pages 1–6, Melbourne, Australia. Association for Computational Linguistics.

Charles R. Harris, K. Jarrod Millman, Stéfan J. van der Walt, Ralf Gommers, Pauli Virtanen, David Cournapeau, Eric Wieser, Julian Taylor, Sebastian Berg, Nathaniel J. Smith, Robert Kern, Matti Picus, Stephan Hoyer, Marten H. van Kerkwijk, Matthew Brett, Allan Haldane, Jaime Fernández del Río, Mark Wiebe, Pearu Peterson, Pierre Gérard-Marchant, Kevin Sheppard, Tyler Reddy, Warren Weckesser, Hameer Abbasi, Christoph Gohlke, and Travis E. Oliphant. 2020. Array programming with NumPy. *Nature*, 585(7825):357–362.

Dan Jurafsky and James H. Martin. 2009. *Speech and language processing*. Pearson Prentice Hall, Upper Saddle River, N.J.

Bo Pang and Lillian Lee. 2004. A sentimental education: Sentiment analysis using subjectivity summarization based on minimum cuts. In *Proceedings of the 42nd Annual Meeting of the Association for Computational Linguistics (ACL-04)*, pages 271–278, Barcelona, Spain.

F. Pedregosa, G. Varoquaux, A. Gramfort, V. Michel, B. Thirion, O. Grisel, M. Blondel, P. Prettenhofer, R. Weiss, V. Dubourg, J. Vanderplas, A. Passos, D. Cournapeau, M. Brucher, M. Perrot, and E. Duchesnay. 2011. Scikit-learn: Machine learning in Python. *Journal of Machine Learning Research*, 12:2825–2830.

Thomas Wolf, Lysandre Debut, Victor Sanh, Julien Chaumond, Clement Delangue, Anthony Moi, Pierric Cistac, Tim Rault, Rémi Louf, Morgan Funtowicz, Joe Davison, Sam Shleifer, Patrick von Platen, Clara Ma, Yacine Jernite, Julien Plu, Canwen Xu, Teven Le Scao, Sylvain Gugger, Mariama Drame, Quentin Lhoest, and Alexander M. Rush. 2020. Transformers: State-of-the-art natural language processing. In *Proceedings of the 2020 Conference on Empirical Methods in Natural Language Processing: System Demonstrations*, pages 38–45, Online. Association for Computational Linguistics.

Natural Language Processing for Computer Scientists and Data Scientists at a Large State University

Casey Kennington
Department of Computer Science
Boise State University
caseykennington@boisestate.edu

Abstract

The field of Natural Language Processing (NLP) changes rapidly, requiring course offerings to adjust with those changes, and NLP is not just for computer scientists; it's a field that should be accessible to anyone who has a sufficient background. In this paper, I explain how students with Computer Science and Data Science backgrounds can be well-prepared for an upper-division NLP course at a large state university. The course covers probability and information theory, elementary linguistics, machine and deep learning, with an attempt to balance theoretical ideas and concepts with practical applications. I explain the course objectives, topics and assignments, reflect on adjustments to the course over the last four years, as well as feedback from students.

1 Introduction

Thanks in part to a access to large datasets, increases in compute power, and easy-to-use programming programming libraries that leverage neural architectures, the field of Natural Language Processing (NLP) has become more popular and has seen more widespread adoption in research and in commercial products. On the research side, the Association for Computational Linguistics (ACL) conference—the flagship NLP conference—and related annual conferences have seen dramatic increases in paper submissions. For example, in 2020 ACL had 3,429 paper submissions, whereas 2019 had 2,905, and this upward trend has been happening for several years. Certainly, lowering barriers to access of NLP methods and tools for researchers and practitioners is a welcome direction for the field, enabling researchers and practitioners from many disciplines to make use of NLP.

It is therefore becoming more important to better equip students with an understanding of NLP to prepare them for careers either directly related to NLP, or which leverage NLP skills. In this paper, I reflect on my experience setting up and maintaining a class in NLP at Boise State University, a large state university, how to prepare students for research and industry careers, and how the class has changed over four years to fit the needs of students.

The next section explains the course objectives. I then explain challenges that are likely common to many university student populations, how NLP is designed for students with Data Science and Computer Science backgrounds, then I explain course content including lecture topics and assignments that are designed to fulfill the course objectives. I then offer a reflection on the three times I taught this course over the past four years, and future plans for the course.

2 Course Objectives

Most students who take an NLP course will not pursue a career in NLP proper; rather, they take the course to learn skills that will help them find employment or do research in areas that make use of language, largely focusing on the medium of text (e.g., anthropology, information retrieval, artificial intelligence, data mining, social media network analysis, provided they have sufficient data science training). My goal for the students is that they can identify aspects of natural language (phonetics, syntax, semantics, etc.) and how each can be processed by a computer, explain the difference between classification models and approaches, be able to map from (basic) formalisms to functional code, and use existing tools, libraries, and data sets for learning while attempting to strike a balance between theory and practice. In my view, there are several aspects of NLP that anyone needs to grasp, and how to apply NLP techniques in novel circumstances. Those aspects are illustrated in Figure 1.

No single NLP course can possibly account for a level of depth in all of the aspects in Figure 1, but a student who has taken courses or has experience in at least two of the areas (e.g., they have taken a

Proceedings of the Fifth Workshop on Teaching NLP, pages 115–124
June 10–11, 2021. ©2021 Association for Computational Linguistics

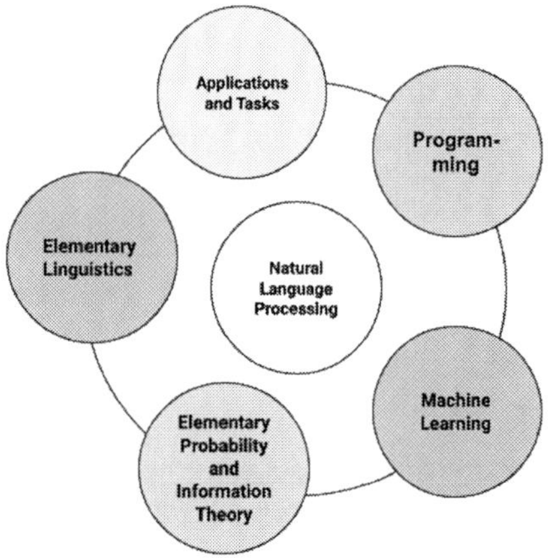

Figure 1: Areas of content that are important for a course in Natural Language Processing.

statistics course and have experience with Python, or they have taken linguistics courses and have used some data science or machine learning libraries) will find success in the course more easily than those with no experience in any aspect.

This introduces a challenge that has been explored in prior work on teaching NLP (Fosler-Lussier, 2008): the diversity of the student population. NLP is a discipline that is not just for computer science students, but it is challenging to prepare students for the technical skills required in a NLP course. Moreover, similar to the student population in Fosler-Lussier (2008), there should be course offerings for both graduate and undergraduate students. In my case, which is fairly common in academia, as the sole NLP researcher at the university I can only offer one course once every four semesters for both graduate and undergraduate students, but also students with varied backgrounds–not only computer science. As a result, this is not a research methods course; rather, it is more geared towards learning the important concepts and technical skills surrounding recent advances in NLP. Others have attempted to gear the course content and delivery towards research (Freedman, 2008) giving the students the opportunity to have open-ended assignments. I may consider this for future offerings, but for now the final project acts as an open-ended assignment, though I don't require students to read and understand recent research papers.

In the following section, I explain how we prepare students of diverse backgrounds to succeed in an NLP course for upper-division undergraduate and graduate students.

3 Preparing Students with Diverse Academic and Technical Backgrounds

Boise State University is the largest university in Idaho, situated in the capital of the State of Idaho. The university has a high number of non-traditional students (e.g., students outside the traditional student age range, or second-degree seeking students). Moreover, the university has a high acceptance rate (over 80%) for incoming first-year students. As is the case with many universities and organizations, a greater need for "computational thinking" among students of many disciplines has been an important driver of recent changes in course offerings across many departments. Moreover, certain departments have responded to the need and student interest in machine learning course offerings. In this section, we discuss how we altered the Data Science and Computer Science curricula to meet these needs and the implications these changes have had on the NLP course.[1]

Data Science The Data Science offerings begin with a foundational course (based on Berkeley's data8 content) that has only a very basic math prerequisite.[2] It introduces and allows students to practice Python, Jupyter notebooks, data analysis and visualization, and basic statistics (including the bootstrap method of statistical significance). Several courses follow this course that are more domain specific, giving the students options for gaining practical experience in Data Science skills relative to their abilities and career goals. One path more geared towards students of STEM-related majors (though not targeting Computer Science majors) as well as some majors in the Humanities, is a certificate program that includes the foundational course, a follow-on course that gives students experience with more data analysis as well as probability and information theory, an introductory machine learning course, and a course on databases. The courses largely use Python as the programming language of choice.

Computer Science In parallel to the changes in Data Science-related courses, the Department of Computer Science has seen increased enrollment and increased request for machine learning-related courses. The department offers several

[1] We do not have a Data Science department or major degree program; the Data Science courses are housed in different departments across campus.

[2] `http://data8.org/`

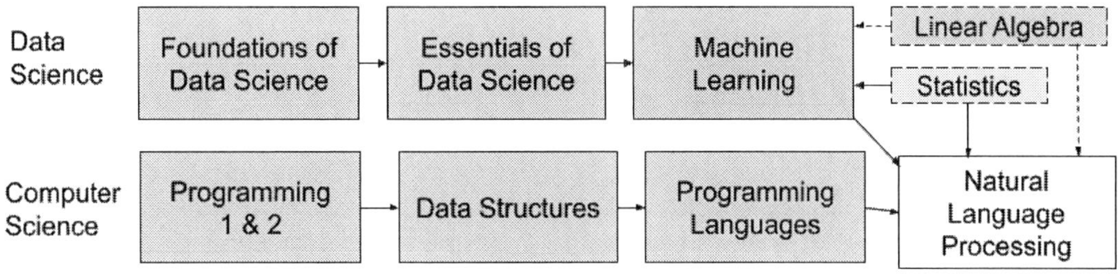

Figure 2: Two course paths that prepare students to succeed in the NLP course: Data Science and Computer Science. Solid arrows denote pre-requisites, dashed arrows denote co-requisites. Solid outlines denote Data Science and Computer Science courses, dashed outlines denote Math courses.

courses, though they focus on upper-division students (e.g., artificial intelligence, applied deep learning, information retrieval and recommender systems). This is a challenge because the main Computer Science curriculum focuses on procedural languages such as Java with little or no exposure to Python (similar to the student population reported in Freedman (2008)), forcing the upper-division machine learning-related courses to spend time teaching Python to the students. This cannot be underestimated–programming languages may not be natural languages, but they are *languages* in that it takes time to learn them, particularly relevant Python libraries. To help meet this challenge, the department has recently introduced a Machine Learning Emphasis that makes use of the Data Science courses mentioned above, along with additional requirements for math and upper-division Computer Science courses.

Preqrequisites Unlike Agarwal (2013) which attempted and introductory course for all levels of students, this course is designed for upper-division students or graduate students. Students of either discipline, Computer Science or Data Science, are prepared for this NLP course, albeit in different ways. Computer Scientists can think computationally, have experience with a syntactic formalism, and have experience with statistics. Data Science students likewise have experience with statistics as well as Python, including data analysis skills. Though the backgrounds can be quite diverse, my NLP course allows two prerequisite paths: all students must take a statistics course, but Computer Science students must take a Programming Languages course (which covers context free grammars for parsing computer languages and now covers some Python programming), and the Data Science students must have taken the introductory machine learning course. Figure 2 depicts the two course paths visually.

4 NLP Course Content

In this section, I discuss course content including topics and assignments that are designed to meet the course objectives listed above. Woven into the topics and assignments are the themes of *ambiguity* and *limitations*, explained below.

4.1 Topics & Assignments

Theme of Ambiguity Figure 3 shows the topics (solid outlines) that roughly translate to a single lecture, though some topics require multiple lectures. One main theme that is repeated throughout the course, but is not a specific lecture topic is *ambiguity*. This helps the students understand differences between natural human languages and programming languages. The *Introduction to Linguistics* topic, for example, gives a (very) high-level overviews of phonetics, morphology, syntax, semantics, and pragmatics, with examples of ambiguity for each area of linguistics (e.g., phonetic ambiguity is illustrated by hearing someone say *it's hard to recognize speech* but it could be heard as *it's hard to wreck a nice beach*, and syntactic ambiguity is illustrated by the sentence *I saw the person with the glasses* having more than one syntactic parse).

Probability and Information Theory This course does not focus only on deep learning, though many university NLP offerings seem to be moving to deep-learning only courses. There are several reasons not to focus on deep learning for a university like Boise State. First, students will not have a depth of background in probability and information theory, nor will they have a deep understanding of optimization (both convex and non-convex) or error functions in neural networks (e.g., cross entropy). I take time early in the course to explain discrete and continuous probability, and information theory. Discrete probability theory is straight forward as it requires counting, something that is intuitive when working with language data represented as text strings. Continuous probability theory, I have found, is more difficult for students to grasp as it relates to machine learning or NLP, but building on students' understanding of discrete probability theory seems to work pedagogically. For example, if we use continuous data and try somehow to count values in that data, it's not clear what should be counted (e.g., using binning), highlighting the importance of continuous probability functions that fit around the data, and the importance of estimating parameters for those continuous functions–an important concept for understanding classifiers later in the course. To illustrate both discrete and continuous probability, I show students how to program a discrete Naive Bayes classifier (using ham/spam email classification as a task) and a continuous Gaussian Native Bayes classifier (using the well-known iris data set) from scratch. Both classifiers have similarities, but the differences illustrate how continuous classifiers learn parameters.

Sequential Thinking Students experience probability and information theory in a targeted and highly-scaffolded assignment. They then extend their knowledge and program, from scratch, a part-of-speech tagger using counting to estimate probabilities modeled as Hidden Markov Models. These models seem old-fashioned, but it helps students gain experience beyond the standard machine learning workflow of mapping many-to-one (i.e., features to a distribution over classes) because this is a many-to-many sequential task (i.e., many words to many parts-of-speech), an important concept to understand when working with sequential data like language. It also helps students understand that NLP often goes beyond just fitting "models" because it requires things like building a trellis and decoding a trellis (undergraduate students are required to program a greedy decoder; graduates are required to program a Viterbi decoder). This is a challenging assignment for most students, irrespective of their technical background, but grasping the concepts of this assignment helps them grasp more difficult concepts that follow.

Syntax The Syntax & Parsing assignment also deserves mention. The students use any parser in NLTK to parse a context free grammar of a fictional language with a limited vocabulary.[3] This helps the students think about structure of language, and while there are other important ways to think about syntax such as dependencies (which we discuss in the course), another reason for this assignment is to have the students write grammars for a small vocabulary of words in a language they don't know, but also to create a non-lexicalized version of the grammar based on parts of speech, which helps them understand coverage and syntactic ambiguity more concretely.[4] There is no machine learning or estimating a probabilistic grammar here, just parsing.

Semantics An important aspect of my NLP class is semantics. I introduce them briefly to formal semantics (e.g., first-order logic), WordNet (Miller, 1995), distributional semantics, and grounded semantics. We discuss the merits of representing language "meaning" as embeddings and the limitations of meaning representations trained only on text and how they might be missing important semantic knowledge (Bender and Koller, 2020). The Topic Modeling assignment uses word-level embeddings (e.g., word2vec (Mikolov et al., 2013) and GloVe (Pennington et al., 2014)) to represent texts and gives them an opportunity to begin using a deep learning library (*tensorflow & keras* or *pytorch*).

We then consider how a semantic representation that has knowledge of modalities beyond text, i.e., images is part of human knowledge (e.g., what is the meaning of the word *red*?), and how recent work is moving in this direction. Two assignments give the students a deeper understanding of these ideas. The transfer learning assignment requires the students to use convolutional neural networks pre-trained on image data to represent objects in images and train a classifiers to identify simple object types, tying images to words. This is extended in the Grounded Semantics assignment where a binary classifier (based on the words-as-classifiers model introduced in Kennington and Schlangen (2015), then extended to work with images with "real" objects in Schlangen et al. (2016)) is trained

[3] I opt for Tamarian: `https://en.wikipedia.org/wiki/Darmok`

[4] I have received feedback from multiple students that this was their favorite assignment.

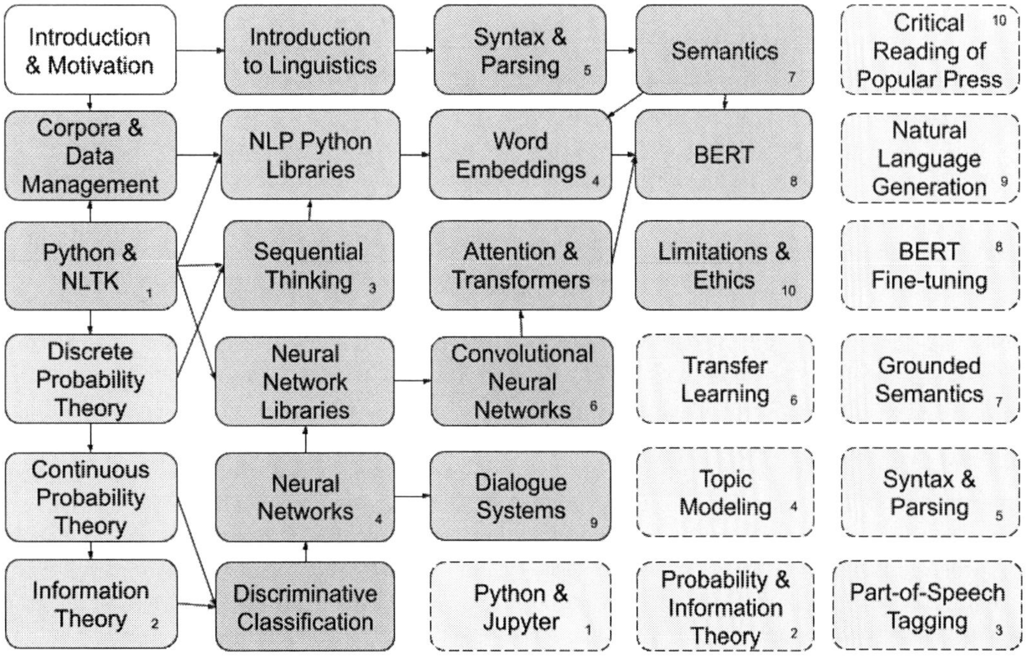

Figure 3: Course Topics and Assignments. Colors cluster topics (green=probability and information theory, blue=NLP libraries, red=neural networks, purple=linguistics, yellow=assignments). Courses have solid lines; topic dependencies are illustrated using arrows. Assignments have dashed lines. Assignments are indexed with the topics on which they depend.

for all words in referring expressions to objects in images in the MSCOCO dataset annotated with referring expressions to objects in images (Mao et al., 2016). Both assignments require ample scaffolding to help guide the students in using the libraries and datasets, and the MSCOCO dataset is much bigger than they are used to, giving them more real-world experience with a larger dataset.

Deep Learning An understanding of deep learning is obviously important for recent NLP researchers and practitioners. One constant challenge is determining what level of abstraction to present neural networks (should students know what is happening at the level of the underlying linear algebra, or is a conceptual understanding of parameter fitting in the neurons enough?). Furthermore, deep learning as a topic requires and understanding of its limitations and at least to some degree how it works "under the hood" (learning just how to use deep learning libraries without understanding how they work and how they "learn" from the data is akin to giving someone a car to drive without teaching them how to use it safely). This also means explaining some common misconceptions like how neurons in neural networks "mimic" real neurons in human brains, something that is very far from true, though certainly the idea of neural networks is inspired from human biology. For my students, we progress from linear regression to logistic regression (illustrating how parameters are being fit and how gradient descent is different from directly estimating parameters in continuous probability functions; i.e., maximum likelihood estimation vs convex and non-convex optimization), building towards small neural architectures and feed-forward networks. We also cover convolutional neural networks (for transfer learning and grounded semantics), attention (Vaswani et al., 2017), and transformers including transformer-based language models like BERT (Devlin et al., 2018), and how to make use of them; understanding how they are trained, but then only assigning fine-tuning for students to experience directly. I focus on smaller datasets and fine-tuning so students can train and tune models on their own machines.

Final Project There is a "final project" requirement. Students can work solo, or in a group of up to three students. The project can be anything

NLP related, but projects generally are realized as using an NLP or machine/deep learning library to train on some specific task, but others include methods for data collection (a topic we don't cover in class specifically, but some students have interest in the data collection process for certain settings like second language acquisition), as well as interfaces that they evaluate with some real human users. Scoping the projects is always the biggest challenge as many students initially envision very ambitious projects (e.g., build an end-to-end chatbot from scratch). I ask students to consider how much effort it would take to do three assignments and use that as a point of comparison. Throughout the first half of the semester students can ask for feedback on project ideas, and at the halfway point in the semester, students are required to submit a short proposal that outlines the scope and timeline for their project. They have the second half of the semester to then work through the project (with a "checkpoint" part way through to inform me of progress and needed adjustments), then they write a project report on their work at the end of the semester with evaluations and analayses of their work. Graduate students must write a longer report than the undergraduate students, and graduate students are required to give a 10-minute presentation on their project. The timeline here is critical: the midway point for beginning the project allows students to have experience with classification and NLP tasks, but have enough time to make adjustments as they work on their project. For example, students students attempt to apply BERT fine-tuning after the BERT assignment even though it wasn't in their original project proposal.

Theme of Limitations As is the case with ambiguity, *limitations* is theme in the course: limitations of using probability theory on language phenomena, limitations on datasets, and limitations on machine learning models. The theme of limitations ties into an overarching ethical discussion that happens at intervals throughout the semester about what can reasonably be expected from NLP technology and whom it affects as more practical models are deployed commercially.

The final assignment *critical reading of the popular press* is based on a course under the same title taught by Emily Bender at the University of Washington.[5] The goal of the assignment is to learn to critically read popular articles about NLP. Given an article, they need to summarize the article, then scrutinize the sources using the following as a guide: can they (1) access the primary source, such as original published paper, (2) assess if the claims in the article relate to what's claimed by the primary source, (3) determine if experimental work was involved or if the article is simply offering conjecture based on current trends, and (4) if the article did not carry out an evaluation, offer ideas on what kind of evaluation would be approrpriate to substantiate any claims made by the article's author(s). Then students should relate the headline of the article to the main text and determine if reading the headline provides an abstract understanding of the article's contents, and determine to what extent the author identified limitations to the NLP technology they were reporting on, what someone without training in NLP might take away from the article, and if the authors identified the people who might be affected (negatively or positively) by the NLP technology. This assignment gives students experience in recognizing the gap between the reality of NLP technology, how it is perceived by others, whom it affects, and its limitations.

We dedicate an entire lecture to ethics, and students are also asked to consider the implications of their final projects, what their work can and cannot reasonably do, and who might be affected by their work.[6]

Discussion Striking a balance between content on probability and information theory, linguistics, and machine learning is challenging for a single course, but given the diverse student population at a public state school, this approach seems to work for the students. An NLP class should have at least some content about linguistics, and framing aspects of linguistics in terms of ambiguity gives students the tools to think about how much they experience ambiguity on a daily basis, and the fact that if language were not ambiguous, data-driven NLP would be much easier (or even unnecessary). The discussions about syntax and semantics are especially important as many have not considered (particularly those who have not learned a foreign

[5] The original assignment definition appears to no longer be public.

[6] Approaching ethics from a framework of limitations I think helps students who might otherwise be put off by a discussion on ethics because it can clearly be demonstrated that NLP models have not just technical limitations and those limitations have implications for real people; an important message from this class is that *all* NLP models have limitations.

language) how much they take for granted when it comes to understanding and producing language, both speech and written text. The discussions on how to represent meaning computationally (symbolic strings? classifiers? embeddings? graphs?) and how a model should arrive at those representations (using speech? text? images?) is rewarding for the students. While most of the assignments and examples focus on English, examples of linguistic phenomena are often shown from other languages (e.g., Japanese morphology and German declension) and the students are encouraged to work on other languages for their final project.

Assignments vary in scope and scaffolding. For the probability and information theory and BERT assignments, I provide a fairly well-scaffolded template that the students fill in, whereas most other assignments are more open-ended, each with a set of reflection and analysis questions.

4.2 Content Delivery

Class sizes vary between 35-45 students. Class content is presented largely either as presentation slides or live programming using Jupyter notebooks. Slides introduce concepts, explain things outside of code (e.g., linguistics and ambiguity or graphical models), but most concepts have concrete examples using working code. The students see code for Naive Bayes (both discriminative and continiuous) classifiers, I use Python code to explain probability and information theory, classification tasks such as spam filtering, name classification, topic modeling, parsing, loading and prepossessing datasets, linear and logistic regression, sentiment classification, an implementation of neural networks from scratch as well as popular libraries.

While we use NLTK for much of the instruction following in some ways what is outlined in Bird et al. (2008), we also look at supported NLP Python libraries including *textblob*, *flair* (Akbik et al., 2019), *spacy*, *stanza* (Qi et al., 2020), *scikitlearn* (Pedregosa et al., 2011), *tensorflow* (Abadi et al., 2016) and *keras* (Chollet et al., 2015), *pytorch* (Paszke et al., 2019), and *huggingface* (Wolf et al., 2020). Others are useful, but most libraries help students use existing tools for standard NLP pre-processing like tokenization, sentence segmentation, stemming or lemmatization, part-of-speech tagging, and many have existing models for common NLP tasks like sentiment classification and machine translation. The *stanza* library has models for many languages. All code I write or show in class is accessible to the students throughout the semester so they can refer back to the code examples for assignments and projects. This of course means that students only obtain a fairly shallow experience for any library; the goal is to show them enough examples and give them enough experience in assignments to make sense of public documentation and other code examples that they might encounter.

The course uses two books, both which are available free online, the NLTK book,[7] and an ongoing draft of Jurafsky and Martin's upcoming 3rd edition.[8] The first assignment (Python & Jupyter in Figure 3) is an easy, but important assignment: I ask the students to go through Chapter 1 and parts of Chapter 4 of the NLTK book and for all code examples, write them by hand into a Jupyter notebook (i.e., no copy and pasting). This ensures that their programming environments are setup, steps them through how NLTK works, gives them immediate exposure to common NLP tasks like concordance and stemming, and gives them a way to practice Python syntax in the context of a Jupyter notebook. Another part of the assignment asks them to look at some Jupyter notebooks that use tokenization, counters, stop words, and n-grams, and asks them questions about best practices for authoring notebooks (including formatted comments).[9]

Students can use cloud-based Jupyter servers for doing their assignments (e.g., Google colab), but all must be able to run notebooks on a local machine and spend time learning about Python environments (i.e., anaconda). Assignments are submitted and graded using okpy which renders notebooks and allows instructors to assign grading to themselves or teaching assistants, and students can see their grades and written feedback for each assignment.[10]

4.3 Adjustments for Remote Learning

This course was relatively straightforward to adjust for remote delivery. The course website and okpy (for assignment submissions) are available to the students at all times. I decided to record lectures live (using Zoom) then make them available with

[7] `http://www.nltk.org/book_1ed/`

[8] `https://web.stanford.edu/~jurafsky/slp3/`

[9] I use the notebooks listed here for this part of the assignment `https://github.com/bonzanini/nlp-tutorial`

[10] `https://okpy.org/`

semester	Python	Ling	ML	DL
Spring 2017	none	none	10%	none
Spring 2019	50%	30%	30%	10%
Spring 2021	80%	30%	60%	20%

Table 1: Impressions of preparedness for Python, Linguistics (Ling), Machine Learning (ML), and Deep Learning (DL).

transcripts to the students. This course has one midterm, a programming assignment that is similar in structure to the regular assignments. During an in-person semester, there would normally be a written final, but I opted to make the final be part of their final project grade.

5 Reflection on Three Offerings over 4 years

Due to department constraints on offering required courses vs. elective courses (NLP is elective), I am only able to offer the NLP course in the Spring semester of odd years; i.e., every 4 semesters. The course is very popular, as enrollment is always over the standard class size (35 students). Below I reflect on changes that have taken place in the course due to the constant and rapid change in the field of NLP, in our undergraduate curriculum, and the implications those changes had on the course. These reflections are summarized in Table 1. As I am, to my knowledge, the first NLP researcher at Boise State University, I had to largely develop the contents of the course on my own, requiring adjustments over time as I better understand student preparedness. At this point, despite the two paths into the course, most students who take the course are still Computer Science students.

Spring 2017 The first time I taught the course, only a small percentage of the students had experience with Python. The only developed Python library for NLP was NLTK, so that and scikit-learn were the focus of practical instruction. I spent the first three weeks of the course helping students gain experience with Python (including *Jupyter, numpy, pandas*) then used Python as a means to help them understand probability and information theory. The course focused on generative classification including statistical n-gram language modeling with some exposure to discriminative models, but no exposure to neural networks.

Spring 2019 Between 2017 and 2019, several important papers showing how transformer networks can be used for robust language modeling were gaining in momentum, resulting in a shift towards altering and understanding their limitations (so called BERTology, see Rogers et al. (2020) for a primer). This, along with the fact that changes in the curriculum gave students better experience with Python, caused me to shift focus from generative models to neural architectures in NLP and to shift to cover word-level embeddings more rigorously. I spent the second half of the semester introducing neural networks (including multi-layer perceptrons, convolutional, and recurrant architectures) and giving students assignments to give them practice in tensorflow and keras. After the 2017 course, I changed the pre-requisite structure to require our programming languages course instead of data structures. This led to greater pareparedness in at least the syntax aspect of linguistics.

Spring 2021 In this iteration, I shifted focus from recurrant to attention/transformer-based models and assignmed a BERT fine-tuning assignment on a novel dataset using *huggingface*. I also introduced *pytorch* as another option for a neural network library (I also spend time on *tensorflow* and *keras*). This shift reflects a shift in my own research and understanding of the larger field, though exposure to each library is only partial and somewhat abstract. I note that students who have a data science background will likely appreciate tensorflow and *keras* more as they are not as object-oriented than *pytorch*, which seems to be more geared towards students with Computer Science backgrounds. Students can choose which one they will use (if any) for their final projects. More students are gaining interest in machine learning and deep learning and are turning to MOOC courses or online tutorials, which has led in some degree to better preparation for the NLP course, but often students have little understanding about the limitations of machine learning and deep learning after completing those courses and tutorials. Moreover, students from our university have started an Artificial Intelligence Club (the club started in 2019; I am the faculty advisor), which has given the students guidance on courses, topics, and skills that are required for practical machine learning. Many of the NLP class students are already members of the AI Club, and the club has members from many academic disciplines.

5.1 Student Feedback

I reached out to former students who took the class to ask for feedback on the course. Specifically, I asked if they use the skills and concepts from the NLP class directly for their work, or if the skills and concepts transferred in any way to their work. Student responses varied, but some answered that they use NLP directly (e.g., to analyze customer feedback or error logs), while most responded that they use many of the Python libraries we covered in class for other things that aren't necessarily NLP related, but more geared towards Data Science. For several students, using NLP tools helped them in research projects that led to publications.

6 Conclusions & Open Questions

With each offering, the NLP course at Boise State University is better suited pedagogically for students with some Data Science or Computer Science training, and the content reflects ongoing changes in the field of NLP to ensure their preparation. The topics and assignments cover a wide range, but as students have become better prepared with Python (by the introduction of new prerequisite courses that cover Python as well as changing some courses to include assignments in Python), more focus is spent on topics that are more directly related to NLP.

Though I feel it important to stay abreast of the ongoing changes in NLP and help students gain the knowledge and skills needed to be successful in NLP, an open question is *what* changes need to be made, and a related question is *how soon*. For example, I think at this point it is clear that neural networks are essential for NLP, though it isn't always clear what architectures should be taught (e.g., should we still cover recurrant neural networks or jump directly to transformers?). It seems important to cover even new topics sooner than later, though a course that is focused on research methods might be more concerned with staying up-to-date with the field, whereas a course that is more focused on general concepts and skills should wait for accessible implementations (e.g., huggingface for transformers) before covering those topics.

With recordings and updated content, I hope to flip the classroom in the future by assigning readings and watching lectures before class, then use class time for working on assignments.[11]

Much of my course materials including notebooks, slides, topics, and assignments can be found on a public Trello board.[12]

Acknowledgements

I am very thankful for the anonymous reviewers for giving excellent feedback and suggestions on how to improve this document. I hope that it followed those suggestions adequately.

References

Martín Abadi, Paul Barham, Jianmin Chen, Zhifeng Chen, Andy Davis, Jeffrey Dean, Matthieu Devin, Sanjay Ghemawat, Geoffrey Irving, Michael Isard, et al. 2016. Tensorflow: A system for large-scale machine learning. In *12th {USENIX} symposium on operating systems design and implementation ({OSDI} 16)*, pages 265–283.

Apoorv Agarwal. 2013. Teaching the basics of NLP and ML in an introductory course to information science. In *Proceedings of the Fourth Workshop on Teaching NLP and CL*, pages 77–84, Sofia, Bulgaria. Association for Computational Linguistics.

Alan Akbik, Tanja Bergmann, Duncan Blythe, Kashif Rasul, Stefan Schweter, and Roland Vollgraf. 2019. Flair: An easy-to-use framework for state-of-the-art nlp. In *NAACL 2019, 2019 Annual Conference of the North American Chapter of the Association for Computational Linguistics (Demonstrations)*, pages 54–59.

Emily M Bender and Alexander Koller. 2020. Climbing towards NLU: On Meaning, Form, and Understanding in the Age of Data. In *Association for Computational Linguistics*, pages 5185–5198.

Steven Bird, Ewan Klein, Edward Loper, and Jason Baldridge. 2008. Multidisciplinary instruction with the natural language toolkit. In *Proceedings of the Third Workshop on Issues in Teaching Computational Linguistics*, pages 62–70, Columbus, Ohio. Association for Computational Linguistics.

François Chollet et al. 2015. Keras. `https://keras.io`.

Jacob Devlin, Ming-Wei Chang, Kenton Lee, and Kristina Toutanova. 2018. BERT: Pre-training of Deep Bidirectional Transformers for Language Understanding. *arXiv*.

[11]This worked well for the Foundations of Data Science course that I introduced to the university; the second time I taught the course, I flipped it and used class time for students to work on assignments, which gave me a better indication of how students were understanding the material, time for one-on-one interactions, and fewer issues with potential cheating.

[12]`https://trello.com/b/mRcVsOvI/boise-state-nlp`

Eric Fosler-Lussier. 2008. Strategies for teaching "mixed" computational linguistics classes. In *Proceedings of the Third Workshop on Issues in Teaching Computational Linguistics*, pages 36–44, Columbus, Ohio. Association for Computational Linguistics.

Reva Freedman. 2008. Teaching NLP to computer science majors via applications and experiments. In *Proceedings of the Third Workshop on Issues in Teaching Computational Linguistics*, pages 114–119, Columbus, Ohio. Association for Computational Linguistics.

C. Kennington and D. Schlangen. 2015. Simple learning and compositional application of perceptually groundedword meanings for incremental reference resolution. In *ACL-IJCNLP 2015 - 53rd Annual Meeting of the Association for Computational Linguistics and the 7th International Joint Conference on Natural Language Processing of the Asian Federation of Natural Language Processing, Proceedings of the Conference*, volume 1.

Junhua Mao, Jonathan Huang, Alexander Toshev, Oana Camburu, Alan L Yuille, and Kevin Murphy. 2016. Generation and comprehension of unambiguous object descriptions. In *Proceedings of the IEEE conference on computer vision and pattern recognition*, pages 11–20.

Tomas Mikolov, Ilya Sutskever, Kai Chen, Greg Corrado, and Jeffrey Dean. 2013. Distributed Representations of Words and Phrases and their Compositionality. In *Proceedings of NIPS*.

George A Miller. 1995. Wordnet: a lexical database for english. *Communications of the ACM*, 38(11):39–41.

Adam Paszke, Sam Gross, Francisco Massa, Adam Lerer, James Bradbury, Gregory Chanan, Trevor Killeen, Zeming Lin, Natalia Gimelshein, Luca Antiga, Alban Desmaison, Andreas Kopf, Edward Yang, Zachary DeVito, Martin Raison, Alykhan Tejani, Sasank Chilamkurthy, Benoit Steiner, Lu Fang, Junjie Bai, and Soumith Chintala. 2019. Pytorch: An imperative style, high-performance deep learning library. In H. Wallach, H. Larochelle, A. Beygelzimer, F. d'Alché-Buc, E. Fox, and R. Garnett, editors, *Advances in Neural Information Processing Systems 32*, pages 8024–8035. Curran Associates, Inc.

F. Pedregosa, G. Varoquaux, A. Gramfort, V. Michel, B. Thirion, O. Grisel, M. Blondel, P. Prettenhofer, R. Weiss, V. Dubourg, J. Vanderplas, A. Passos, D. Cournapeau, M. Brucher, M. Perrot, and E. Duchesnay. 2011. Scikit-learn: Machine learning in Python. *Journal of Machine Learning Research*, 12:2825–2830.

Jeffrey Pennington, Richard Socher, and Christopher Manning. 2014. Glove: Global Vectors for Word Representation. In *Proceedings of the 2014 Conference on Empirical Methods in Natural Language Processing (EMNLP)*, pages 1532–1543.

Peng Qi, Yuhao Zhang, Yuhui Zhang, Jason Bolton, and Christopher D Manning. 2020. Stanza: A python natural language processing toolkit for many human languages. *arXiv preprint arXiv:2003.07082*.

Anna Rogers, Olga Kovaleva, and Anna Rumshisky. 2020. A Primer in BERTology: What we know about how BERT works. *arXiv*.

David Schlangen, Sina Zarriess, and Casey Kennington. 2016. Resolving References to Objects in Photographs using the Words-As-Classifiers Model. In *Proceedings of the 54th Annual Meeting of the Association for Computational Linguistics*, pages 1213–1223.

Ashish Vaswani, Noam Shazeer, Niki Parmar, Jakob Uszkoreit, Llion Jones, Aidan N Gomez, Lukasz Kaiser, and Illia Polosukhin. 2017. Attention is all you need. *arXiv preprint arXiv:1706.03762*.

Thomas Wolf, Lysandre Debut, Victor Sanh, Julien Chaumond, Clement Delangue, Anthony Moi, Pierric Cistac, Tim Rault, Rémi Louf, Morgan Funtowicz, Joe Davison, Sam Shleifer, Patrick von Platen, Clara Ma, Yacine Jernite, Julien Plu, Canwen Xu, Teven Le Scao, Sylvain Gugger, Mariama Drame, Quentin Lhoest, and Alexander M. Rush. 2020. Transformers: State-of-the-art natural language processing. In *Proceedings of the 2020 Conference on Empirical Methods in Natural Language Processing: System Demonstrations*, pages 38–45, Online. Association for Computational Linguistics.

On Writing a Textbook on Natural Language Processing

Jacob Eisenstein
Google Research
jeisenstein@google.com

Abstract

There are thousands of papers about natural language processing and computational linguistics, but very few textbooks. I describe the motivation and process for writing a college textbook on natural language processing, and offer advice and encouragement for readers who may be interested in writing a textbook of their own.

1 Introduction

As natural language processing reaches ever-greater heights of popularity, its students can learn from blogs and tutorials, videos and online courses, podcasts, social media, open source software projects, competitions, and more. In this environment, is there still any room for textbooks? This paper describes why you might write a textbook about natural language processing, how to do it, and what I learned from writing one.

Summary of the book. This paper will not focus on the details of my textbook (Eisenstein, 2019), but I offer a brief summary for context. My main goal was to create a text with a formal and coherent mathematical foundation in machine learning, which would explain a broad range of techniques and applications in natural language processing. The first section of the book builds up the mathematical foundation from linear classification though neural networks and unsupervised learning. The second section extends this foundation to structure prediction, with classical algorithms for search and marginalization in sequences and trees, while also introducing some ideas from morphology and syntax. The third section treats the special problem of semantics, which distinguishes natural language processing from other applications of machine learning. This section is more methodologically diverse, ranging from logical to distributional semantics. The final section treats three of the primary application areas: machine translation, information extraction, and text generation. Altogether this comprises nineteen chapters, which is more than could be taught in a single semester. Rather, the teacher or student can select subsets of chapters depending on whether they wish to emphasize machine learning, linguistics, or applications. The preface sketches out a few paths through the book for various types of courses.

2 Motivation and related work

In this section, I offer some reasons for writing a textbook, compare textbooks with alternative educational formats, and provide a few words of encouragement for prospective authors.

2.1 Why you might want to write a textbook

The first requirement is that you expect to enjoy the type of work involved: reading the most impactful papers in the field, synthesizing and curating the ideas these papers contain, and presenting them in a way that is accessible and engaging for students. One of the main contributions of a textbook over the original research material is the unification of terminology and mathematical notation, so it will help if you have strong opinions about this and an impulse toward consistency. Finally, writing a good textbook requires reading great textbooks to understand what makes them work, and I enjoyed having a reason to spend more time with some of my favorites (e.g., MacKay, 2003; Blackburn and Bos, 2005; Cover and Thomas, 2012; Sipser, 2012; Murphy, 2012).

A more respectable reason to write a textbook is to clarify and amplify your vision for the field. The writing process forces you to try to understand things from multiple perspectives and to identify connections across diverse methods, problems, and concepts. If you are an opinionated researcher or teacher, there are probably ideas that you think haven't gotten the credit they deserve or haven't

Proceedings of the Fifth Workshop on Teaching NLP, pages 125–130
June 10–11, 2021. ©2021 Association for Computational Linguistics

been presented in the right way. Maybe you think students should know more about some method or set of problems: for example, I felt that learning to think about NLP by doing paper-and-pencil exercises could help students avoid wasting a lot of time writing code that was conceptually flawed. A textbook is the perfect vehicle for grinding such axes, as long as you don't take it too far and you keep the focus on what will benefit the reader.

One more reason to write a textbook is that we really do need them: only a small handful of NLP textbooks have ever been written. It is true that the textbook market is somewhat "winner-take-all": it is easiest to build a course around a textbook that is already widely in use, and hard to get teachers to change their materials. But different types of courses and students have different needs, and mature fields have dozens of books that target each of these audiences. Compared with the difficulty of finding a niche among the thousands of research papers written each year, a well-written NLP textbook is almost guaranteed to offer something valuable to a large number of readers.

2.2 Why I did it

Honesty requires some additional introspection about my real motivations. The project started because I felt unprepared to teach many topics in natural language processing, and could think of no better preparation than writing out some notes and derivations in my own words. I find it hard to focus on lectures that are based on slides, and I have noticed that many students seem to have the same difficulty. So I tried to write notes that would enable me to teach from a whiteboard.[1]

A second motivation was to create a resource for my students. When I started teaching in 2012, there was really only one textbook that was sufficiently complete and contemporary to offer in a college-level NLP course: Jurafsky and Martin (2008, J&M).[2] But as an incoming faculty member, I was particularly eager to train graduate students as potential research assistants, and J&M was less mathematical than I would have liked for this purpose. My first approach was to have students read contemporary research papers and surveys, but this requires training, and students struggled with inconsistencies in notation and terminology across papers. I needed something that would give students a bridge to contemporary research, and decided I would have to write it myself.

These reasons added up to a set of course notes that I posted on Github, but not a textbook. After periodic nudges from editors over a period of several years (see Table 1), and some experience reviewing books and book proposals, I finally decided to submit a proposal of my own in 2017. At this time I was close to submitting my tenure materials, and writing a book seemed like a welcome change of pace. I had become friends with a group of professors in the humanities and social sciences who were sweating over their own book projects at the time, and I envied their focus on solo long-term work, which seemed so different from my life of bouncing from one student-led project to the next. And finally, I flattered myself to think that I would be able to write the book quickly from the material that I had amassed in five years of teaching — read on to learn whether this prediction was accurate. Overall, the book arose from a combination of impostor syndrome and irrational optimism, a recipe that may be at the heart of many writing projects.

2.3 Why not do something else?

When people find out that you are writing a textbook, you may receive suggestions for all sorts of better ways to communicate the same information. In the 2010s, there was great interest in online courses — particularly at Georgia Tech, which was then my home university — and I was urged to produce videos for such a course on natural language processing. Another possibility would have been to write a blog, which would be easier to keep current than a textbook, and would permit readers to post comments and questions (e.g., Ruder, 2021). Going further, tools like Jupyter notebooks (Kluyver et al., 2016) offer exciting new ways to combine writing, math, and code. Some intrepid authors have even written entire textbooks as collections of these interactive documents (e.g., VanderPlas, 2016). With all these alternatives, why write a traditional textbook on "dead trees," (as one of my students put it)? Some reasons are more personal and others are practical. Here are three:

Longevity. Although much of the textbook will be obsolete in a few years, some parts may stand the test of time; there are topics for which I still

[1] A specific inspiration to my early notes were the teaching materials from Michael Collins, e.g., `http://www.cs.columbia.edu/~mcollins/loglinear.pdf`.

[2] There are also some outstanding books that were either too old (Manning and Schütze, 1999) or not quite aligned with my goals for the course (e.g., Bender, 2013; Bird et al., 2009; Goldberg, 2017; Smith, 2011).

turn to my copy of Manning and Schütze (1999). Even if my book does not offer the best explanation of anything that anyone cares about in twenty years, I am glad to know that people will probably be able to read it if they want to. With more innovative online media, there is no such guarantee. Course videos may be available far into the future, but they are difficult to produce well, requiring an entirely different set of skills than the amateur typesetting capabilities that most academics acquire in the course of their studies.

Quality. The publication process brings in several people who help you write the best possible book: an editor who helps you choose the material and the high-level approach, reviewers who make sure the presentation is clear and correct, and a copy editor who finds writing errors. Perhaps because textbooks are rare, I also found that colleagues were very generous when asked to lend their expertise.

Finality. The field of natural language processing will surely continue to grow and evolve, and online media offers the temptation to try to keep pace with these changes. But if you agree to be bound by the conventional publishing process, there will come a day where you send a file to the publisher and are unable to make any further changes. While some authors seem to be happy (or at least willing) to continually revise through many editions over several decades (e.g., Russell and Norvig, 2020), I wanted the option to move on to other things.

While textbooks can be expensive, open access online editions are increasingly typical. In my case, I was able to negotiate a free online edition in exchange for a small portion of the royalties.

2.4 Yes, you

Before committing, I confessed to my prospective editor one of my deepest fears about the project: the best-known textbooks on natural language processing (Manning and Schütze, 1999; Jurafsky and Martin, 2008) were written by true luminaries. Who was I to try to compete with them? Being a crafty and experienced editor, she replied that perhaps those authors were not so luminous before their textbooks, and wouldn't I like to write one and join them in the firmament? Although I am not so crafty, even I could see through this ploy. What ultimately gave me the courage to proceed was the realization that if I didn't write this *particular* textbook, then no one else would. AI summer was then coming into full bloom, and the true luminaries had plenty of other things to keep them occupied. In any case, there is no minimum amount of luminosity required for writing a textbook: publishers will ask that you give some evidence that you know what you're talking about, but the main criterion is to have a compelling vision for a book that hasn't been written yet.

3 Methodology

Publishers seem keenly aware of the need for more textbooks in natural language processing and in AI more generally, and I found several editors that were eager to talk at conferences. I selected MIT Press because of their track record in publishing some of my favorite computer science textbooks. Other factors that you may wish to consider are the length of the review and production process, and the publisher's position towards open access. I was lucky to get feedback on the contract from another editor and from colleagues who have written books in other fields, but I did not think of negotiating with regard to electronic editions and translations. Fortunately the publisher was generous on these points, as they turned out to be a significant fraction of the revenue for the book. In any case, in the current environment of high demand for AI expertise, the financial compensation is not competitive with other uses of the same amount of time. You may find that it makes more sense to negotiate on aspects of the book and publishing process, such as length, open access, and support.

The publisher requires four main inputs from the author: a proposal, a complete draft for review, a "finished version" for copy editing and composition, and markup of page proofs. In the rest of the section, I'll describe how I approached each of these inputs. A timeline is given in Table 1.

3.1 Proposal

The publisher required a proposal with two complete chapters (which were entirely rewritten later), a detailed table-of-contents for the rest of book, and a discussion of the imagined readership and the books that readers currently have to choose from. You will also give an estimate for some factors that affect the price: how long the book will be, how many figures to include, and whether color is required; and you will be asked to provide a time-

Fall 2012	**Started teaching natural language processing and writing lecture notes.**
July 2014	First contact with an editor.
2014-2017	Periodic nudges from the editor to please finish my book proposal someday.
March 2017	**Book proposal done and sent out for review.**
May 2017	Book proposal reviewed and accepted.
June 2017	Signed agreement with publisher.
Summer 2017-2018	Did most of the writing.
Early summer 2018	Solicited informal reviews of chapters from subject experts.
June 2018	**Manuscript draft sent out for formal reviews.**
Summer 2018	Wrote most of the exercises while awaiting reviews.
July 2018	Received reviews, started revisions.
November 2018	**Revised manuscript sent out for production.**
Winter 2019	Received and reviewed copy edits.
May 2019	**Received and reviewed page proofs.**
Summer 2019	I was supposed to make slide decks while waiting for the book to come out.
October 2019	**Book is published.**

Table 1: A rough timeline. Key inputs from section 3 are highlighted in bold.

line, which no one takes too seriously.[3] As with anything else, it helps to see other proposals that have been successful, and you may ask your editor for positive examples. I spent a significant amount of time on the example chapters, and relatively little on the proposal itself, although it did help me to identify the overall structure of the book.

3.2 Draft

If the proposal is accepted, it's time to start writing. The purpose of this stage is to produce something that can be sent to the reviewers. In my case, the editor did not require the exercises or figures to be done at this stage; I have heard that other presses will solicit reviews on a chapter-by-chapter basis. After getting to a complete draft of each chapter, I also solicited informal reviews from friends and colleagues, which both improved the content and gave me far more confidence about the chapters that did not align with my expertise.

At first I tried to schedule the writing to align with teaching — for example, writing the chapter on parsing while teaching the same unit — but I wasn't able to keep up, and several chapters had to be left to the following summer. I hesitate to offer much writing advice to this audience, but I will pass along one thing I learned from Mark Liberman, when I asked how he was such a prolific blogger:[4] it's possible to learn to write well if you constrain yourself to write quickly, but it's much more difficult to learn to write quickly while constraining yourself to write well. So write quickly, and eventually the quality will catch up.

One regret about this stage is that I did not adopt the publisher's formatting templates. I had already written many pages of course notes, and when I couldn't immediately get them to compile against the publisher's format, I decided to put this off until later. Naturally that only made things much more difficult in the end, and I didn't use all that much of my original material anyway.

There are several reasons why my estimate of the completeness of the original course notes was too optimistic. While teaching, you are likely to emphasize the aspects of the subject that you know best. This means that the remaining parts to write are exactly those that are most difficult for you. In the classroom, you can rely on interactive techniques such as dialog and demonstrations to overcome weaknesses in the exposition of technically-challenging material, but the textbook must stand alone. Finally, the requirements for consistency, clarity, and accuracy of attribution in a textbook are much higher than the standard that I had reached in my course notes, and although the difference may seem small to many readers, it represents quite a lot of work for the writer. In total, I kept hardly any of the original text, although I was able to reuse the high-level structure of roughly half of the chapters.

[3] As my editor put it, "if missing deadlines was a crime, the prisons would be full of authors."

[4] `https://languagelog.ldc.upenn.edu`

3.3 Revision(s)

The reviews were generally positive, but one reviewer was quite critical of the early chapters; although the publisher didn't require it, I made substantial changes based on this feedback. At this point I also tried to add a few notes about very recent work, such as BERT (Devlin et al., 2019), which appeared on arXiv while I was doing the revisions. Had the original reviews been more negative, the publisher might have required another round before accepting my revisions, but luckily this wasn't required in my case. The reviewers were very helpful, but I am skeptical that any of them read the whole thing, and I recommend seeking external reviews, especially for the later chapters that the reviewers are likely to skip or skim.

3.4 Proofs

The remaining steps involve details of the writing style and typesetting. At this stage I handed over the source documents to the production team, and could only communicate by adding notes to a PDF. This may be less of a technical requirement and more an incentive to prevent authors from introducing significant new content. The copy editing stage identified many writing problems, but the copy editor was unable to check the math. The publisher offered to pay for a math editor, but I was unable to find someone willing to do it. Fortunately, many of the mathematical errors had already been identified by students of my course. This stage also involved a bit of haggling about minor issues like whether it would be necessary for citations to include page numbers from conference proceedings, and when it was appropriate to use a term of art that violated the house style, such as "coreference" instead of "co-reference."

Once the copy edits are complete, a LaTeX professional was able to compile the document using the publisher's format. This created a number of problems with the typesetting of the math, which were somewhat painstaking to check and resolve, and which could have been avoided if I had used the publisher's templates from the beginning. At this point the publisher is highly resistant to any changes to the content, but I did get them to fix some glaring errors that I found at the last minute.

4 Evaluation

What worked. It is difficult to be objective about a project of this scope. I am always happy to learn that the book is being used in a course or for self-study, and was thrilled about translations into Chinese and Korean. The text seems best suited to classes that are similar to mine, where the primary goal is to train future researchers, who need a mathematical foundation in the discipline. I have been told that the exercises are particularly helpful, and I have received many requests for solutions, which I am happy to provide to teachers. There have been fewer reports of errors than I had expected, which I attribute to the careful reading of several classes of students while I was teaching from the unpublished notes.[5] Offering the PDF online seems to have been an essential factor in the adoption of the textbook, especially given that the most popular alternative (J&M) is also freely available.

What could have been better. By the time the book appeared in print, there had been a number of significant changes in both the theory and practice of natural language processing. While this was expected, it is nonetheless hard not to be disappointed not to have put more emphasis on the topics that increased in importance — I'll say a bit more on this in the final section. Some readers feel that the term "introduction" in the title is misleading with regard to the amount of mathematical background that is expected. While the text assumes only multivariate calculus (and attempts to be clear about this expectation), the pace of the opening chapters is difficult for students who are out of practice. My editor was probably correct that adoption would be greater if I provided slides that professors could teach from, but I couldn't bring myself to make time for this tedious task after finishing the book.

5 Future work

As the field of natural language processing continues to progress, it is tempting to update the textbook with the latest research developments. For example, multilinguality and multimodality would deserve significantly more emphasis in a second edition, and a revision would have to reflect the maturation of applications such as question answering and dialog. But while some changes could be addressed by adding or modifying a few chapters, others — particularly the shift from conventional supervised learning to more complex methodologies like pretraining, multi-task learning, distilla-

[5] I maintain an errata page at `https://github.com/jacobeisenstein/gt-nlp-class/blob/master/notes/errata.md`

tion, and prompt-based learning — seem to require a more fundamental rethinking of the book's underlying structure, particularly in a textbook that emphasizes a coherent mathematical foundation. Any such revisions would have to grow out of classroom teaching experience, which did so much to determine the shape of the first edition.

Acknowledgments. Thanks to William Cohen, Slav Petrov, and the anonymous reviewers for feedback.

References

Emily M Bender. 2013. *Linguistic fundamentals for natural language processing: 100 essentials from morphology and syntax*, volume 6 of *Synthesis lectures on human language technologies*. Morgan & Claypool Publishers.

Steven Bird, Ewan Klein, and Edward Loper. 2009. *Natural language processing with Python: analyzing text with the natural language toolkit*. O'Reilly Media, Inc.

Patrick Blackburn and Johan Bos. 2005. *Representation and inference for natural language: A first course in computational semantics*. CSLI Publications.

Thomas M Cover and Joy A Thomas. 2012. *Elements of Information Theory*. John Wiley & Sons.

Jacob Devlin, Ming-Wei Chang, Kenton Lee, and Kristina Toutanova. 2019. BERT: Pre-training of deep bidirectional transformers for language understanding. In *Proceedings of the 2019 Conference of the North American Chapter of the Association for Computational Linguistics: Human Language Technologies, Volume 1 (Long and Short Papers)*, pages 4171–4186, Minneapolis, Minnesota. Association for Computational Linguistics.

Jacob Eisenstein. 2019. *Introduction to natural language processing*. MIT press.

Yoav Goldberg. 2017. Neural network methods for natural language processing. *Synthesis lectures on human language technologies*, 10(1):1–309.

Dan Jurafsky and James H Martin. 2008. *Speech and language processing*, 2nd edition. Prentice Hall.

Thomas Kluyver, Benjamin Ragan-Kelley, Fernando Pérez, Brian Granger, Matthias Bussonnier, Jonathan Frederic, Kyle Kelley, Jessica Hamrick, Jason Grout, Sylvain Corlay, Paul Ivanov, Damián Avila, Safia Abdalla, Carol Willing, and Jupyter development team. 2016. Jupyter notebooks — a publishing format for reproducible computational workflows. In *Positioning and Power in Academic Publishing: Players, Agents and Agendas*, pages 87–90. IOS Press.

David J. C. MacKay. 2003. *Information theory, inference and learning algorithms*. Cambridge university press.

Christopher Manning and Hinrich Schütze. 1999. *Foundations of statistical natural language processing*. MIT press.

Kevin P Murphy. 2012. *Machine learning: a probabilistic perspective*. MIT press.

Sebastian Ruder. 2021. Recent advances in language model fine-tuning. `https://ruder.io/recent-advances-lm-fine-tuning/`.

Stuart Russell and Peter Norvig. 2020. *Artificial intelligence: a modern approach*, 4th edition. Pearson.

Michael Sipser. 2012. *Introduction to the Theory of Computation*. Cengage learning.

Noah A Smith. 2011. Linguistic structure prediction. *Synthesis lectures on human language technologies*, 4(2):1–274.

Jake VanderPlas. 2016. *Python data science handbook: Essential tools for working with data*. O'Reilly Media, Inc.

Learning How To Learn NLP: Developing Introductory Concepts Through Scaffolded Discovery

Alexandra Schofield
Harvey Mudd College
xanda@cs.hmc.edu

Richard Wicentowski
Swarthmore College
rwicent1@swarthmore.edu

Julie Medero
Harvey Mudd College
julie@cs.hmc.edu

Abstract

We present a scaffolded discovery learning approach to introducing concepts in a Natural Language Processing course aimed at computer science students at liberal arts institutions. We describe some of the objectives of this approach, as well as presenting specific ways that four of our discovery-based assignments combine specific natural language processing concepts with broader analytic skills. We argue this approach helps prepare students for many possible future paths involving both application and innovation of NLP technology by emphasizing experimental data navigation, experiment design, and awareness of the complexities and challenges of analysis.

1 Introduction

Discovery learning describes a pedagogical framing where, instead of introducing students to a skill and then using assessments to explicitly practice that skill, students are given a broad objective and "discover" pertinent concepts and skills in pursuit of that objective. Though pedagogical research yields unimpressive results for pure discovery learning (Mayer, 2004), several works support the effectiveness of *guided* discovery learning (Alfieri et al., 2011), where students are provided scaffolding for how to develop their solutions and regular opportunities for feedback or validation. This type of instructional approach offers the opportunity to exercise creativity and to take more ownership of their own sensemaking process.

In this paper, we present a proof of concept of the merits of scaffolded discovery learning by describing our implementation of four guided discovery learning exercises[1] to anchor the first four weeks of an undergraduate natural language processing course. We also detail why we have found this scaffolded discovery learning approach especially well-suited to an undergraduate NLP course.

2 Motivation

There are several strategic benefits to a discovery learning approach for NLP. First, the traditional computer science approach to NLP instruction tends to emphasize programming and/or core algorithms first (Bird, 2008), which requires students to jump immediately into implementing widely accepted algorithms for particular tasks. While this may lead to a more satisfying performance outcome, it may miss the opportunity for students to engage with why particular choices, such as how to tokenize text or how to smooth an n-gram model, actually make sense from a linguistic perspective. These skills are important when transferring to new domains, where the optimal choices might change and require further assessment.

Second, the choice of which model is the mostly "widely accepted" has been shown to change rapidly. Examining the curricular recommendations made by the ACM/IEEE Joint Task Force for Computing Curricula over time, we see speech recognition and parsing as emphasized topics in 2001, but no specific discussion of n-gram models (ACM/IEEE, 2001). In contrast, probabilistic models and ngrams appear in the 2013 version, while speech recognition disappears as an emphasized topic and parsing remains on the syllabus in vaguer terms (ACM/IEEE, 2013). While familiarity with these different problem spaces is helpful for building context and approaches to new problem domains, it is hard to predict if the depth of knowledge required to fully implement a conditional random field (CRF) or a deep neural net for machine translation will be useful beyond the next few years. In contrast, our discovery-learning labs focus on how to set up experimental data and protocols, select and interpret appropriate metrics, use those metrics to investigate what textual phe-

[1] Materials for these four assignments are available for use at https://github.com/DiscoverNLP.

Proceedings of the Fifth Workshop on Teaching NLP, pages 131–137
June 10–11, 2021. ©2021 Association for Computational Linguistics

nomena they actually embody, and react to that knowledge with possible design interventions. We have found these skills not only generalize better across different models and problem domains, but also dominate the actual time spent doing our NLP work as researchers.

Third, this strategy of teaching is more compatible with the structure of the curricula at the undergraduate-only institutions where we teach. Upper-level courses such as natural language processing have shallow prerequisites and students have uneven backgrounds in math, computer science and linguistics. This challenge is shared by both computer science and linguistics undergraduate programs (Bird, 2008) and graduate courses aimed at an information studies audience (Hearst, 2005; Liddy and McCracken, 2005). Emphasizing skills of evaluation and model discovery over detailed model analyses helps ensure that students comfortable with data structures and some probability will be able to succeed and develop meaningful skills in the course. In our context, it has the additional benefit of inviting a liberal arts approach to critique the nature of what we evaluate in NLP tasks, as well as to consider the implications of the deployment of language technologies.

3 Learning Objectives

We present four labs as a central element of the first four weeks of a natural language course. In developing these exercises, we emphasize three skills we hope students develop through these assignments: analysis of quantitative results, text exploration, and generalizing concepts to new models. While some of these fall into the classic "text processing first" paradigm of course offered as an applied linguistics approach by Bird (2008), it does not do so at the exclusion of understanding the "why" of related algorithms and models. Notably, none of these skills specify particular models in natural language processing, though the labs we present do have some alignment with different classic NLP course topics. This is a deliberate alternative approach: by de-emphasizing outcomes focused on "knowing" particular algorithms and models, we provide more opportunity to practice skills to approach and interpret new models that students may choose to explore later in the course.

Analysis of quantitative results. Our work aims to support a progression not in terms of complexity of models, but in the levels of critique students apply to computational work on text. By building from some of the basic challenges of what it means to read, process, and write text in a computer through the development of increasingly complex metrics, students naturally have the opportunity to progress from making comments based on initially observed phenomena to making the case for whether results are surprising using typical metrics of the field. Unlike work that primarily privileges meeting certain minimum accuracy thresholds, these exercises intentionally include analyses of unimpressive results, helping to emphasize important lessons about how seemingly large quantitative differences don't always indicate significance in the vast, sparse universe of language.

Exploration of the text. Natural language processing benchmarks often present results in ways that obscure the contents of the data being evaluated, especially in cases where test data is totally hidden. Students new to the field of NLP often do not have strong intuitions around how much variation exists even in a limited problem domain. Examining system inputs and outputs helps them develop intuitions about language data and what it means to be "unusual" in a highly sparse space. Our discovery approach helps reinforce the importance of including both quantitative experimental results and qualitative discussions using examples about model behavior with respect to the text, as both contribute to an understanding of what a model has (or hasn't) done.

Thinking beyond individual models. An important component of practicing natural language processing is implementing models and comparing their performance. However, current "state of the art" models often are built using a combination of different fairly detailed neural architectural choices. Engaging with implementing these can require either many prerequisite courses, many days of in-class time to establish working knowledge of neural networks for sequential data, or a strategy of teaching how to code the models that eschews why to use these pieces. Further, with little confidence that these models won't be obsolete in two years, it can be an expensive investment to set up curricular materials for these topics without knowing whether they will still merit reuse the next time the course is offered. Because our approach de-emphasizes the specific models implemented in favor of understanding broader skills around evaluation and comparison, we believe it will better prepare students to teach themselves and to ask meaningful research questions when approaching new work.

4 Course Format

The format of the two courses using these labs include both a lecture-focused larger class format and a smaller discussion-based format. In both, students are expected to read some text from the textbook, Jurafsky and Martin (2020), supplemented by papers on relevant NLP topics. Outside of course readings, the lab work constitutes the vast majority of the work completed outside of class for the first half of the semester.

In both formats, we reserve one day a week for specifically setting up and starting lab assignments. Students attend "lab day" in order to start work on the lab exercise for that week. The lab relies on the concepts discussed in class. Though the lab assignment is started during the lab period, the expectation is that the lab work will be completed outside of class and due the following week.

5 Lab Assignment Progression

The following subsections describe the progression of four laboratory assignments intended for the first four weeks of the course. Each lab assignment has a learning outcome related to analytical skills in natural language processing. Each of the four labs presented also focuses on introducing content from Jurafsky and Martin (2020).

These assignments are implemented in Python, with starter code provided through GitHub. The assignments can be coupled with autograders for the code managed through Gradescope.[2] When used, the autograders (which account for less than half the points in the student's final write-up) can serve as extra scaffolding, as they provide a useful on-demand tool for students to check whether their code is correct before writing their analysis.

Each lab is accompanied by an extensive lab write-up, which breaks the exploration topic into individual implementation goals, check-ins, and questions for students to address as they venture through the assignment. These are designed to be self-contained: while references to concepts or definitions described in the textbook reading may appear, most formulas and terms specific to the questions in the lab are re-introduced as part of the write-up. The text alternates between providing textual definitions and descriptions, coding instructions, and analysis questions. As the lab progresses, the questions grow more open-ended, culminating in prompts to make sense of results and what they signal about how well a model fits the text.

5.1 Lab 1: Regex Chatbot

In this lab, students develop a chatbot using regular expressions, either using Slack or Discord in our class offerings.[3] While the requirements of the assignment are fairly basic (for instance, the regular expressions must use groups and quantifiers), students are primarily graded on a write-up describing the chatbot and its performance. Students are expected to document with screenshots examples of conversations that worked well or poorly and to analyze what sorts of features might be missing.

Preparation Students are expected to read the regular expressions subsection of the J&M textbook (§2.1). Students must also complete the first portion and at least one challenge puzzle from a regular expressions puzzle game called Regex Golf.[4].

Outcomes Having completed this assignment, students should be able to develop and test Python regular expressions, as well as to outline and illustrate a qualitative analysis of the capabilities and limitations of a new model. This assignment also encourages students to focus their time on thoughtful analysis instead of optimal performance prior introducing clear numerical metrics of performance. For instance, the sample of a student write-up in Figure 1 shows introspection related to a relatively simple pig Latin bot on how punctuation adds wrinkles to the program. These observations about what cases can lead to additional complexity help set up how we attend to variation in case, punctuation, Unicode, and more general human language variation in datasets for future labs. Though regular expressions are technically covered in another required course in the CS major as a theory topic, we find it important to solidify in an applied context, as tokenization is a necessary part of processing pipelines for the remainder of the course, a conclusion we share with Hearst (2005).

[2] `https://www.gradescope.com/`

[3] A side benefit of starting with this assignment is that, for courses that use one of these systems for Q&A, it encourages participation early among students.

[4] From Erling Ellinsen: `https://alf.nu/RegexGolf`

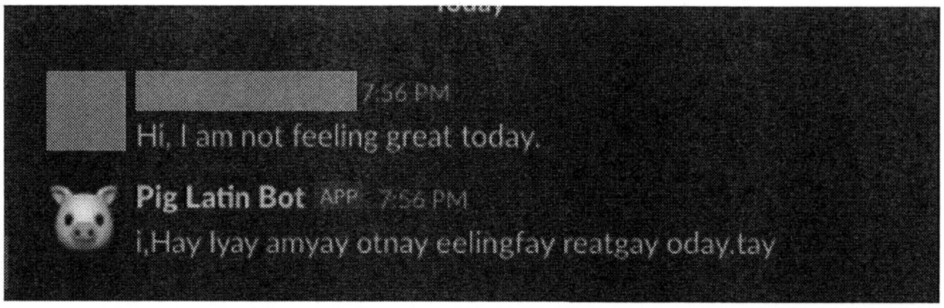

Here, however is a case where our SlackBot does poorly. It does not respond as intended, as we can see that it does not fix the capitalization of the first word. Moreover, the bot assumes that punctuation marks are a part of the word and includes them in the Pig Latin translation. If I had more time, I would be able to address this by having the regular expression ensure that the last character is a letter. Additionally, to fix the capitalization issue, I would need to check if the first letter of the word is capitalized, and if so, add its lower case version in the translation but then capitalize the first letter of the translated word.

Figure 1: A sample student write-up for Lab 1 describing a case where their bot failed to generate formulaic pig Latin and proposing improvements to address that case.

5.2 Lab 2: Tokenization and Segmentation

In this lab, students are first guided step-by-step through the basics of making a tokenizer in order to compute word frequencies in English texts from Project Gutenberg. Reflections include discussion of the effect of punctuation and lower-casing on which words appear most frequently. From there, students move on to improve a rule-based sentence segmenter for several portions of the Brown corpus using simple regular expressions. In this exercise, students report their precision, recall, and F1 scores, and reflect on which rules worked well, which did not, and why. Throughout both pieces, students explore the text, focusing on which text does not behave as expected.

Preparation Students are expected to prepare with textbook reading on text normalization (§2.2-2.4) as well as classification metrics (§4.7).

Outcomes Having completed this assignment, students should be able to perform standard string manipulations in Python. Students also will identify behaviors in text collections that fall outside typical prescriptive grammar rules, e.g. that sentences in the Brown corpus may start with a lowercase letter or end with a colon. Students are often tempted to add rules to their system for every sentence boundary, even those that are due to annotation errors. The analysis portion of this lab leads them to consider issues of overfitting for the first time, since adding rules for those edge cases leads to worse performance on held-out data. To complete the lab, students will need to combine these observations with quantitative results regarding word frequencies and classification metrics to describe what they have observed about their methods. Students will additionally reinforce Lab 1 skills of regular expression creation and identifying strengths and weakness in new systems.

5.3 Lab 3: Zipf's Law and N-gram Models

In this lab, students first look through the same Project Gutenberg texts to assess how closely the unigram frequency patterns match those projected by Zipf's law. Students then develop functions to extract unigram, bigram and trigram frequencies from the texts. They use these functions to compare features found in an unrelated data set. In the last offering of this course, we utilized the Hyperpartisan news dataset (Kiesel et al., 2019) in order to understand how many types and tokens are unique to hyperpartisan or non-hyperpartisan-labeled news. Students explored these same evaluations on a random reshuffling of the data to understand the magnitude of "unique" attributes that can arise even when comparing texts from the same source.

Preparation Students are expected to prepare with textbook reading on n-gram language models (§3.1-3.4).

Outcomes Having completed this assignment, students should be able to develop code to extract n-gram frequencies from text and predict unigram frequency distributions from Zipf's law. This requires interpreting relative and absolute frequencies and their reasonable values: a common error

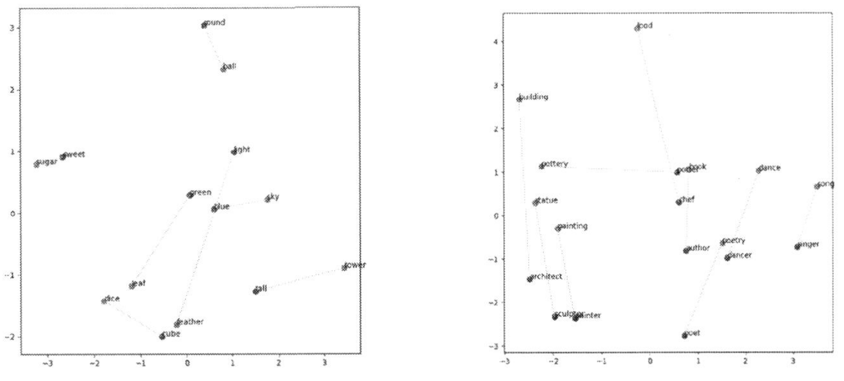

(a) Properties of objects

(b) Creators and creations

Figure 2: Two examples of alternate analogy tasks developed by students for Lab 4.

scenario as students attempt to compare empirical versus theoretical behavior is to plot absolute theoretical word frequencies against relative empirical word frequencies, as displayed in Figure 3. Further, they should be able to provide qualitative and quantitative analysis of rare and common features and their effect on different frequency statistics.

The datasets used for this lab are too large for naïve file-reading solutions that load the whole file into memory at once. Students learn to iteratively process the data, which prepares them for working with large files in later labs and course projects. As they work with these files, students gain some practice leveraging existing libraries (such as `lxml`[5], `spaCy` (Honnibal et al., 2020), and `matplotlib` (Hunter, 2007)) to process text and plot data.

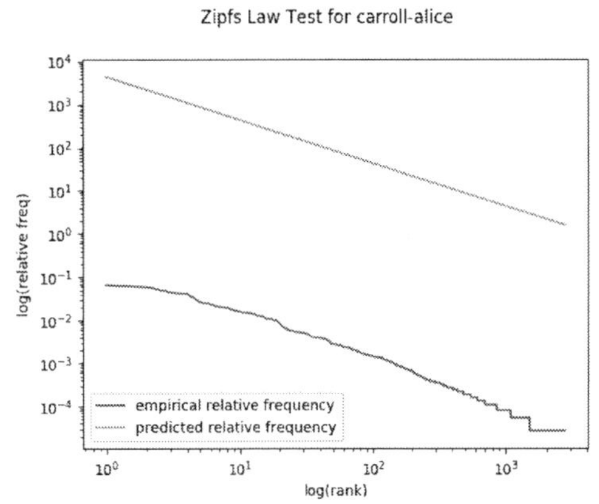

Figure 3: An incorrect plot for Lab 3, caused by a student conflating relative and absolute frequencies. Autograders and lab check-in points allow students to engage with these points of confusion while still catching errors before students write their analyses.

5.4 Lab 4: Word Embeddings

In this lab, students use GloVe embeddings (Pennington et al., 2014) to experiment with relationships between word vectors, including word similarities and word analogies. Students first practice loading in text vectors and saving them as a compressed `numpy` matrix. Subsequently, they develop code to rank similar words for a selection of related words, as well as to test whether certain relations (e.g. gender, number, comparative vs superlative) have consistent vector differences as rendered in 2d plots using PCA. Finally, students develop their own relations and word lists to test the consistency of this method.

Preparation Students are expected to prepare with textbook reading on vectors space models (§6.1-6.5) and their evaluation (§6.10-6.12). Section 6.8 on word2vec or an introduction to GloVe may boost confidence.

Outcomes Having completed this assignment, students should be able to perform mathematical operations common to vector space models, such as computing cosine similarity, vector norms, and average vector differences. Students will know how to use `numpy` operations to speed up computation (Harris et al., 2020) and dimensionality reduction to visualize higher-dimensional behavior. Additionally, students should know how to develop and test a hypothesis about word vector geometries using appropriate metrics, visualizations, and qualitative insights. These hypotheses can lead to broader understanding of what types of relationships work well as word embedding analogies, too, including

[5] `https://lxml.de/`

how relationships that are not one-to-one may fail (Figure 2a) and how polysemy adds wrinkles to word analogies (Figure 2b).

6 Observations

In many ways, this format has helped us to feel liberated in how we approach topics later in the semester. In the most recent offering of the course, for instance, the latter half focuses on student projects and presentations on student-determined topics covering a range of popular tasks like machine translation and question answering and more wide-ranging topics like text-to-speech systems and computational social science. In other semesters, the course has continued with structured weekly (or bi-weekly) lab assignments, often culminating in a lab assignment that introduces a shared task that students then work on as a final project. Overall, we find that the foundational skills introduced in the first four weeks prepare students well for all of these paths through the rest of the course.

This approach admittedly releases the opportunity to do a deeper technical dive with the class into modern models; while students tend to discuss LSTMs, BERT, and other popular modern models, they are not expected to fully present these topics in their presentations. While we had initially worried about whether this would provide too little infrastructure to make sense of neural models, we have been happy with how students use the skills we emphasized earlier to uncover known controversies in the field of NLP. We have witnessed advanced discussions initiated by the students about topics such as how strong baselines can be in question-answering datasets, the possible shortcomings of metrics such as BLEU, ROUGE, and PYRAMID, and what it would mean to reach human parity for machine translation.

Taking a discovery approach is not without risks, especially when students may get stuck or confused. We have learned some lessons about where more guidance may be needed for students. First, unsurprisingly, file I/O often can be remarkably picky, and we have found that the I/O portions of these labs can be fairly brittle when students make choices that may have been reasonable in previous classes with fairly rudimentary file processing. Further illustration around ways to load and save data, manipulate `numpy` and `spaCy` objects, and otherwise use libraries can greatly reduce time students spend stuck on smaller bugs instead of NLP questions. Additionally, students often ask a number of questions about how much analysis is sufficient and which aspects to focus on, often not finding engagement with the text intuitive. Sample write-ups from the first lab or two may help illustrate this, as well as more development on the prompts for the write-up to elicit thoughtful analyses.

7 Conclusions

We hope that the description of this class format and assignment progression helps motivate the feasibility of a discovery-based approach to teaching natural language processing. We are delighted to share the initial assignment instructions, lab files, and student Gradescope image publicly on Github at `https://github.com/DiscoverNLP`, with additional files for autograding through Gradescope available on request.

8 Acknowledgements

We would like to thank the students at both Swarthmore College and Harvey Mudd College who participated in and gave feedback to this class, including the students who gave permission for their work to be shared in this paper.

References

ACM/IEEE Joint Task Force on Computing Curricula. 2001. Computing curricula 2001. `https://www.acm.org/education/curricula-recommendations`.

ACM/IEEE Joint Task Force on Computing Curricula. 2013. Computing curricula 2013. `https://www.acm.org/education/curricula-recommendations`.

Louis Alfieri, Patricia J Brooks, Naomi J Aldrich, and Harriet R Tenenbaum. 2011. Does discovery-based instruction enhance learning? *Journal of Educational Psychology*, 103(1):1.

Steven Bird. 2008. Defining a core body of knowledge for the introductory computational linguistics curriculum. In *Proceedings of the Third Workshop on Issues in Teaching Computational Linguistics*, pages 27–35, Columbus, Ohio. Association for Computational Linguistics.

Charles R. Harris, K. Jarrod Millman, Stéfan J. van der Walt, Ralf Gommers, Pauli Virtanen, David Cournapeau, Eric Wieser, Julian Taylor, Sebastian Berg, Nathaniel J. Smith, Robert Kern, Matti Picus, Stephan Hoyer, Marten H. van Kerkwijk, Matthew Brett, Allan Haldane, Jaime Fernández del

Río, Mark Wiebe, Pearu Peterson, Pierre Gérard-Marchant, Kevin Sheppard, Tyler Reddy, Warren Weckesser, Hameer Abbasi, Christoph Gohlke, and Travis E. Oliphant. 2020. Array programming with NumPy. *Nature*, 585(7825):357–362.

Marti Hearst. 2005. Teaching applied natural language processing: Triumphs and tribulations. In *Proceedings of the Second ACL Workshop on Effective Tools and Methodologies for Teaching NLP and CL*, pages 1–8, Ann Arbor, Michigan. Association for Computational Linguistics.

Matthew Honnibal, Ines Montani, Sofie Van Landeghem, and Adriane Boyd. 2020. *spaCy: Industrial-strength Natural Language Processing in Python*. Zenodo.

J. D. Hunter. 2007. Matplotlib: A 2d graphics environment. *Computing in Science & Engineering*, 9(3):90–95.

Dan Jurafsky and James H Martin. 2020. *Speech and Language Processing*, 3rd (draft) edition. Prentice Hall.

Johannes Kiesel, Maria Mestre, Rishabh Shukla, Emmanuel Vincent, Payam Adineh, David Corney, Benno Stein, and Martin Potthast. 2019. SemEval-2019 task 4: Hyperpartisan news detection. In *Proceedings of the 13th International Workshop on Semantic Evaluation*, pages 829–839, Minneapolis, Minnesota, USA. Association for Computational Linguistics.

Elizabeth Liddy and Nancy McCracken. 2005. Hands-on NLP for an interdisciplinary audience. In *Proceedings of the Second ACL Workshop on Effective Tools and Methodologies for Teaching NLP and CL*, pages 62–68, Ann Arbor, Michigan. Association for Computational Linguistics.

Richard E Mayer. 2004. Should there be a three-strikes rule against pure discovery learning? *American Psychologist*, 59(1):14.

Jeffrey Pennington, Richard Socher, and Christopher Manning. 2014. GloVe: Global vectors for word representation. In *Proceedings of the 2014 Conference on Empirical Methods in Natural Language Processing (EMNLP)*, pages 1532–1543, Doha, Qatar. Association for Computational Linguistics.

The Online Pivot: Lessons Learned from Teaching a Text and Data Mining Course in Lockdown, Enhancing online Teaching with Pair Programming and Digital Badges

Beatrice Alex
Literatures, Languages and Cultures
University of Edinburgh
Edinburgh
Scotland, UK
balex@ed.ac.uk

Clare Llewellyn
Social and Political Science
University of Edinburgh
Edinburgh
Scotland, UK
clare.llewellyn@ed.ac.uk

Pawel Michal Orzechowski **Maria Boutchkova**
University of Edinburgh Business School
University of Edinburgh
Scotland, UK
Pawel.Orzechowski@ed.ac.uk Maria.Boutchkova@ed.ac.uk

Abstract

In this paper we provide an account of how we ported a text and data mining course online in summer 2020 as a result of the COVID-19 pandemic and how we improved it in a second pilot run. We describe the course, how we adapted it over the two pilot runs and what teaching techniques we used to improve students' learning and community building online. We also provide information on the relentless feedback collected during the course which helped us to adapt our teaching from one session to the next and one pilot to the next. We discuss the lessons learned and promote the use of innovative teaching techniques applied to the digital such as digital badges and pair programming in break-out rooms for teaching Natural Language Processing courses to beginners and students with different backgrounds.

1 Introduction

It was spring 2020 and it felt like we were in crisis mode. We wanted to teach a text and data mining (TDM) pilot course but because of social distancing measures we could not do it in a physical classroom. We had to learn new ways of interacting online and using a multitude of different technologies and we needed to do it fast. We had been planning this course for a while before Covid-19 hit. We were designing a TDM for Humanities and Social Science students but because of the situation we had to adapt the way we delivered it. Rather than hybrid teaching as intended, accommodating in-classroom, online synchronous and online asynchronous students, we had to fully commit to online methods in a matter of a few weeks. We decided to plunge headlong into the digital teaching world.

The easiest way would have been to post videos of a traditional style lectures – it is very tempting to take this approach. We felt, however, that it was important that we maintained what is good about teaching when everyone is in the same room, the collaboration, its social aspects, the feedback, all of which you lose when a student sits on their own in a room watching a pre-recorded lecture.

We decided to run a TDM boot camp to virtually test our new course which we were planning as part of the Edinburgh Futures Institute (EFI) postgraduate programme.[1] We wanted to not only teach fundamental methods for text mining corpora to programming novices but also teach ourselves how to become better practitioners in teaching in an online world.

In this paper, we will describe our methods and experience for porting an in-person TDM course into the online world. In the next section we will present related publications on teaching Natural Language Processing or TDM courses. We then describe the academic backgrounds of the teaching team (Section 3.1) and provide an overview of our course (Section 3.2). Sections 3.3 and 3.4 explain how we taught and adapted it in two online pilot runs delivered in June and September 2020. We

[1] EFI is a new institute at the University of Edinburgh which will support interdisciplinary research and teaching for the whole institution. https://efi.ed.ac.uk

Proceedings of the Fifth Workshop on Teaching NLP, pages 138–148
June 10–11, 2021. ©2021 Association for Computational Linguistics

provide information on how we collected relentless feedback during and after each course and include a detailed account of one participant of the first pilot and how it has affected her teaching (Section 4). Finally, we summarise what we learned from these experiences (Section 5) and lay out future plans for our TDM course (Section 6).

2 Related Work

There are two aspects that we consider of importance in relation to this work, the course content, Natural Language Processing (NLP), and the environment, teaching online during a pandemic. In this section we explore both topics.

NLP educators choose which aspects to teach based on multiple constraints such as class length, student experience, recent advancements, program focus, and even personal interest.

Our TDM course is fundamentally designed to be cross-disciplinary as we are teaching NLP and coding to students from multiple schools and backgrounds including linguistics, social sciences and business. Jurgens and Li (2018) point out that NLP courses are designed to reflect, amongst other things, the background and experience of the students. Agarwal (2013) explains that in courses such as these the majority of students, who he calls "newbies in Computer Science", have never programmed before. He highlights that we can increase experience through homework tasks which we did both before the course and in-between each session. Hearst (2005) states that in these circumstances it is not important to place too much emphasis on the theoretical underpinnings of NLP but to focus on providing instructions for students on what is possible and how they can use it on their own in the future. We based our approach on using the NLTK[2] and spaCy[3] Python libraries as well as used examples inspired by Bird et al. (2009, 2005). We aim to explain how text analysis works step-by-step using clear and simple examples. We thereby aspire to develop and broaden humanities and social science students' data-driven training and give them an understanding of how things work inside the box, something for which there is still a significant need in their core disciplines (McGillivray et al., 2020).

Teaching text analysis to non-computer scientists has been explored in texts such as Hovy (2020). For our course we had to consider the variety of backgrounds and experiences that this would encompass and needed to use a pre-course learning task and office hours to provide a more level knowledge starting point. We also had to design the course to keep more advanced students engaged while not intimidating learners who may find it more challenging. We used core material to explain principle concepts (such as tokens, tokenisation, and part-of-speech (POS) tagging etc.) but with a hands-on approach. We avoided too much technical detail and put the material in the context of projects we have worked on ourselves to demonstrate how each analysis step becomes useful in practice.

As we taught our TDM course online in the context of a worldwide pandemic, we also report on related work in the area of online teaching, and with respect to the challenges in which we are teaching. Massive open online courses (MOOC) generally focus on providing online access to learning resources to a large number and wide range of participants. This has led to a desire to automate teaching and innovate digital interaction techniques in order to engage with large numbers of students. Whilst our intention was to teach a limited number of students, we hoped to use and draw upon innovation in this area in order to improve the experience for our students. E-learning and technology should not be seen as an attempt to replace or automate human teaching, although this can often be a fear articulated by teachers. In a discussion of automation within teaching Bayne (2015) argues that we can design online teaching and still place human communication at the centre with technology enhancing the learning of the student. Bayne suggests that the human teacher, the student and the technology can be intertwined. We asked students to engage with digital objects and the technology to enhance their learning journey. As teachers we do not merely support the digital learner but we remain at the centre of teaching the course.

Fawns et al. (2019) point out that online learning is a key growth area in higher education, which is even more true since the pandemic started, but that it is harder to form relationships in online courses. Therefore, we saw it as important to develop online dialogue between students in order to form communities which can improve these relationships. Building a community online can be harder but it is possible. We tried to achieve this through using a combination of traditional learning such as lectures

[2]https://www.nltk.org

[3]https://spacy.io

and task-based learning such as pair programming exercises. Online learning tends to be interrupted as we are in our homes or elsewhere and have responsibilities that can take us away from the online space, bandwidth issues, dropping children at school, flatmates interrupting, phone calls, even the door bell ringing. Our teaching practices needed to be accepting of and adapted to this context.

Ross et al. (2013) discuss the issues of presence and distance in online learning. Interruptions in students' concentration are a common event when learning online and we must use resilience strategies to maintain a 'nearness' to our students. This includes recognising that these events are normal and that engaging is an effort, identifying affinities and creating a socialness, valuing that distraction can change our perspective and this is helpful and designing openings, events that allow and encourage student to come together and engage. Whilst designing the course we kept these ideas in focus in order to allow us to develop and enhance our online relationships and our students' learning.

3 A Virtual Learning Experience

3.1 The Team

Our team is made up of three early career academics at the University of Edinburgh. Two teaching fellows have a background in Natural Language Processing with PhDs in Computational Linguistics. The third teaching fellow has a PhD in Computer Science and frequently teaches programming to different types of audiences, including business students as well as students outside of higher education. The author list of this paper also includes a fourth (last) author who was a participant of our first pilot, is a lecturer herself, and who has provided us with useful feedback for future iterations of this course (see Section 4.2).

3.2 Course Overview

In our data-driven society, it is increasingly essential for people throughout the private, public and third sectors to know how to analyse the wealth of information society creates each day. Our TDM course gives participants who have no or very limited coding experience the tools they need to interrogate data. This course is designed to teach non-coders how to analyse textual data using Python as the main programming language. It takes them through the required steps needed to be able to analyse and visualise information in large sets of textual document collections, or corpora.

The course takes place over three three-hour sessions and each session introduces participants to a new topic through a short lecture. The topics build on the previous sessions and at the end of each session there is time for discussion and feedback. In the first session we start with Python for reading in and processing text and teach how individual documents are loaded and tokenised. We work with plain text files but do raise the issue that textual data can be stored in different formats. However, to keep things simple we do not cover other formats in detail in the practical sessions.

In the second session we show how this is done using much larger sets of text and add in visualisations. We used two data sets as examples, the Medical History of British India (of Scotland, 2019) made available by the National Library of Scotland[4] and the inaugural addresses of all American Presidents from 1789 to 2017. We show how participants can create concordance lists, token frequency distributions in a corpus and over time as well as lexical dispersion plots and how they can perform regular expression searches using Python. In this session we also explain that textual data can be messy and that a lot of time can be spent on cleaning and preparing data in a way that is most useful for further analysis. For example, we point students at stop words and punctuation in the results and explain how to filter them when creating frequency-based visualisations.

During the third session we cover POS-tagging and named entity recognition. This last session concludes with a lesson on visualisations of text and derived data by means of text highlighting, frequency graphs, word clouds and networks (see some examples in Figure 1). The underlying NLP tools used for this course are NLTK 3 and spaCy which are widely use for NLP research and development. This is also where we put some of the course material in context of our own research to show how it can be applied in practice in a real project. For example, we mentioned our previous work on collecting topic-specific Twitter datasets for further analysis (Llewellyn et al., 2015), on geoparsing historical and literary text (Clifford et al., 2016; Alex et al., 2019a) and on named entity recognition for radiology reports (Alex et al., 2019b; Gorinski et al., 2019).

[4]https://data.nls.uk/data/digitised-collections/a-medical-history-of-british-india/

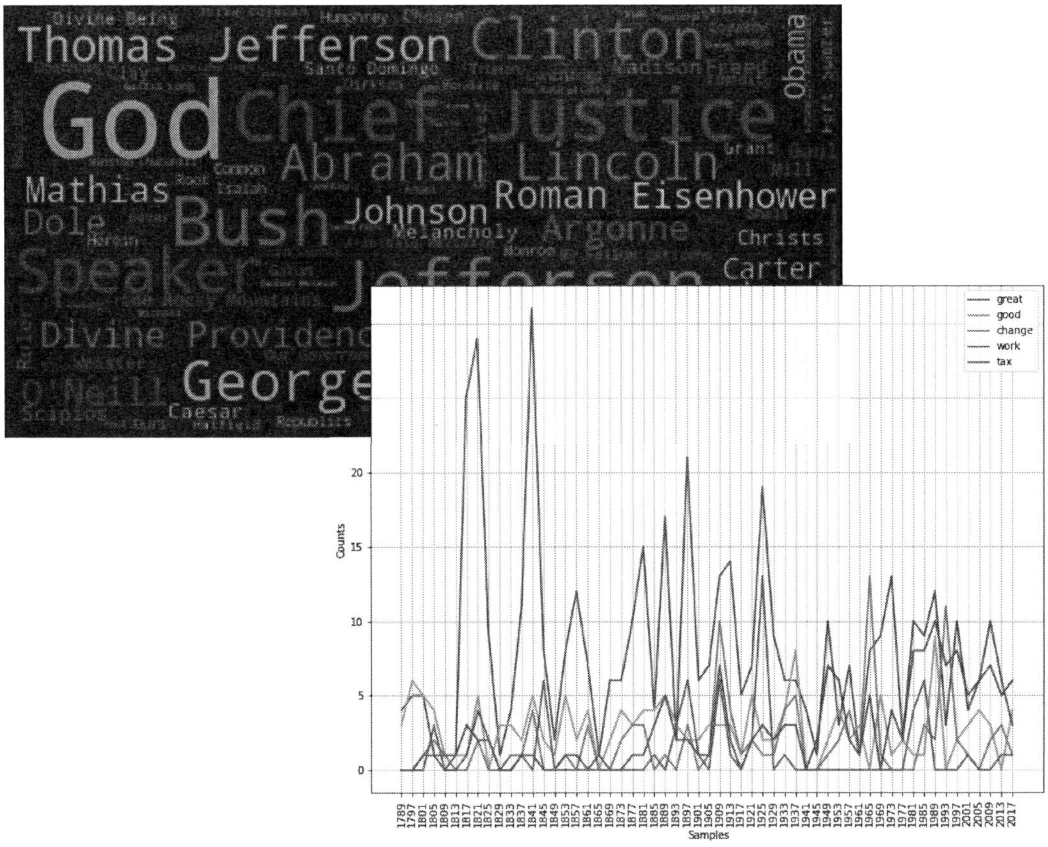

Figure 1: Visualisations of text explorations created by the students.

In the two pilots, we ran this course over three afternoon sessions on Monday, Wednesday and Friday, with an office hour on the days in-between to sort out any potential technical issues and answer questions. The main learning outcome is that by the end of the course the participants will have acquired initial TDM skills which they can use in their own research and build on by taking more advanced NLP courses or tutorials. A main goal of this course is to teach the material in a clear step-by-step way so all Python code and the examples are specific to each task but do not go in-depth into complicated programming concepts which we believe would confuse complete novices.

3.3 Pilot 1

In the first pilot we wanted to test the content of this course but also different methods for teaching online. We are all likely to be teaching virtually more often in the future even once the pandemic subsides. For example, EFI was planning to run hybrid courses to students across the world, even prior to COVID-19. In this new world, we believe that online and hybrid teaching is here to stay alongside teaching students in the classroom. Higher education will need to determine their offer of different experiences to students be they on site or participating online synchronously or asynchronously.

We limited the first pilot to 25 participants. The backgrounds of students who signed up for our course were mixed coming from Law, Linguistics and Business. Everyone was either a student or a member of staff at the University of Edinburgh, where we had advertised the course, including every level from professor to undergraduate, joining from around the world. Some students even participated from different time zones.

On each day we started with a short presentation discussing the TDM theory of what was being taught in the practical session that followed. In the first pilot this was a live lecture, not recorded, allowing us to adapt the content to questions that came up during the course. When one teacher spoke the other two managed the video chat, answering questions or dealing with specific problems from students, and raising questions to the speaker. This was something we found was essential as it was very easy to lose flow and get distracted without this help. We learned then that it would have been extremely challenging to teach this course live online single-handedly and after each session expressed appreciation that there were three of us helping each other.

We used a variety of technologies provided by the university. Learn,[5] our in-house virtual learning environment (VLE), was used to provide access to course materials. We met with students virtually using the Blackboard Collaborate software[6] which is accessible through Learn. Aside from the video itself, we used text chat, the virtual whiteboard, polls, the ability to raise a hand, breakout groups, file sharing, and screen sharing, all functionalities which have become second nature after a year of pandemic but which when we ran the first pilot were for the most part still fairly unfamiliar to many participants. We also used Noteable,[7] the University of Edinburgh's in-house notebook platform, to provide a virtual programming environment (VPE) with Jupyter Notebooks,[8] and used GitHub[9] to provide students access to the course material and code. We note that the students did not have to learn how to use GitHub, which would be a big ask for coding novices, but merely had to paste the GitHub link of the corresponding material into Noteable which then automatically loaded the material in the form of a notebook.

Each day the students were given two sets of worked through problems using the VPE which they used directly through the VPL in their own browser. We found this to be a really important tool for everyone as it reduced the need for students to download and set up software on different operating systems and alleviated us from doing a lot of technical support to get students set up and running for all the practical parts of the course.

During the sessions the students were given a link to a GitHub repository from which they could pull new notebooks onto the VPE at the beginning of each session. The notebooks include a combination of explanations, code to run and mini or extended programming tasks. For each approximately hour-long coding session students were assigned a random buddy and which they were put in a break-out room within the Collaborate video call. By now we are used to teaching and/or learning online and have likely experienced joining break-out rooms but at the time when we ran the first pilot most of our participants had never been in a break-out room before. So that experience took some getting used to. We described it as *feeling like being put in a separate room with your buddy. You can chat and share screens without being overheard by other people.* If the students got stuck on a particular coding problem or line of code and could not solve the issue together, they could raise a virtual hand and an instructor would drop into the room to help and answer questions or resolve programming issues. We also regularly popped into the rooms to see how everyone was doing, something which was well received by the students.

One of our team members is a strong proponent of pair programming (Williams et al., 2000; Hanks et al., 2011), where two students work together on a single machine to solve problems. This allows each pair of students to learn from each other as well as from their teacher(s) and thereby helps to broaden participation and to dispel the myth that programmers work on their own (Williams, 2006). We wanted to see if it was possible to take this approach into a virtual teaching environment. In addition to the students learning TDM skills, it also provided an opportunity for social interaction which was particularly welcome when we first piloted our course at the tail end of the first wave of COVID-19 in the UK and after weeks of strict lockdown with no or little opportunity to meet and interact with people outside one's own household.

One advantage of Blackboard Collaborate is that instructors are able to see visually when the people in break-out rooms are chatting to each other. This helped us to gauge if students embraced our pair programming experiment or if they preferred to work quietly "side-by-side" but connected virtually.

After each practical session we pulled everyone back into the shared room and asked participants to fill in a quick survey to give us feedback. We answered any questions, had a quick break, and then moved onto the next notebook with a new buddy. We wrapped up each session with a short Q&A and another round of feedback.

[5]`https://www.learn.ed.ac.uk`

[6]`https://help.blackboard.com/Learn/Instructor/Interact/Blackboard_Collaborate`

[7]`https://noteable.edina.ac.uk`

[8]`https://jupyter.org`

[9]`https://github.com`

3.4 Pilot 2

By the time of the second pilot in September 2020, we had gotten a lot more used to online meetings and two members of the teaching team had trained in a summer course on hybrid teaching called An Edinburgh Model for Teaching Online. This time we allowed 30 participants to sign up with over half of them from Scottish Government and the commercial sector, alongside university students and staff.

The main change we made to our first pilot, without altering the course content, is that we restructured the course material into teaching with digital badges (Gibson et al., 2015; Muilenburg and Berge, 2016) which are used in gamification of education (Dicheva et al., 2015; Ostashewski and Reid, 2015). The principles that guided us were: flexibility, compartmentalisation and empowering the learner. Each badge is built around a Threshold concept (Land et al., 2005), a core step or skill (a 'eureka' moment) that opens the doors to further learning. Using a clear name and symbol, each badge signposts students' takeaways and how it fits within the top level learning journey (see Figure 2).

The macro-structure in which badges form our course is complemented by a micro-structure of each badge: background theory and instructional content, code-along videos, notebooks with worked examples, exercises of increasing difficulty, relentless feedback, pair work and mini coding problems (with solutions). Badges build on top of each other, forming branches and enabling optional, further learning. Additionally, the modular micro-structure, enables easier switching between platforms or teaching modes (e.g. videos versus slides) and multiplies the benefits of improvements. Badges proved to be a promising format for delivering teaching of this course, especially in times of change, disruption and pivoting.

We wanted to give us and our course participants more flexibility, so we recorded all of the short lectures presented at the start of each badge and situated before each coding session in the course. This allowed students to come back to the recorded lecture materials later-on. It also gave us more flexibility answering questions in the chat, solving technical issues in the background and discussing the running of a given badge in a teaching team break-out room while participants were watching the video lecture.

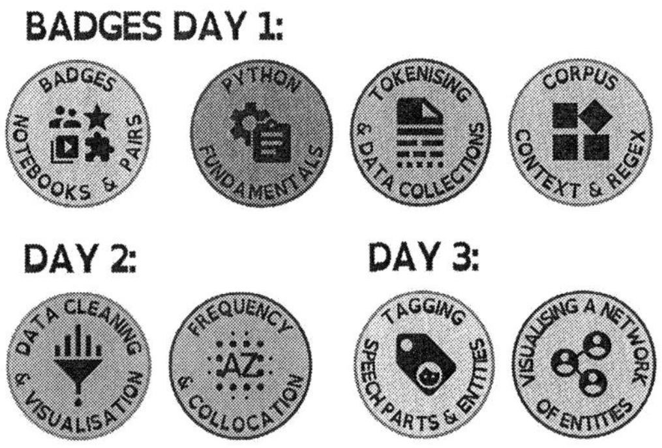

Figure 2: The badges used in our TDM course. We created them using Android Material Design Icons which are open source under Apache License 2.0.

4 Feedback

4.1 Relentless Feedback

In both pilots we collected relentless feedback. This feedback loop helped us to address questions raised and go over things that were unclear. We found it was really important to be flexible and adapt to what the students wanted. The twice-a-session mini-feedback form was really helpful for that and we made it very clear which parts of the course on day 2 and 3 were in response to participants' feedback (see feedback analysis in Figure 3).

For example, a comments we received in the first pilot was that the students would prefer a quick recap of the previous session, which we then started doing and was a great way to link sessions and get the course material fresh in everyone's minds. Given the feedback, we also worked through the first section of a notebook together, so everyone had a clear idea of what to do.

The relentless feedback and our response is one of the reasons we believe we had such a high participant retention rate which we were very pleased about. The pilots was free of charge, non-compulsory and ran over three afternoons. At least two thirds of the students who joined at the start of the week completed the last session on Friday.

We received constructive criticism but overall had very positive feedback on the course which, especially after the first pilot, made us feel very motivated having just had completed teaching our first online course. One participant thought it was "Fantastic!" in our final feedback survey. Another wrote "The pair learning is excellent! Jupiter [sic] notebooks are a great tool. The real-time interactivity is super rewarding." Others reported that the

	AVG	MODE	day1_s1	day1_s2	day2_s1	day2_s2	day3_s1
difficulty	3.2	3	3.1	3.3	2.8	3.6	3.5
progress/learning	4.2	4	3.7	4.4	4.3	4.3	4.7
mood	4.3	5	4.1	4.4	4.4	4.3	4.6
collaboration	3.9	5	3.9	4.1	3.8	3.5	4.3

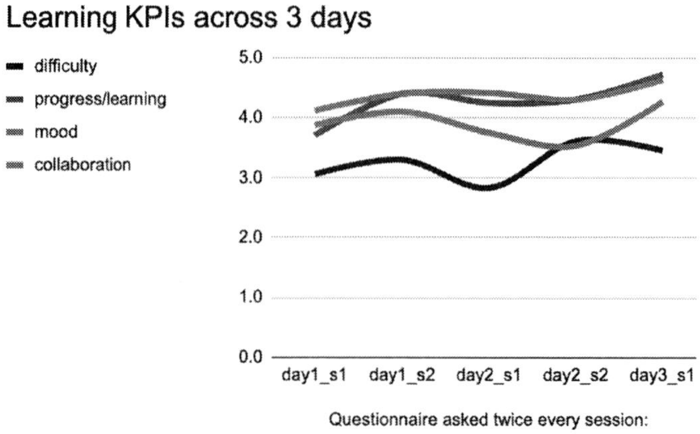

"Fantastic! The pair learning is excellent! Jupiter notebooks are a great tool. The real time interactivity is super rewarding."

Figure 3: Feedback analysis for all surveys over the course of the boot camp and a quote from one student (with permission to share). We asked students to record difficulty of the course, their progress and learning, their mood and how they felt about their collaboration in pairs as key performance indicators (KPIs) throughout the course.

lecturers and the "humour and playfulness of the examples" made the course "really great, especially for someone completely new to coding." Yet another person commented that they would use the skills they learned in gathering data for their undergraduate dissertation about their research project.

4.2 Detailed Student Feedback

The following account is a more detailed reaction to our course provided by one of the student who participated in the first pilot of the TDM course and who we include as an author on this paper:

I was one of the mature students on the first pilot of the TDM Workshop – an academic myself with quantitative methods and coding experience in Stata and MatLab but not in Python, nor any previous experience with text mining or natural language processing.

I appreciated the feedback requests at the end of each session via Microsoft Office forms and the immediate showcasing of the results for the whole class. Whenever there were bandwidth issues, the teaching team coordinated instantaneously and took over from each other.

The part of the course that taught me the most were the pair breakout rooms where we worked through computational Jupyter notebooks. The annotation of the exercises was invaluable, as were the videos showing one of the instructors working through a notebook themselves and importantly running into an error and explaining how we use the error message as guidance to fix the code. During the breakout sessions having the three instructors drop in and answer any questions was an excellent balance of allowing the students independence while also feeling supported. Working with different partners every time was also very valuable. When taking an active role and talking through the lines of code and my understanding of the outcome, I was able to check in with my partner and

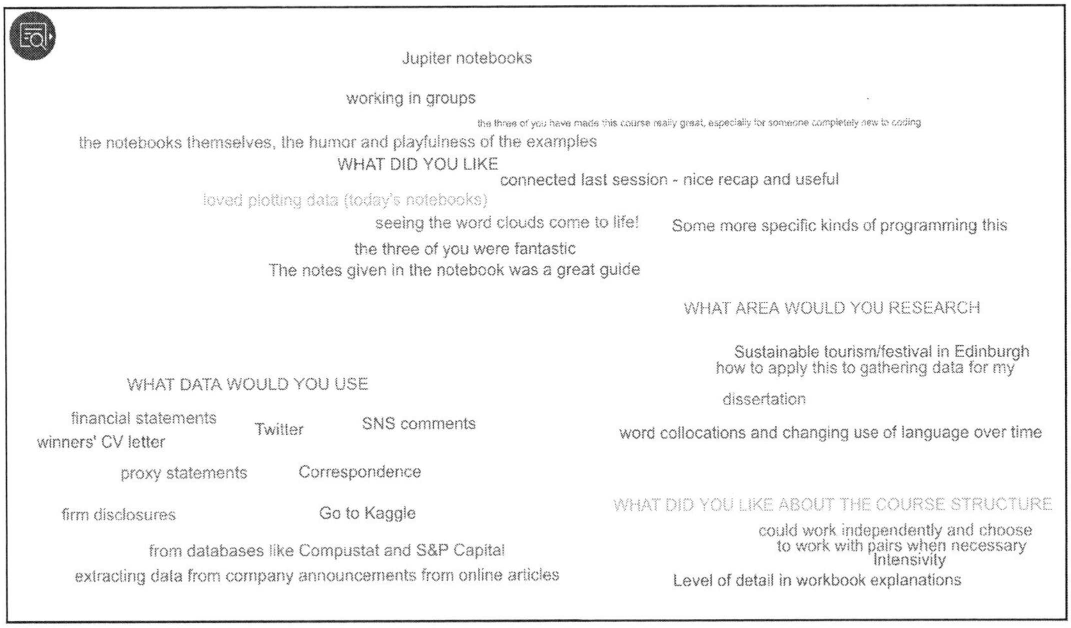

Figure 4: Whiteboard with feedback generated by students in the course.

be exposed to their style and approach to learning. Similarly, when taking the passive role and witnessing their way to working through a computational notebook, I could take away ideas of how to explain my thinking and understanding of the code in different ways.

The distribution of new material via GitHub was very efficient. The interactions via the virtual whiteboard created playfulness and joy in the learning process. Although I did not participate in the second pilot and was not exposed to the Badges, I see them as another element of enhancing the playfulness of the process.

The TDM Workshop I participated in took place relatively early in the pandemic before "Zoom fatigue" had set it and participants were excited to engage. A year later, full-time students appear to have become more resistant to engaging in voice and/or visual participation.

There were some points that required improvement, for example typos in the annotation of the computational notebooks or some time being eaten up by technical troubleshooting. However, even these created an atmosphere of immediacy, flexibility and a sense of "We are all in this together".

Overall, I benefited immensely from taking the first pilot. Not only do I now have an idea of text mining tools and how to use them but I was also inspired by and adopted the computational notebooks in my own teaching of Investments in the Autumn of 2020. I also implemented regular feedback, which I felt provided the element of playfulness and joy, in an even more interactive platform with gifs, wordclouds and animations (using Mentimeter[10]).

5 Lessons Learned

Despite on-the-whole positive comments, we still found teaching in an online environment quite odd. We felt that we lost the sense of whether the students were engaged, learning and enjoying the experience because most participants had their cameras switched off so we could not see their faces or body language. The feedback did help, even simply asking students to 'raise your hand if you can hear me', but it still remains odd to us to talk to a blank screen without seeing everyone.

We did not get everything right. The technology did not always work but luckily one teaching team member is quite experienced in fixing software-related issues. We would have struggled without it. Initially we also did not give enough thought to accessibility; we just assumed the software would deal with that - it did not. We learned that we have to ask all students before the course if they might have issues in accessing course materials or video calls and make time to deal with any technical issues that could arise as a result.

[10] `https://www.mentimeter.com`

We learned that students can be shy when it comes to talking to each other and putting on their webcams. We found ice breaker questions upfront, can be answered playfully on a whiteboard, very helpful for putting students at ease and have some fun. We used some simple things that made a lot of difference. We played music in the room before the class so when students joined, they knew we were there and that their speakers were on. We made extensive use of the virtual whiteboard to gather anonymous feedback really fast in addition to frequent short surveys (see Figure 4). We also included questions in the notebooks that buddies had to work on together to encourage discussion. The notebooks contained essential TDM coding tasks and more complex tasks for the curious. This allowed some students to extend their learning without others feeling they were left behind.

We also found that the amount of content that we could cover grew as the course went on. There were initial issues with the technology which needed fixing and as we were all getting used to the new way of teaching. The conversation also became more natural as time went on. At first it was quite odd to drop into the break-out rooms but by the second session this became easier and we were all chatting a lot more. The majority of students really liked the pair programming, they liked the flexibility and the content. They really felt they were part of the course in a way that is not always experienced online.

As instructors, we found that teaching in this way, switching between modes, lecturing, answering the chat, live coding and responding to issues is really cognitively challenging. It is hard work and cannot easily be done by one individual. The technologies we use are complex and can fail but they are for the most part intuitive and provide a wide range of ways to teach and interact. We learned that online teaching is exhausting but done right it can still be really rewarding. We all enjoyed the interactions and felt part of a little community. After the course we did a debriefing and each wrote down three things we liked about the course and something we wished we could have achieved (see page Appendix on 11).

We, the TDM course teachers on this paper, have, in the same way as the author who participated in the course, benefited immensely from what we learned through these pilots before delving into our online teaching in the first term of 2020/21.

6 Summary and Future Work

In this paper, we have reflected of how we ported a TDM course online as a result of the global pandemic caused by COVID-19. We described the content of the course and how we adapted it over two pilot runs. We particularly found different features of Blackboard Collaborate useful for teaching, especially the use of a virtual whiteboard and dividing the class up into break-out rooms. Students responded positively to learning in pairs and to course materials broken down into digital badges. Finally, the relentless feedback we collected throughout each session and after the course helped us as teachers to improve the course and how we teach it. To make a course like this a good learning experience, it is really important to build community and get students to talk not just to the teachers but to each other as they would in a classroom.

Being caught in lockdown encouraged us to innovate, and our experience demonstrates what is possible to achieve virtually despite the limitations. Experiencing the learning in a classroom is difficult to replicate online, however, we are confident that these types of virtual environments will play a role in education beyond this pandemic, to complement and enhance traditional learning.

Going forward we would like to experiment with teaching this course in different ways: asynchronously to students joining from different time zones, to much larger groups to understand where the limits are in terms of number of participants given staff capacity, or in a writer-retreat type setup where the instructors touch base with students several times during the day. We will also look at how this course can be pivoted back to on-campus teaching for students who can join in person and once the current pandemic slows down, lockdown restrictions are relaxed and on-campus teaching resumes. We are pleased to announce that this course will be part of the post-graduate programme taught at EFI.

Acknowledgements

We thank Professor Laura Cram for supporting us in the long-term development of this course as part of EFI's PGT training programme. Our course was built on and expands material developed for a Library Carpentries course[11] with the support of the Centre for Data, Culture and Society.[12] We

[11] `http://librarycarpentry.org/lc-tdm/`
[12] `https://www.cdcs.ed.ac.uk`

would also like to thank Siobhan Dunn and her colleagues at EFI for managing the registration for our courses and Marco Rossi at the University of Edinburgh Business School's Student Development Team for offering the course to their students.

References

Apoorv Agarwal. 2013. Teaching the basics of NLP and ML in an introductory course to information science. In *Proceedings of the Fourth Workshop on Teaching NLP and CL*, pages 77–84, Sofia, Bulgaria. Association for Computational Linguistics.

Beatrice Alex, Claire Grover, Richard Tobin, and Jon Oberlander. 2019a. Geoparsing historical and contemporary literary text set in the City of Edinburgh. *Language Resources and Evaluation*, 53(4):651–675.

Beatrice Alex, Claire Grover, Richard Tobin, Cathie Sudlow, Grant Mair, and William Whiteley. 2019b. Text mining brain imaging reports. *Journal of Biomedical Semantics*, 10(1):1–11.

Sian Bayne. 2015. Teacherbot: interventions in automated teaching. *Teaching in Higher Education*, 20(4):455–467.

Steven Bird, Ewan Klein, and Edward Loper. 2005. NLTK tutorial: Introduction to natural language processing. *Creative Commons Attribution*.

Steven Bird, Ewan Klein, and Edward Loper. 2009. *Natural language processing with Python: Analyzing text with the natural language toolkit*. " O'Reilly Media, Inc.".

Jim Clifford, Beatrice Alex, Colin M Coates, Ewan Klein, and Andrew Watson. 2016. Geoparsing history: Locating commodities in ten million pages of nineteenth-century sources. *Historical Methods: A Journal of Quantitative and Interdisciplinary History*, 49(3):115–131.

Darina Dicheva, Christo Dichev, Gennady Agre, and Galia Angelova. 2015. Gamification in education: A systematic mapping study. *Journal of Educational Technology & Society*, 18(3):75–88.

Tim Fawns, Gill Aitken, and Derek Jones. 2019. Online learning as embodied, socially meaningful experience. *Postdigital Science and Education*, 1(2):293–297.

David Gibson, Nathaniel Ostashewski, Kim Flintoff, Sheryl Grant, and Erin Knight. 2015. Digital badges in education. *Education and Information Technologies*, 20(2):403–410.

Philip John Gorinski, Honghan Wu, Claire Grover, Richard Tobin, Conn Talbot, Heather Whalley, Cathie Sudlow, William Whiteley, and Beatrice Alex. 2019. Named entity recognition for electronic health records: A comparison of rule-based and machine learning approaches. ArXiv.

Brian Hanks, Sue Fitzgerald, Renée McCauley, Laurie Murphy, and Carol Zander. 2011. Pair programming in education: A literature review. *Computer Science Education*, 21(2):135–173.

Marti A Hearst. 2005. Teaching applied natural language processing: Triumphs and tribulations. In *Proceedings of the Second ACL Workshop on Effective Tools and Methodologies for Teaching NLP and CL*, pages 1–8.

Dirk Hovy. 2020. *Text Analysis in Python for Social Scientists: Discovery and Exploration*. Cambridge University Press.

David Jurgens and Lucy Li. 2018. A Look Inside the Pedagogy of Natural Language Processing. 25/09/2018. Accessed on 23/04/2021.

Ray Land, Glynis Cousin, Jan HF Meyer, and Peter Davies. 2005. Threshold concepts and troublesome knowledge (3): implications for course design and evaluation. *Improving student learning diversity and inclusivity*, 4:53–64.

Clare Llewellyn, Claire Grover, Beatrice Alex, Jon Oberlander, and Richard Tobin. 2015. Extracting a topic specific dataset from a Twitter archive. In *International Conference on Theory and Practice of Digital Libraries*, pages 364–367. Springer.

Barbara McGillivray, Beatrice Alex, Sarah Ames, Guyda Armstrong, David Beavan, Arianna Ciula, Giovanni Colavizza, James Cummings, David De Roure, Adam Farquhar, et al. 2020. The challenges and prospects of the intersection of humanities and data science: A white paper from The Alan Turing Institute.

Lin Y Muilenburg and Zane L Berge. 2016. *Digital badges in education: Trends, issues, and cases*. Routledge.

National Library of Scotland. 2019. A Medical History of British India. Accessed on 23/04/2021.

Nathaniel Ostashewski and Doug Reid. 2015. A history and frameworks of digital badges in education. In *Gamification in education and business*, pages 187–200. Springer.

Jen Ross, Michael Sean Gallagher, and Hamish Macleod. 2013. Making distance visible: Assembling nearness in an online distance learning programme. *International Review of Research in Open and Distributed Learning*, 14(4):51–67.

Laurie Williams. 2006. Debunking the nerd stereotype with pair programming. *Computer*, 39(5):83–85.

Laurie Williams, Robert R Kessler, Ward Cunningham, and Ron Jeffries. 2000. Strengthening the case for pair programming. *IEEE software*, 17(4):19–25.

A Appendix: Three Stars and a Wish

Clare:

★ I liked that we were all willing to try anything and go beyond our comfort zone and fail

★ I liked the way we naturally supported each other and took different roles, and swapped those roles

★ I enjoyed learning the technology – something I thought I'd hate!

I wish we could find a way to make the students more interactive, chat, turn their cameras on.

Pawel:

★ Relentless feedback: asking 30s pulse-checking questionnaires twice a day; we used Office Forms.

★ Staff room: easy and persisting internal comms channel within the course development team; we used Teams.

★ Poetic licence: the person who created the final version of the notes was allowed to make adjustments to the content, so they fit the format.

Our greatest ally was the tech that just worked. I wish we could also provide core hybrid experience of being in the same room.

Beatrice:

★ Great team of people, great combination of skills

★ Brilliant to see feedback from students coming in

★ I learned a lot about teaching online

I wish I could witness the learning better online.

Teaching NLP outside Linguistics and Computer Science classrooms: Some challenges and some opportunities

Sowmya Vajjala
National Research Council, Canada
sowmya.vajjala@nrc-cnrc.gc.ca

Abstract

NLP's sphere of influence went much beyond computer science research and the development of software applications in the past decade. We see people using NLP methods in a range of academic disciplines from Asian Studies to Clinical Oncology. We also notice the presence of NLP as a module in most of the data science curricula within and outside of regular university setups. These courses are taken by students from very diverse backgrounds. This paper takes a closer look at some issues related to teaching NLP to these diverse audiences based on my classroom experiences, and identifies some challenges the instructors face, particularly when there is no ecosystem of related courses for the students. In this process, it also identifies a few challenge areas for both NLP researchers and tool developers.

1 Introduction

Until a few years ago, it was common to see NLP courses predominantly taught in either Computer Science or Linguistics departments, attended primarily by students from both the departments. In the past few years, there has been an increasing interest in NLP across disciplines. This is also reflected in the arrival of focused NLP courses such as "Clinical NLP"[1] and "Introduction to Computational Literary Analysis"[2].

This trend is by no means specific to NLP alone. There has been a growing interest in including courses related to computing/programming in many liberal arts and sciences departments over the past few years. Guzdial (2021) lists three reasons why many departments want such courses for their students: to support new discoveries through computational methods; to use new modes of interactive communication through apps, simulated environments etc.; to study the cultural, social and political influence of models and how to improve them. This need resulted in the creation of data science programs open for all students from various colleges/departments. Naturally, the introduction of such programs started discussion around what should be included in such *generic* data science introductory curricula (Krishnamurthi and Fisler, 2020). An introductory course in NLP is commonly offered either as an elective or as a part of the main coursework in most such data science course/minor/certificate programs in universities. Such a course is also a common component in industry facing certification programs offered outside of university settings.

However, popular textbooks and course materials on NLP are not created taking these diverse audiences and their motivations into consideration. They cover a range of topics in depth, requiring a deeper technical background that students coming from diverse academic backgrounds may not possess. While there are some recent efforts to write books focused to specific groups of students (Jockers, 2014; Hovy, 2020), they tend to focus on a smaller subset of topics within NLP.

Further, most courses and textbooks focus on the algorithms, with much less attention given to other essentials such as data collection, text extraction, pre-processing and other practical issues one will encounter when working on new research problems (and datasets), or while deploying NLP systems in some application scenario. Considering that many students take these courses with goals unrelated to performing NLP research later (e.g., using NLP in their disciplinary research, working for a software company, etc.), this lack of appropriate materials can be seen as a potential gap between current NLP teaching and what is required. Additionally, while research progress feeds into the development of course syllabi, we don't see the opposite i.e., teaching experiences informing NLP research.

[1] https://www.coursera.org/learn/clinical-natural-language-processing
[2] https://icla2020.jonreeve.com/

Proceedings of the Fifth Workshop on Teaching NLP, pages 149–159
June 10–11, 2021. ©2021 Association for Computational Linguistics

In this background, this paper summarizes my experiences with teaching multiple NLP courses to a diverse student body (STEM, humanities, social sciences) both at undergrad and graduate level, and identifies some challenge areas for classroom instruction. At the same time, it also identifies some relatively understudied problems in NLP research and some issues to consider for tool developers. In short, the contributions of the paper can be summarized as follows:

- It identifies the challenges of teaching a range of student audiences outside of linguistics and computer science departments.
- It identifies a few challenge areas for NLP research and practice, which should be addressed to further the use of NLP methods and techniques beyond computer science and related disciplines.

The rest of this paper is organized as follows: Section 2 gives a brief overview of existing work on teaching NLP to put this paper's contributions in context. Section 3 describes the NLP courses I taught with diverse goals and for diverse audiences, in detail. The next section then identifies some challenges in terms of teaching for all these different contexts (Section 4). Section 5 elaborates on how these teaching experiences help us identify some challenge areas for NLP researchers as well as tool developers. Section 6 summarizes and concludes the paper.

2 Teaching NLP - A short review

Since the first Teaching NLP workshop almost two decades ago, there has been some discussion in the community on various issues related to NLP pedagogy through the TeachCL/TeachingNLP workshop series,[3] and other events such as Teach4DH.[4]. Published work on teaching NLP can be broadly classified into four groups:

1. Sharing insights about building new CL programs in various intra- and inter-disciplinary contexts (e.g., Lonsdale, 2002; Dale et al., 2002; Koit et al., 2002; Baldridge and Erk, 2008; Zinsmeister, 2008; Reiter et al., 2017)
2. Focused discussion about the challenges in the design of single courses, sometimes targeting a broader/diverse audience (e.g., Liddy and McCracken, 2005; Xia, 2008; Madnani and Dorr, 2008; Agarwal, 2013; Navarro-Colorado, 2017)
3. Development and usage of specific tools/games/strategies for teaching NLP (e.g., Bontcheva et al., 2002; Lin, 2008; Bird et al., 2008; Hockey and Christian, 2008; Levow, 2008; Barteld and Flick, 2017)
4. Discussion around the design of linguistic problems for North American Computational Linguistics Open Competition (NACLO)[5] and other events (e.g., Bozhanov and Derzhanski, 2013; Littell et al., 2013).

However, to my knowledge, there hasn't been much discussion on the gap between what we learn in the classroom versus how you use it later (whether in research or practice), how we should adapt the syllabus depending on the audience for the course, and on how teaching experiences can potentially inform NLP research and practice. I addressed these issues in this paper, based on my experiences with teaching NLP.

3 Description of NLP Courses

This section describes the teaching scenarios in which I taught NLP between 2016-2021, which form the basis for the observations discussed in this paper. Full semester courses described below were taught at an American university during 2016-18, and the online, compact courses were taught at two German universities during 2020-21. All classrooms were small in size ($<$ 30 students) and there were no teaching assistants. Inspired by Bird (2008)'s classification of student's background and goals for using NLTK [6], and Fosler-Lussier (2008)'s grouping of students taking NLP courses, a grouping of my NLP teaching contexts, is shown in Table 1, taking student background and course goals into consideration. The "General" courses, as the name indicates, target a broader audience, while "Focused" courses were created to address specific student needs.

The rest of this section presents a detailed overview about the courses taught under these

[3]https://www.aclweb.org/anthology/venues/teachingnlp/

[4]https://teach4dh.github.io/

[5]https://nacloweb.org/

[6]Table 3.1 in http://www.nltk.org/book/ch00.html

	General	Focused
Undergrad	A non-technical course intended to give an overview of language and computers, open for all disciplines	An introductory course taught as a part of data science curriculum for Liberal Arts and Sciences (LAS) majors
Grad/Advanced undergrad	Two general NLP courses with a focus on various algorithms and applications	Two introductory NLP courses for specific graduate groups (applied linguists and economists)

Table 1: NLP Teaching Contexts in terms of student groups

groups. I hope to achieve the following goals through this long overview:

1. share some insights about what to include/exclude in the syllabus/exercises, when we are developing a new NLP course for a non-traditional audience

2. provide a useful context to the challenges that will be discussed later in the paper.

3.1 Undergrad-General (U-Gen):

I taught one course[7] which could be classified as a general undergraduate course that is open for all. This is based on the textbook by Dickinson et al. (2012), which is used to teach several such "Language and Computers" courses around the world. Students in this course came from all years of undergraduate curriculum, but were dominated by freshmen and sophomores from Sciences and Engineering. The course had an opt-in programming component for enthusiastic students, but otherwise, generic enough that all freshmen undergraduate students from any discipline can follow.

Syllabus: The topics covered followed the book's structure, with more contemporary information. For example, the topic "tutoring systems" included a discussion of software such as DuoLingo, and the topic "dialog systems" included discussion on virtual assistants such as Siri, Cortana etc. The focus in using these tools in this classroom is to explain how such systems work, and evaluate their performance in real world contexts, rather than on teaching how to build such systems. Two sessions were spent on giving a non-technical overview of NLP with some discussion on recent trends and on the broader impact of NLP on other areas of study.

Evaluation: The assignments in this course required students to explore a few existing NLP tools/demos (e.g., corenlp.run) or browse existing corpora (e.g., corpus.byu.edu). The students also did a group presentation that involved using a readily available day to day software which has some NLP component and summarizing its performance with concrete examples and qualitative measures. The final exam for this course had two parts: the first part required the students to write a report performing a error analysis of two commercial systems doing the same task (e.g., machine translation, speech recognition, etc.) and the second part asked them to write a perspective essay on the impact of language technologies on the society.

3.2 Undergrad-Focused (U-Focused)

I taught one course[8] which was one of the electives in an undergraduate data science minor program. This was open to students from all departments under the school of Liberal Arts & Sciences. It was taught twice and attracted students from a wide range of disciplines including, but not limited to: Literature, Sociology, Journalism, Management, World Languages, Linguistics and Computer Science.

Syllabus: The goal of this course was to introduce students to methods of discovering language patterns in text documents and applying them to solve practical text analysis problems in their disciplines. The course required students to write a few programs, although the knowledge of program-

[7] https://github.com/nishkalavallabhi/LING120-Fall2017/

[8] https://github.com/nishkalavallabhi/LING410X-Spring18

ming was not a pre-requisite. Since many of these students were getting familiarized with using R as a part of their curricula (for statistics courses), and I viewed it as a language in which they can make some progress without having to gain expertise in programming simultaneously, the course was taught in R. Relevant programming concepts and data structures were introduced in the context of the topics of the course, on the fly. Jockers (2014) was used as the main textbook for this course, since it assumed no programming background from its target audience (Literature students), and it used R.

In terms of course organization, a few sessions were spent on introducing students to the basics of installing and using R, specifically with the goal of working with textual data in mind. The next topic discussed methods to collect, extract and clean texts/corpora. This was followed by teaching about doing basic exploratory corpus analysis along with keyword and key phrase extraction approaches. The next topics focused on text classification and topic modeling - both of which are the most commonly used methods with textual data across disciplines. The final topic for the course discussed various means of visualizing textual data.

Evaluation: The course included assignments that followed the topic structure, and required students to write small R programs to extract text patterns, scrape data from different forms of documents (e.g., webpages, twitter), extracting keywords, ngrams etc., following step by step process making alterations to pre-written code for training a text classifier and a topic model, and building basic visualizations of textual data (e.g., word clouds, dispersion plots etc). All assignments relied on learning to use existing R libraries instead of focusing on building everything from scratch. The students did a group presentation which involved visualizing textual data. The final exam consisted of doing a small project and submitting the term paper. The students were required to pick an interesting dataset for a problem they encountered in their own discipline, and use one of the methods they learnt in the course.

3.3 Grad/Advanced undergrad-General (G-Gen)

I taught two courses that are the closest to a typical Natural Language Processing course taught in universities across the world: the first course followed the standard structure in traditional textbooks, and the second course focused specifically on how to do NLP in the absence of large annotated datasets. Students in both courses primarily consisted of advanced undergrad or graduate students coming from linguistics and computer science, with varying degrees of background in programming, linguistics, and computer science. All students passed at least one programming course prior to attending these courses.

Statistical NLP: The course's objective was to teach some of the common algorithms and techniques that form the foundation for modern day NLP. Accordingly, starting with regular expressions and language models, the topics we dealt with included part of speech tagging, parsing, discourse, information extraction, text classification and other NLP applications, and ended with introducing text embedding representations along with an overview of neural network architectures. Jurafsky and Martin (2008) and Goldberg (2017) were used as the prescribed textbooks. Assignments focused on implementing some of the popular NLP algorithms from scratch, and final project involved modeling one of the common tasks such as text classification or information extraction using existing datasets and producing a technical report describing the same.

NLP without data[9] : The objective of this course was to address a real world scenario that is not typically addressed in NLP courses - how do we apply NLP methods in the absence of annotated training data. Hence, after giving a broad overview of NLP and its uses both in real world and for other disciplines, and discussing in detail about NLP system development pipeline and text representation, the course focused on the following topics:

1. Corpus collection, text extraction and exploratory analysis
2. Automatically labeling data and performing data augmentation
3. Working with small datasets and transfer learning

This course was taught remotely, as a compact, intensive 1 month online course in January 2021 (9 hours per week, for 3 weeks) due to the current

[9] `https://github.com/nishkalavallabhi/SfSCourseJan2021`

pandemic situation. It primarily relied on a collection of blog posts, research papers, code tutorials and python notebooks from various sources, as no available textbook specifically addressed this topic. It had two assignments, which required students to explore the usage of existing NLP tools to perform given tasks and to "generate" labeled data for information extraction, and write up a report evaluating their approaches with some error analysis. There was a group presentation, where students had to pick from a selected collection of recent research articles on the course's topics. Finally, there was an optional term paper (for extra credits), where the students can pick a resource scarce NLP scenario and apply what they learnt in this course to address it.

3.4 Grad/Adv.undergrad-Focused (G-Focused)

I taught two introductory NLP courses that were specific to graduate students - one for applied linguistics Masters/PhD students and the other for Economics Masters/PhD students.

NLP for Applied Linguists Applied linguistics graduate program in the university where this course was taught consisted of students studying corpus linguistics, computer assisted language teaching/learning, and technical communication. Since the use of language processing tools in these areas is increasing day by day, the goal of this course was to teach some text processing methods that can be directly applicable in their dissertation research. Accordingly, the course introduced various NLP techniques from regular expressions to using parsers, in the context of technologies for language learning and corpus analysis e.g., spelling/grammar checkers, pattern extractors for corpus analysis etc. Bird et al. (2008) and Jurafsky and Martin (2008) were used as the textbooks for this course, along with Church (1994).

The course had five assignments which involved writing small programs covering the topics of the course, and a group project, followed by a one-to-one oral exam to assess student understanding of the relevance of the course to their area of study.

NLP for Economists[10]: This was originally planned to be a one week intensive course, but was taught online over three weeks due to the pandemic situation in Fall 2020. It also included instruction on Python fundamentals. The syllabus for the topic comprised of four broad topics:

1. Introduction: An overview of NLP and its usefulness in Economics; Python fundamentals
2. Python & textual data, which focused on data collection, text extraction, pre-processing and text representation
3. NLP methods for economics, covering exploratory corpus analysis, text classification, topic modeling, and giving an overview of others such as information extraction and text summarization
4. NLP in Economics - research paper readings and discussion

The students had to do 3 assignments covering the first three topics which involved writing small python programs to use existing tools and write an analysis of how they work for their domain data. They also did a group presentation picking a paper that used NLP methods to address research questions in economics, chosen most often from their own disciplinary journals, instead of NLP conferences. Students also had to submit a term paper which involved creation of a problem statement describing a new economics problem that can be addressed using NLP methods. No specific textbook was used for the course, although several recommendations were listed in the syllabus. The course videos and slides, and links to publicly available online content were the primary materials for the course, as there was no appropriate textbook available to suit the needs of this audience.

As it can be seen from all the above course descriptions, the courses addressed a range of audiences, and accordingly, differed in the way the course was organized as well as the topics that were covered. Most of these courses can be called "non-traditional" NLP courses, considering their contents and intended audience. In the following section, I will elaborate on some of the general and course specific challenges I faced in the design and delivery of these courses.

4 Challenges for Teaching

While all the courses received generally good student feedback towards the end, there are several issues that could have been managed better. Some of these issues arise because I am teaching a diverse, non-conventional NLP audience, and hence,

[10] `https://econnlpcourse.github.io/`

we don't have readily available solutions yet. Each course, of course, comes with its own challenges. In this section, I will discuss some of the more general teaching challenges I faced across all courses, and how I addressed them.

Student goals and Course Contents: For many of the courses described in the previous section, the students did not have an ecosystem of related courses in their curriculum because there are no NLP focused research groups or teaching programs in the university. For all except *G-Gen* courses, any NLP course is potentially a one off course that covers programming, NLP, and anything remotely concerned with computing for the students. The student goals accordingly are related to either just fulfilling a course requirement, or gaining some quick actionable insights that they can use right away, or show relevant skills when they apply for a job soon. In this background, I found it particularly challenging to adapt the syllabi such that they get readily usable practical skills, along with a solid foundation to explore the topics further on their own if needed.

An approach that seemed to work is to tie each concept of the course to a practical use case (either a software application or some research problem in another discipline) and give assignments that are closer to their real-world scenarios. In the *U-Gen* course, group activities involving apps the students regularly use such as Duolingo, Google Search, Siri etc generated a lot of interesting questions in the class. In the *G-Focused* courses, providing an overview about relevant disciplinary research that uses NLP, and encouraging discussions about how the students can use NLP in their research turned out to be useful. The NACLO exercises helped to introduce the challenges while working with textual data, in a way that holds students' attention and generated interesting discussions, in all the four cells in Table 1.

Faculty goals and Course Contents: As mentioned above, many students lacked the eco-system of related courses (all except *G-Gen*). Thus, a lot of surrounding topics that are not typically a part of NLP courses had to be covered in these classes. Specifically, these topics revolved around concepts of software programming, and the mathematics needed to understand some of the basic NLP methods. Two questions I constantly grappled with in terms of my own teaching goals for *U-Focused* and *G-Focused* courses courses were - how much mathematics/programming/linguistics should be included? how can I encourage good programming/software engineering practices while still focusing on teaching the students to solve NLP related problems?

For the first question, keeping mathematics and linguistics to the bare minimum, situating all programming related exercises in the context of NLP/textual data, and providing additional resources/tutorials for those interested in knowing more math/linguistics behind NLP helped . For the second question, I tried to write clean, well-commented code for classroom examples as much as possible, and showed variations of writing the same piece of code, on top of the exercises in the prescribed textbook, discussing why we may chose one over the other. I also encouraged students to review each other's submissions and post discussions about programming in the forum for some of these courses. Both these teaching strategies created some awareness about programming practices among the students.

However, there were always students who wanted more/less of math/linguistics/programming during the classroom session itself, or in the form of assignments, especially in *G-Gen* and *G-Focused* courses. Some students felt enough challenged, some were overwhelmed. This issue is by no means specific to my experiences, and has been documented in past work on teaching NLP too (Brew et al., 2005; Koit et al., 2002). I addressed this by providing optional, additional (ungraded) programming exercises and reading materials in all the courses.

In terms of programming practices, I found it particularly challenging to introduce the idea of version control for code for students in *U-Focused* and *G-Focused* classrooms. The students without prior background in any form of programming found it difficult to understand Git. I emphasized its importance and spent a small amount of time discussing why version control is useful, and how to do it, and provided a few tutorial references. While none of the students used version control during the courses, I hope that as they gain more experience, they will understand its relevance and adopt in practice.

Textbooks and the real world: If we ask ourselves - what will the students do with what they learn in these courses, provided they manage to stick to NLP?, we can think about three options: a) pursue further studies/research focused on NLP b) pursue further studies/research in their own discipline, using NLP methods in their work c) work in a company on NLP projects. Among these, we can safely assume that the last two are the most likely scenarios for the audience I taught.

In my experience as a software engineer and as a data scientist in industry, and while collaborating with researchers from other disciplines, some of the most common issues I encountered are:

- How do we collect and label the data needed to train NLP models?
- How can we do a clean and accurate extraction of text from various file formats?
- What are the efficient ways of selecting models going beyond standard intrinsic evaluation measures (e.g., considering external measures, deployment costs, maintenance issues etc)

Most of this issues are also commonly experienced by NLP researchers, if they work on a new problem or on creating a new corpus resource. Yet, none of these issues are discussed even cursorily in available/standard NLP textbooks, which means that the students have to rely on a lot of online blogs and other resources.

I addressed these issues by including topics such as: what does a NLP system development pipeline look like? and how is NLP used beyond CS research and software development scenarios? in the introductory "NLP overview" sessions itself in *G-Gen* classrooms, introducing the students to the challenges one faces at each step. In the rest of the course too, I addressed these issues in more detail as needed, providing code examples, and including real-world case studies. Particularly, one course described in this paper, "NLP without annotated dataset", entirely focused on the first issue mentioned earlier.

In *U-Focused* and *G-Focused* classrooms, I added a detailed overview of how NLP is used in various disciplines as a research method, and organized student group discussions with contemporary research papers in these disciplines. Even in the relatively simpler *U-Gen* course scenario, we ran into the issue of the existing textbook being outdated, which required me to look for new materials on the topic. As mentioned earlier, I addressed this issue by introducing discussions and assignments on more contemporary developments about the textbook's topics.

I found it particularly challenging to cover all of these aspects in one course, while also giving enough background in core NLP topics, though. In future, it would be useful to develop some structured reading material/tutorials/workbooks that can serve as goto sources on these topics, rather than asking the students to just explore on their own from a wide range of available material on the web.

Graded Resources: Another recurring challenge I ran into relates to the availability of appropriate textbooks. While I found introductory textbooks that suited some of the classes, the students in the *G-Focused* group repeatedly mentioned the lack of a progressively difficult self-learning path. As they rightly pointed out, we either have introductory books which gave a basic idea of selected topics (e.g., Jockers, 2014), or very advanced textbooks (e.g., Jurafsky and Martin, 2008), but nothing in between. The issue of lack of resources was also highlighted by Hearst (2005) in the context of teaching an applied NLP course. Although this was to some extent addressed by some of the more practically oriented books published by O'Reilly Media[11] and Manning Publications[12], they still addressed industry facing scenarios, which did not always account for these students' needs.

Teaching diverse audience: All except the *G-Gen* courses described in this paper had either students coming from diverse disciplines, or a homogeneous group belonging to a non-STEM discipline. In such cases, it is important that the students understand the relevance of the course to their own discipline. This can be challenging, if we, as the instructors, don't know what are some interesting challenges in the various disciplines. The need to target courses to the student background was also discussed in the past in Baldridge and Erk (2008). To this end, I had several informational chats with the faculty members from these disciplines, to understand the use cases for NLP in their research, apart from reading research that used NLP methods in the respective disciplines. This was definitely useful in making NLP more relevant to the student groups. Co-teaching such courses with faculty from other disciplines is an idea to explore in future, provided the class is homogeneous, and both instructors are willing to invest time and energy into learning the methods of the other discipline.

[11] https://www.oreilly.com/

[12] https://www.manning.com/

These are some of the challenges I faced in teaching NLP and how I addressed them. However, all these issues are by no means completely answered, and more discussion is needed in this direction. Teaching NLP workshops, and sharing of teaching resources (and anecdotes) can be a starting point towards addressing these issues.

5 Challenges beyond the Teaching context

Generally, we see some discussion about how research informs teaching and the choice of topics in a course. We may notice the evolution of the standard Natural Language Processing course over the past two decades, in terms of the topics covered[13]. We also see a lot of discussion around challenges encountered in teaching itself, as seen in the Teaching NLP papers in the past. However, when teaching to *outside* audience, we can uncover hitherto under-studied research questions that are potentially more relevant while doing NLP outside of computer science and linguistics. I will focus on such issues in this section, by splitting it into two groups: NLP research and tool development.

5.1 NLP Research

The questions raised by the students in *G-Focused* courses identified some under-studied issues in contemporary NLP research, which are described below:

Predictions and Causality: In NLP, we generally work with various representations of textual data, and build predictive models. Though there is an increasing body of research on understanding the predictions, it is not common to see a causal analysis. However, in some disciplines, such causal relationship is important for any prediction. While teaching an economics classroom, we repeatedly ran into these discussions about drawing causal inference for a text classifier or a topic modeling decision. These led a student to a question - will NLP ever be really useful in economics research beyond being a fancy new technique?

There is some existing work that uses causal analysis along with NLP methods in economics literature (Gentzkow et al., 2019), but there is not much within NLP research in that direction, focusing on specific applications. Although there is some recent interest among NLP researchers on causal inference (Veitch et al., 2020; Keith et al., 2020), we do not yet have off the shelf teaching resources to incorporate such aspects into the classroom, to my knowledge. More NLP research and inter-disciplinary collaborations in this direction may lead to the creation of the much needed teaching and software resources to address this important issue in future.

Text as secondary data: Unlike typical NLP focused problems, text is a form of secondary data for many other disciplines (e.g., economics, again). Thus, their expectation is that the primary source of information for model predictions should come from the primary data sources. While discussing feature representations for text, we repeatedly ran into the issue of how to effectively combine these different feature representations coming from primary and secondary sources. It is certainly possible to concatenate representations or create multimodal representations and let the model figure out feature importance, as we commonly do in NLP research. However, the students questioned this approach and asked for methods to develop models such that their primary feature representations were given importance over textual representation.

I am not aware of a commonly used approach for the same, that can be incorporated directly in a course through theory or practical exercises. However, I believe we should acknowledge that the students are more familiar with research methods from their own disciplines and want to use NLP within that framework, rather than completely switch to "the NLP way" of building models. New research on using text representation as a secondary feature vector along with primary features may be a step in the direction of addressing this issue.

Construct validity of text representations: Construct validity refers to whether a feature actually measures what it is supposed to measure. In language testing literature, construct validity is frequently studied in the context of automated language assessment software. In the Applied Linguistics graduate course, we discussed automatic essay scoring and spelling/grammar correction systems briefly, as use cases of NLP in language assessment and teaching. During these discussions, the students, who typically came from a language assessment background, questioned the lack of traditional steps such as exploratory analyses to understand the corpus, and evaluating the construct

[13]NLP Pedagogy interviews by David Jurgens and Lucy Li shorturl.at/bntR5

validity of the feature representations we use in NLP. While we see some discussion around these issues in the context of real world NLP system development (e.g., Sheehan, 2017; Beigman Klebanov and Madnani, 2020), we don't see much discussion about such issues in research describing the development of new NLP methods or in NLP textbooks. As we see NLP being used more and more outside its typical contexts, perhaps, it is time for us as NLP researchers to consider these issues while analyzing models and their performance.

All these are important problems beyond teaching NLP, for NLP researchers in general, and in the inter-disciplinary research context in particular. As Connolly (2020) suggests, supplementing computing related courses with methods, and perspectives from social sciences may give new insights for NLP researchers into addressing these issues. This will benefit teaching NLP contexts beyond the traditional audience, and also enrich NLP research in future.

5.2 Tool Development

In all the courses taught outside of classrooms dominated by STEM students (i.e., all except *G-Gen*), I frequently ran into the issue of insufficient documentation for NLP tools the students want to use. From my personal experience, this situation is constantly improving. Yet, it is far from ideal. Despite being actively involved with using various NLP tools in daily life, it is not uncommon for many of us to face some challenges with software usage.

This is even harder for those without that background with DIY software. Especially, tools that work across all commonly used operating systems are not very easy to find, but are essential when we want to use them in classrooms. It was particularly challenging even as an instructor, while teaching the data science minor course which used R. Since the students preferred to use their own machines, it was not possible to enforce a common operating system/library versions setup. So, I addressed this issue by guiding the students with links to videos on installation of various tools on all common operating systems where possible, and using alternative libraries where this did not work. Other issues the students raised were about the lack of proper graphical user interfaces and visualization methods for NLP tools. While I could not offer any clear solutions for these issues, tool developers should perhaps keep a broader, potentially non-technical users in mind when they release and document their tools in future.

What is described in this section is merely a snapshot of some of the teaching NLP challenges that go beyond the teaching context, and need the attention of other members of the NLP community - researchers and tool developers. The list mentioned in this section is by no means exhaustive, and more discussion is needed in this direction especially in the current situation where NLP is taught and used by many disciplines beyond linguistics and computer science.

6 Conclusion

In this paper, I summarized my experiences with teaching NLP courses for diverse groups of undergraduate and graduate students and identified a few challenge areas for teaching such courses. I also discussed few challenge areas for NLP researchers and tool developers, addressing which can help improve both teaching NLP and the ease of applying NLP in research areas beyond linguistics and computer science. It should be acknowledged though, that this discussion is more qualitative than quantitative in nature. Perhaps doing a survey of the students of such courses a couple of years later about how they are using NLP compared to what they learnt in a classroom could be one way to measure these observations in a more quantitative manner. I hope that this paper will contribute to the growing body of work on NLP Teaching, and also lead to further discussion on an increased focus on the inter-disciplinarily relevant aspects of NLP teaching, research and practice.

Acknowledgements

Firstly, I thank the workshop committee for organizing this workshop. Comments from all the three anonymous reviewers, and my colleagues - Rebecca Knowles, Gabriel Bernier-Colborne and Taraka Rama were immensely useful in bringing the paper from the first draft to the final version - I thank them all for their time and thoughts on this paper. Finally, I thank the students in all these courses, and the three universities (Iowa State University, USA; Ludwig Maximilian University of Munich, Germany; Eberhard Karls University of Tübingen, Germany) that gave me the opportunities to teach them.

References

Apoorv Agarwal. 2013. Teaching the basics of nlp and ml in an introductory course to information science. In *Proceedings of the Fourth Workshop on Teaching NLP and CL*, pages 77–84.

Jason Baldridge and Katrin Erk. 2008. Teaching computational linguistics to a large, diverse student body: courses, tools, and interdepartmental interaction. In *Proceedings of the Third Workshop on Issues in Teaching Computational Linguistics*, pages 1–9.

Fabian Barteld and Johanna Flick. 2017. Lea-linguistic exercises with annotation tools. In *Teach4DH@ GSCL*, pages 11–16.

Beata Beigman Klebanov and Nitin Madnani. 2020. Automated evaluation of writing – 50 years and counting. In *Proceedings of the 58th Annual Meeting of the Association for Computational Linguistics*, pages 7796–7810, Online. Association for Computational Linguistics.

Steven Bird. 2008. Defining a core body of knowledge for the introductory computational linguistics curriculum. In *Proceedings of the Third Workshop on Issues in Teaching Computational Linguistics*, pages 27–35.

Steven Bird, Ewan Klein, Edward Loper, and Jason Baldridge. 2008. Multidisciplinary instruction with the natural language toolkit. In *Proceedings of the Third Workshop on Issues in Teaching Computational Linguistics*, pages 62–70, Columbus, Ohio. Association for Computational Linguistics.

Kalina Bontcheva, Hamish Cunningham, Valentin Tablan, Diana Maynard, and Oana Hamza. 2002. Using GATE as an environment for teaching NLP. In *Proceedings of the ACL-02 Workshop on Effective Tools and Methodologies for Teaching Natural Language Processing and Computational Linguistics*, pages 54–62, Philadelphia, Pennsylvania, USA. Association for Computational Linguistics.

Bozhidar Bozhanov and Ivan Derzhanski. 2013. Rosetta stone linguistic problems. In *Proceedings of the Fourth Workshop on Teaching NLP and CL*, pages 1–8, Sofia, Bulgaria. Association for Computational Linguistics.

Chris Brew, Markus Dickinson, and Detmar Meurers. 2005. "language and computers": Creating an introduction for a general undergraduate audience. In *Proceedings of the Second ACL Workshop on Effective Tools and Methodologies for Teaching NLP and CL*, pages 15–22.

Kenneth Ward Church. 1994. Unix™ for poets. *Notes of a course from the European Summer School on Language and Speech Communication, Corpus Based Methods*.

Randy Connolly. 2020. Why computing belongs within the social sciences. *Communications of the ACM*, 63(8):54–59.

Robert Dale, Diego Mollá Aliod, and Rolf Schwitter. 2002. Evangelising language technology: A practically-focussed undergraduate program. In *Proceedings of the ACL-02 Workshop on Effective Tools and Methodologies for Teaching Natural Language Processing and Computational Linguistics*, pages 27–32, Philadelphia, Pennsylvania, USA. Association for Computational Linguistics.

Markus Dickinson, Chris Brew, and Detmar Meurers. 2012. *Language and computers*. John Wiley & Sons.

Eric Fosler-Lussier. 2008. Strategies for teaching "mixed" computational linguistics classes. In *Proceedings of the Third Workshop on Issues in Teaching Computational Linguistics*, pages 36–44.

Matthew Gentzkow, Bryan Kelly, and Matt Taddy. 2019. Text as data. *Journal of Economic Literature*, 57(3):535–74.

Yoav Goldberg. 2017. Neural network methods for natural language processing. *Synthesis lectures on human language technologies*, 10(1):1–309.

Mark Guzdial. 2021. What liberal arts and sciences students need to know about computing.

Marti A Hearst. 2005. Teaching applied natural language processing: Triumphs and tribulations. In *Proceedings of the Second ACL Workshop on Effective Tools and Methodologies for Teaching NLP and CL*, pages 1–8.

Beth Ann Hockey and Gwen Christian. 2008. Zero to spoken dialogue system in one quarter: Teaching computational linguistics to linguists using regulus. In *Proceedings of the Third Workshop on Issues in Teaching Computational Linguistics*, pages 80–86, Columbus, Ohio. Association for Computational Linguistics.

Dirk Hovy. 2020. *Text Analysis in Python for Social Scientists: Discovery and Exploration*. Cambridge University Press.

Matthew L Jockers. 2014. *Text Analysis with R for Students of Literature*. Springer.

Dan Jurafsky and James Martin. 2008. *Speech & language processing*. Pearson Education.

Katherine Keith, David Jensen, and Brendan O'Connor. 2020. Text and causal inference: A review of using text to remove confounding from causal estimates. In *Proceedings of the 58th Annual Meeting of the Association for Computational Linguistics*, pages 5332–5344, Online. Association for Computational Linguistics.

Mare Koit, Tiit Roosmaa, and Haldur Õim. 2002. Teaching computational linguistics at the University of Tartu: Experience, perspectives and challenges. In *Proceedings of the ACL-02 Workshop on Effective Tools and Methodologies for Teaching Natural*

Language Processing and Computational Linguistics, pages 85–90, Philadelphia, Pennsylvania, USA. Association for Computational Linguistics.

Shriram Krishnamurthi and Kathi Fisler. 2020. Data-centricity: a challenge and opportunity for computing education. *Communications of the ACM*, 63(8):24–26.

Gina-Anne Levow. 2008. Studying discourse and dialogue with SIDGrid. In *Proceedings of the Third Workshop on Issues in Teaching Computational Linguistics*, pages 106–113, Columbus, Ohio. Association for Computational Linguistics.

Elizabeth Liddy and Nancy McCracken. 2005. Hands-on NLP for an interdisciplinary audience. In *Proceedings of the Second ACL Workshop on Effective Tools and Methodologies for Teaching NLP and CL*, pages 62–68, Ann Arbor, Michigan. Association for Computational Linguistics.

Jimmy Lin. 2008. Exploring large-data issues in the curriculum: A case study with MapReduce. In *Proceedings of the Third Workshop on Issues in Teaching Computational Linguistics*, pages 54–61, Columbus, Ohio. Association for Computational Linguistics.

Patrick Littell, Lori Levin, Jason Eisner, and Dragomir Radev. 2013. Introducing computational concepts in a linguistics olympiad. In *Proceedings of the Fourth Workshop on Teaching NLP and CL*, pages 18–26, Sofia, Bulgaria. Association for Computational Linguistics.

Deryle Lonsdale. 2002. A niche at the nexus: situating an NLP curriculum interdisciplinarily. In *Proceedings of the ACL-02 Workshop on Effective Tools and Methodologies for Teaching Natural Language Processing and Computational Linguistics*, pages 46–53, Philadelphia, Pennsylvania, USA. Association for Computational Linguistics.

Nitin Madnani and Bonnie J. Dorr. 2008. Combining open-source with research to re-engineer a hands-on introductory NLP course. In *Proceedings of the Third Workshop on Issues in Teaching Computational Linguistics*, pages 71–79, Columbus, Ohio. Association for Computational Linguistics.

Borja Navarro-Colorado. 2017. A quick intensive course on natural language processing applied to literary studies. In *Teach4DH@ GSCL*, pages 37–42.

Nils Reiter, Sarah Schulz, Gerhard Kremer, Roman Klinger, Gabriel Viehhauser, and Jonas Kuhn. 2017. Teaching computational aspects in the digital humanities program at university of stuttgart–intentions and experiences. *Humanities*, 1:6.

Kathleen M Sheehan. 2017. Validating automated measures of text complexity. *Educational Measurement: Issues and Practice*, 36(4):35–43.

Victor Veitch, Dhanya Sridhar, and David Blei. 2020. Adapting text embeddings for causal inference. In *Conference on Uncertainty in Artificial Intelligence*, pages 919–928. PMLR.

Fei Xia. 2008. The evolution of a statistical NLP course. In *Proceedings of the Third Workshop on Issues in Teaching Computational Linguistics*, pages 45–53, Columbus, Ohio. Association for Computational Linguistics.

Heike Zinsmeister. 2008. Freshmen's cl curriculum: the benefits of redundancy. In *Proceedings of the Third Workshop on Issues in Teaching Computational Linguistics*, pages 19–26.

Teaching NLP with Bracelets and Restaurant Menus: An Interactive Workshop for Italian Students

Ludovica Pannitto
University of Trento
ludovica.pannitto@unitn.it

Lucia Busso
Aston University
l.busso@aston.ac.uk

Claudia Roberta Combei
University of Bologna
claudiaroberta.combei@unibo.it

Lucio Messina
Independent Researcher
lucio.messina@autistici.org

Alessio Miaschi
University of Pisa
alessio.miaschi@phd.unipi.it

Gabriele Sarti
University of Trieste
gsarti@sissa.it

Malvina Nissim
University of Groningen
m.nissim@rug.nl

Abstract

Although Natural Language Processing (NLP) is at the core of many tools young people use in their everyday life, high school curricula (in Italy) do not include any computational linguistics education. This lack of exposure makes the use of such tools less responsible than it could be and makes choosing computational linguistics as a university degree unlikely. To raise awareness, curiosity, and longer-term interest in young people, we have developed an interactive workshop designed to illustrate the basic principles of NLP and computational linguistics to high school Italian students aged between 13 and 18 years. The workshop takes the form of a game in which participants play the role of machines needing to solve some of the most common problems a computer faces in understanding language: from voice recognition to Markov chains to syntactic parsing. Participants are guided through the workshop with the help of instructors, who present the activities and explain core concepts from computational linguistics. The workshop was presented at numerous outlets in Italy between 2019 and 2021, both face-to-face and online.

1 Introduction

Have you used Google this week? This question would kick off the activity that we describe in this paper every time we delivered it. And a number of follow-up comments would generally appear. *What for? Translating, getting some help for homework, looking for info, writing collaboratively - and getting spelling correction!*

In our workshops, we talk to groups of teenagers – even if someone has not personally used any of those tools on a daily basis, it is utmost unlikely that they have never interacted with a vocal assistant, wondered how their email spam filter works, used text predictions, or spoken to a chat-bot. Also, applications that do not require a proactive role of the user are growing: most of us, for example, are subject to targeted advertising, profiled on the content we produce and share on social media.

Natural Language Processing (NLP) has grown at an incredibly fast pace, and it is at the core of many of the tools we use every day.[1] At the same time, though, awareness of its underlying mechanisms and the scientific discussion that has led to such innovations, and even NLP's very existence as a scientific discipline is generally much less widespread and is basically unknown to the general public (Grandi and Masini, 2018).

A concurrent cause to this lack of awareness resides in the fact that in more traditional high-school formal education systems, such as the Italian one, "young disciplines" such as Linguistics and Computer Science tend to be overlooked. Grammar, that in a high-school setting is the closest field to Linguistics, is rarely taught as a descriptive discipline; oftentimes, it is presented as a set of norms that one should follow in order to speak and write correctly in a given language. While this approach has its benefits, it is particularly misleading when it comes to what actual linguistic research is about. Similarly, Computer Science is often misread by the general public as an activity that deals with computers, while aspects concerning information technology and language processing are often ne-

[1] In this discussion, and throughout the paper, we conflate the terms Natural Language Processing and Computational Linguistics and use them interchangeably.

Proceedings of the Fifth Workshop on Teaching NLP, pages 160–170
June 10–11, 2021. ©2021 Association for Computational Linguistics

glected. This often leads to two important consequences. First, despite the overwhelming amount of NLP applications, students and citizens at large lack the basic notions that would allow them to fully understand technology and interact with it in a responsible and critical way. Second, high-school students might not be aware of Computational Linguistics as an option for their university degree. Oftentimes, students that enrol in Humanities degrees are mainly interested in literature and they only get acquainted with linguistics as discipline at university. At the same time, most Computer Science curricula in Italian higher education rarely focus on natural language-based applications. As a result, Computational Linguistics as such is practically never taught before graduate studies.

As members of the Italian Association for Computational Linguistics (AILC, `www.ai-lc.it`) we have long felt the need to bridge this knowledge gap, and made dissemination a core goal of the Association. As a step in this direction, we have developed a dissemination activity that covers the basic aspects of what it means to process and analyze language computationally. This is the first activity of its kind developed and promoted by AILC, and to the best of our knowledge, among the first in Italy at large.

This contribution describes the activity itself, the way it was implemented as a workshop for high school students in the context of several dissemination events, and how it can serve as a blueprint to develop similar activities for yet new languages.

2 Genesis and Goals

We set to develop an activity whose main aim would be to provide a broad overview of language modeling, and, most importantly, to highlight the open challenges in language understanding and generation.

Without any ambition to present and explain the actual NLP techniques to students, we rather focused on showing how language, which is usually conceptualized by the layperson as a simple and monolithic object, is instead a complex stratification of interconnected layers that need to be disentangled in order to provide a suitable formalization.

In developing our activity, we took inspiration from the *word salad* Linguistic Puzzle, as published in Radev and Pustejovsky (2013):

> Charlie and Jane had been passing notes in class, when suddenly their teacher Mr. Johnson saw what was going on. He rushed to the back of the class, took the note Charlie had just passed Jane, and ripped it up, dropping the pieces on the floor. Jane noticed that he had managed to rip each word of the message onto a separate piece of paper. The pieces of paper were, in alphabetical order, as follows: *dog, in, is, my, school, the*. Most likely, what did Charlie's note originally say?

The problem includes a number of follow up questions that encourage the student to reflect upon the boundaries of sentence structure. In particular, we found that the *word salad* puzzle would give us the opportunity to introduce some of the core aspects of Computational Linguistics' research. Approaching the problem with no previous knowledge helps raising some crucial questions, such as: *what are the building blocks of our linguistic ability that allow us to perform such a task?*, *how much knowledge can we extract from text alone?*, *what does linguistic knowledge look like?*

Since the workshop here presented is the first activity of this kind in the Italian context, we took inspiration from games and problems such as those outlined in Radev and Pustejovsky (2013) and used for the North American Computational Linguistics Olympiads, similar to the ones described in Van Halteren (2002) and Iomdin et al. (2013). Particularly, we were inspired by the institution of (Computational) Linguistic Olympiads in making our workshop a problem-solving game with different activities, each related to a different aspect of computational language processing. Linguistic Olympiads are now an established annual event in many parts of the world since they first took place in Moscow in 1965. In these competitions students (generally of high-school age) are faced with linguistic problems of varying nature, that require participants to use problem-solving abilities to uncover underlying patterns or rules in the data. For an in-depth discussion of the history and diffusion of Linguistic Olympiads in the world, see Derzhanski and Payne (2010) and Littell et al. (2013).

In the choice of algorithms to include in our dissemination activity, we decided to leave aside neural networks and instead focus on traditional statistical approaches, both for historical reasons and for the fact that these convey more clearly the distinction between different layers of linguistic information and their roles in language modeling. A

Activity		Aim
1. Get to know a (computational) linguist	10'	collaboratively build a definition for *linguistics* as a study field
2. Are computers able to *hear*?	15'	familiarize with the concept of *simulation* of humans' speech perception abilities
3. Are computers able to *read*?	30'	introduce corpora as sources of linguistic knowledge and statistical patterns as structural aspects of language
4. Do computers *know* grammar?	30'	introduce human annotation and meta-linguistic knowledge as powerful research tools
5. Becoming a computational linguist	5'	evaluate pros and cons of the two presented approaches, future directions and discuss about what's needed to become a computational linguist

Table 1: Sections of the activity, with their planned duration and a broad aim for each of them.

brief discussion of most recent NLP technologies, including the application of neural networks, is included in the final part of the workshop (Sec. 3.5).

The activity is targeted at students in their last year of middle school (13 years of age) or older. While we believe 13 is a good entry point, there isn't an actual upper-bound, since the activity can be enjoyed by people of any older age (though in practice participation was mainly offered to schools, with the oldest students being 18-19). We thought this would be the appropriate target audience of this workshop for two main reasons. On the one hand, we believe that coming to the activity with a richer metalinguistic background, typically acquired during the first Italian school cycle, would be beneficial for the attendees to better grasp the differences between the scientific approach to language and the more prescriptive approach they are exposed to in school. On the other hand we also conceived the activity as a way of helping students in their future study choices: we therefore included both students attending their last year of middle school and therefore about to choose a high school curriculum as well as high school students, the latter in order to provide them with more options for their university choices.

3 The activity

We planned our dissemination activity for a 90 minutes time slot, divided into five parts, as detailed in Table 1.

3.1 Get to know a (computational) linguist

The first 15 minutes of the workshop are organized both as an ice-breaker activity for the attendees, and as a brief introduction to linguistics and computational linguistics more specifically.

During the introduction we tried to demystify some common misconceptions about linguistics, (i.e., *a linguist knows many languages*, *linguists get sometimes confused with speech therapists*, *a linguist will correct my grammar*, etc.): we presented participants with a list of possible definitions, and they had to identify appropriate ones. We broadly defined linguistics as the study of language as a biological, psychological, and cultural object. Computational Linguistics was then introduced both as a commercial and engineering-oriented field, as well as a purely scientific research discipline.[2]

We also briefly discussed *linguistic questions* with participants as an example of the kind of problems that a linguist tries to approach during their research activity. These included: "How many ways of pronouncing *n* do we have in Italian?", "Do numbers from one to ten exist in all languages?".

For the following parts of the activity, the introduction to each sub-part was dedicated to a reflection upon what it means for us humans to *hear*, *read* and *understand grammar*, and whether there is a difference when the same tasks are performed by computers.

3.2 Are computers able to *hear*?

As vocal assistants such as Alexa, Siri, Google Home etc. have become increasingly popular, we chose them as tangible examples of NLP technologies to kick-off the games. The aim of this section

[2]We relied on the definition reported in `https://www.thebritishacademy.ac.uk/blog/what-computational-linguistics/`.

of the workshop was to demonstrate two points:

- computers do not necessarily solve linguistic tasks the way we solve them; they are therefore *simulating* our abilities without *replicating* them;
- consequently, the concepts of *easy* and *difficult* tasks have to be carefully revised when applied to language models.

We introduced the McGurk effect (McGurk and MacDonald, 1976), to clarify how hearing language is a complex task in itself, involving a broad set of aspects beyond simple sound perception, such as the visual system as well as the expectations regarding the upcoming input. Computers on the other hand *hear* on the basis of an audio signal that is processed (Figure 1), at least in the most traditional and well-established architectures, without access to higher level linguistic knowledge or information from the communicative context.

We then briefly presented speech recognition as a direct optimization task (i.e., given an audio signal, find the word in a given database that maximises the probability of being associated to that signal) and introduced one of the major challenges that speech recognition models are still facing, namely the ability to adapt to different speech styles (i.e., speakers of different language varieties and dialects, non-native speakers, speakers with impairments etc.).

In order to further demonstrate this, we tested the attendees' ability to adapt their hearing skills to different speech varieties by making them hear conversations in various Italian regional accents.[3] While we asked attendees to guess the name of the region of the speakers, the actual aim was to show how we easily adapt to understand speech, differently from speech recognition systems.

3.3 Are computers able to *read*?

From this moment on, the attendees worked on written text. The activity described in this section was aimed at showing how salient aspects related to language structure can be derived from the statistical properties of language.

Following the "Word Salad" puzzle (Radev and Pustejovsky, 2013), the ability of *reading* was presented as follows: given a set of words, are we able to rearrange them in a plausible sentence-like order? We demonstrated how this is an easy task

[3]Conversations were extracted from corpus CLIPS (Albano Leoni et al., 2007).

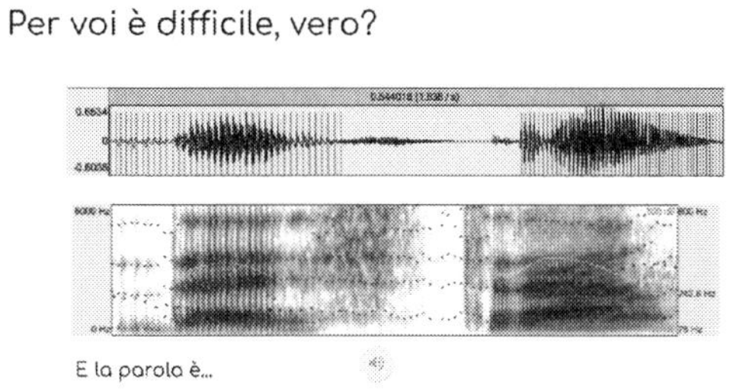

Figure 1: Representation of the audio signal for the italian word *destra* (en. *right*). This was used to show how information coming from audio signals can be represented in a way that easily allows the computer to perform a pattern matching task, but would be impossible to process for humans.

for human beings, when one deals with a language they are familiar with (Figure 2), while, generally one may not be able to perform the same task in case of unknown languages (Figure 3), where each possible ordering seems equally plausible.

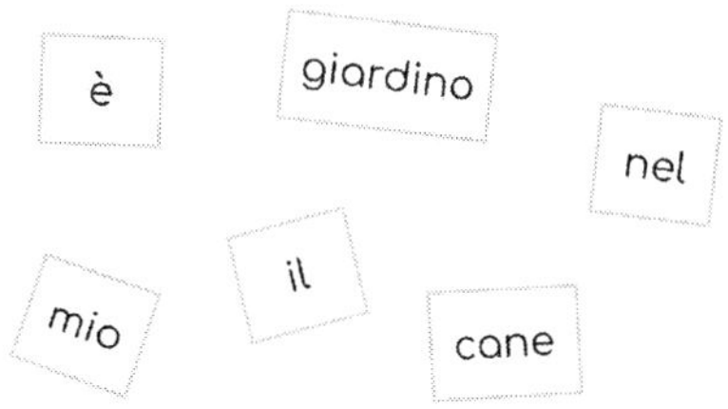

Figure 2: A set of Italian words (from the top left corner, en. *is, garden, in, my, the, dog*): when asked to rearrange them into a sentence, participants would first come up with the most likely ordering (i.e., *il mio cane è nel giardino*, en. *my dog is in the garden*) and if prompted they would then produce more creative sentences (i.e., *il cane nel giardino è mio*, en. *the dog in the garden is mine*). They would however never consider ungrammatical sequences as possible sentences.

We therefore gave the attendees a deck of unknown, mysterious tokens (left card in Figure 4) and asked them to come up with the most plausible sentence that contained all of them. The cards represented either Italian or English words (participants were divided into two teams, each one dealing with a different *masked* language) which had however been transliterated into an unknown alphabet. While this was obviously an impossible task to solve, it gave us the opportunity to introduce a notion of probability in the linguistic realm. We cast it as the expectation that we humans bear on

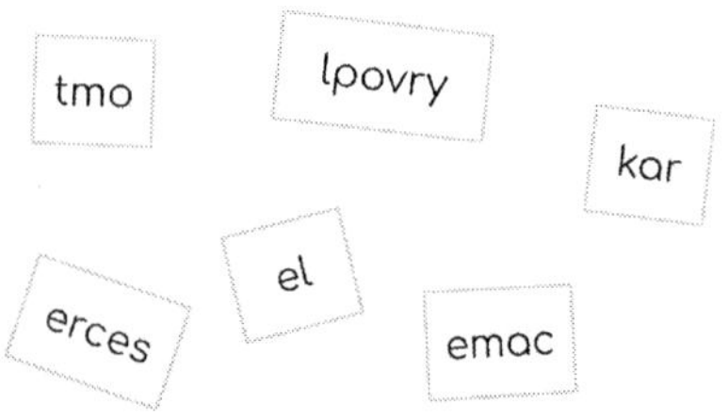

Figure 3: The figure depicts the same situation as Figure 2, this time with non-words.

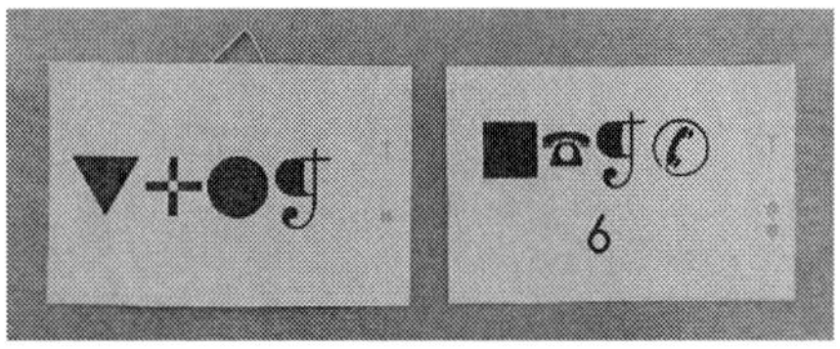

Figure 4: Example cards, both showing a word. Left: a card for the first activity, with a button loop to thread it in a sentence. Right: a card for the second activity, with part of speech (number) at the bottom.

the appearance of a specific linguistic sequence, and the subsequent need for a source of linguistic knowledge to implement the same notion.

When asked to perform the same task on the words of Figure 2, participants produced sentences in a quite consistent order, and the most prototypical sentences (e.g., *il mio cane è nel giardino*, en. *my dog is in the garden*) were usually elicited before some less typical ones (e.g., *il cane nel giardino è mio*, en. *the dog in the garden is mine*), while agrammatical sentences (i.e., random permutations) were never produced.

We justified their responses by explaining that humans accumulate a great amount of linguistic knowledge throughout their lifetime that helps them refine these expectations, while machines are instead in principle unbiased towards having any specific preference. This observation allowed us to introduce participants to the notion of *corpus* as a large collection of linguistic data that mimics the amount of data we are exposed to as humans.

Each team was then provided with a corpus written in an unknown language (approximately 60 sentences hand-crafted by transliterating a portion of the “Snow White” tale into a mysterious alphabet Figure 5). Concurrently, we introduced a simple algorithm to tell apart sentence-like orderings of the provided tokens from the random ones.

The algorithm, which we called *The bracelet method* (Figure 6), is based on the Markov Chain

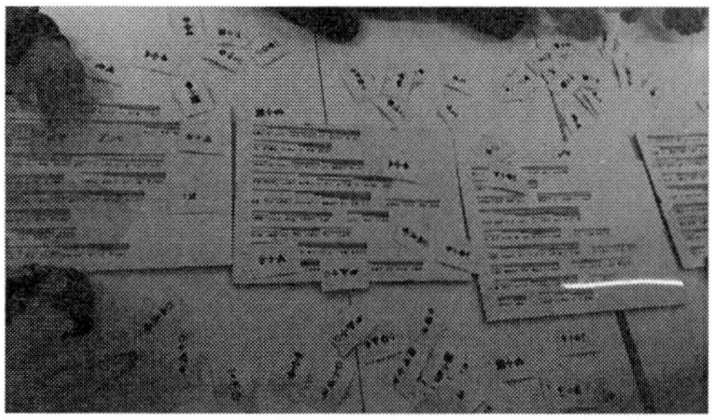

Figure 5: The figure shows one of the corpora that was given to participants, 5 A3 tables containing approx. 60 transliterated sentences from the “Snow White” fairy tale, and tokens with buttonholes that had to be searched in the corpus and threaded into sentences.

procedure: in a scenario similar to that of lining pearls up to form a bracelet, participants could decompose the task of forming up a sentence into smaller tasks. To make the operation more concrete, we equipped each card with a button loop as shown in Figure 4: this way cards could be physically threaded together to form a sentence.

The first step consisted in choosing the first word, for the beginning of the sentence. Since participants were facing a language they didn’t know, they were not aware of language structures nor of the meaning of the tokens. In such a situation, they could decide whether it was plausible to use a given word at the beginning of a sentence just by looking up in the corpus sentences that began the same way. If they found at least one sentence that began with the same word, it meant that that was a licit position and they could use it to start the sentence.

The activity continued as follows: sticking to the bracelet metaphor, participants needed to select and insert the following "pearl" into the thread: ideally the pearl should pair well with the previous one, as we might want to avoid colour mismatch (e.g., it is well known that blue and green do not go well together). The metaphor highlights therefore a core aspect that holds true for language as well, namely that we can condition our choice on a variable number of previous choices, and this will influence the complexity of the obtained pattern.

The activity resulted in a number of sentence-bracelets, as shown in Figure 7, that were then kept aside to be translated at the end of the workshop.

3.4 Do computers *know* grammar?

While the previous game highlighted the importance of statistical information in NLP, in accor-

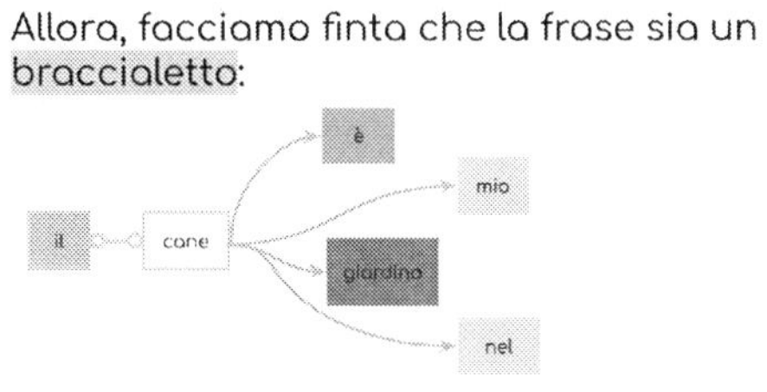

Figure 6: The *bracelet method* applied on the Italian words *è, mio, giardino, nel* (en. *is, my, garden, in*). The algorithm is based on bigram co-occurrences, so the choice for each word is based solely on the previously chosen one. Colors indicate probabilities, which are computed based only on the previously chosen word *cane* (en. *dog*). The first token, *il* (en. *the*), appears grayed as it is ignored for the choice.

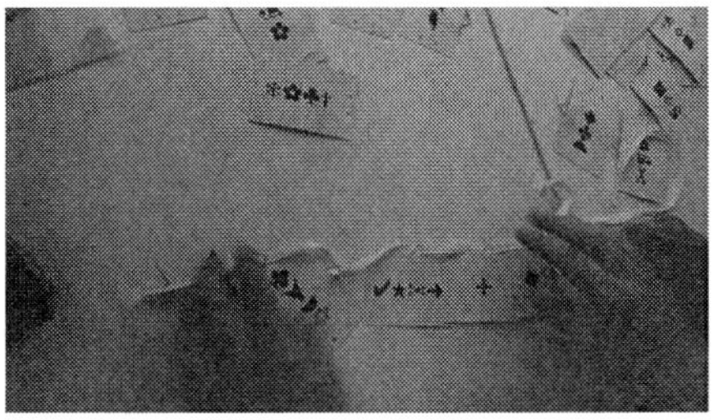

Figure 7: The figure shows the result of a bracelet sequence: tokens are threaded together based on co-occurrences in the corpus.

Figure 8: Each block in the image corresponds to a possible Italian full meal, consisting of: first course (e.g. *fusilli al pomodoro*), second course (e.g. *pollo agli asparagi*) and dessert (e.g. *pannacotta*).

Figure 9: Step-by-step process to assess the validity of a given menu. In the top-right corner the rules for creating a full meal are shown . Categories are defined recursively until each course that constitute the full menu is obtained and therefore reduced to the initial category of a *pasto* (en. *meal*).

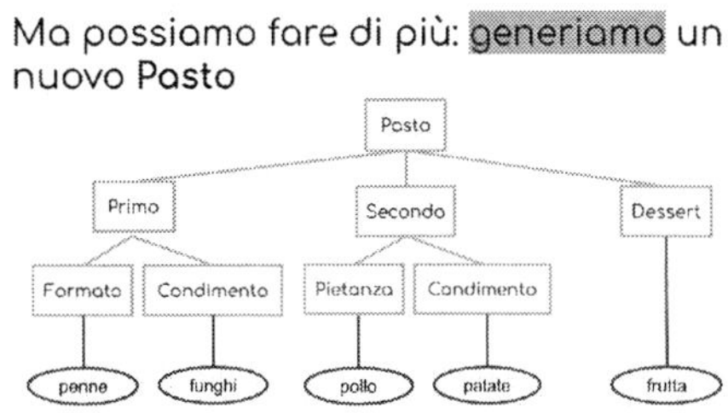

Figure 10: Process flow for creating a new meal from the initial category *pasto* (en. *meal*) up to the leaves containing terminal symbols such as *penne*, *funghi*, *pollo* etc. (en., a type of *pasta*, *mushrooms*, *chicken*). The rules used to generate are the same used for the reduction process, reported in Figure 9.

dance with the overall aim of the activity, we also wanted to introduce some of the algorithms that are more deeply rooted in the linguistic tradition.

In order to do so, we introduced the notion of grammar as a descriptive abstraction over a set of examples. Out of the linguistic context, to exemplify this notion of grammar metaphorically, we presented participants with a set of possible restaurant menus (Figure 8), and encouraged them to come up with the general rule that the restaurant owner must have had in mind when choosing those combinations. All menus were built as a traditional Italian full meal, composed by two main dishes and a dessert. We perpetuated the metaphor showing how, once a set of rules is defined, these can be used both to decide if a new menu is likely to be part of the same set (Figure 9) and also to generate new meals (Figure 10).

This metaphor, which was readily grasped by most participants, was useful to show how different components can be combined together in a meaningful way, as it happens in grammar. Before moving back to the corpus, we showed them what a formal grammar of the menus could look like.

We had previously annotated the corpus with

syntactic and morpho-syntactic information (i.e., part of speech), as shown in Figures 5 and 12. We therefore asked participants to extract from the corpus a possible grammar, namely a set of attested rules and use them to generate a new sentence.

In order to write the grammar, participants were given several physical materials: felt strips reproducing the colors of the annotation, a deck of cards with numbers (identifying parts of speech) and a deck of "=" symbols (Figure 11).

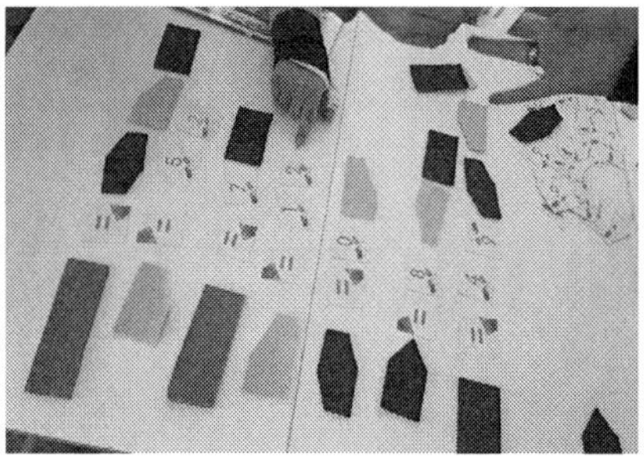

Figure 11: A set of rules extracted during the activity from the corpus. Each rule is made of felt strips for phrases, cards with numbers indicating parts of speech, and "=" cards.

With a new deck of words (Figure 4, right panel), not all of which present in the corpus, participants had to generate a sentence using the previously composed rules.

3.5 Becoming a computational linguist

At this point, participants had created a number of sentences by means of the two techniques described above. It is now time to discover that the mysterious languages they worked on were actually English and Italian. This was achieved in practice by superimposing a Plexiglas frame on the A3 corpus pages (Figure 13): the true nature of the corpora was this way revealed as the participants could see the original texts (in Italian and English) and translate the sentences they had created previously.

The outcome of the activity stimulated discussion amongst the participants, highlighting pros and cons of each approach and how could they be integrated into real-life technologies. Our workshop ended with a brief description of more recent NLP technologies and their commercial applications, such as recommender systems, automatic translation, text completion, etc.

Since the target audience consisted mostly of middle- and high-school students, we offered an overview of what it takes to become a computational linguist and where one could study computational linguistics in Italy.

Figure 12: Example of categories (it. *Categorie*), e.g. phrases and POS tags, and rules (it. *Regole*) for the sentence *"lo specchio rispose a la regina"* (en. *the mirror answered to the queen*).

Figure 13: A trial session of the workshop (the picture shows some of the tutors explaining the game to AILC members): the original language of the corpus has just been revealed by superimposing Plexiglas supports on the corpus tables.

4 The workshop in action

The activity – here outlined in its complete and original form – was presented in various outlets during the last year and a half.

It was initially designed for the 2019 edition of the "Bergamo Scienza" Science Festival[4], where it was presented live to over 450 participants in the course of two weeks. A simplified "print-and-play" version of the workshop was also presented at the 2020 edition of the SISSA[5] Student Day.

Due to the Covid-19 pandemic, all other presentations of the activity had to be moved online. Transposing the workshop crucially meant striving to maintaining the interactive nature of the activities without the possibility of meeting face to face.

[4] https://festival.bergamoscienza.it/
[5] https://www.sissa.it/

To do so, we integrated our original presentation on Google slides with the interactive presentation software Mentimeter[6] - which we used for questions, polling and quizzes. The corpus and tokens were presented via a web interface created especially for this purpose[7].

The interface presented the masked corpus, complete with POS tags and syntactic annotations. For the bracelet activity participants were automatically assigned a number of tokens which they could use to build a sentence by simply dragging and dropping them. (Figures 14 and 15).

This online version was crafted in the first place to be presented at "Festival della Scienza"[8] (Figure 16), a science festival primarily aimed at school students held each year in Genoa, where multiple 45' sessions of the workshop were run over the course of two days. The fourth activity (Section 3.4) involved "bootstrapping" syntactic rules based only on our color-based annotation. To simplify online interaction, we only used the unmasked Italian version of the corpus and participants played collectively, helping each other to build sentences and grammatical rules: rules were collected through a Mentimeter poll, while a sentence was generated in a guided demonstration by the presenter of the workshop.

Overall, the workshop transposed really well online, and was extremely well-received in this version as well. The online modality also allowed us to present it to a more vast and varied audience than just students: a version for the general public was presented at *European Researchers' Night* (*Bright Night*[9]) at the University of Pisa, thanks to a collaboration with the Computational Linguistics Laboratory[10] and ILC-CNR[11] in November 2020, a dedicated session was run for the High school ITS Buzzi[12] (Prato, Italy) in December 2020, and during the second edition of the Science Web Festival[13] in April 2021.

5 Reusability: this activity as a blueprint

As mentioned in Section 1, our activity was inspired by a collection of English-language problems created for students participating in the Computational Linguistics Olympiad (Radev and Pustejovsky, 2013).

We adapted the original activity to the Italian language and context. While we tried to choose widely shared linguistic principles to communicate, the operation of adapting the game to a different language obviously requires language specific choices and details, which would have to be re-evaluated when porting the activity to yet new languages. Particularly, since the materials have been developed for Italian, it might be the case that transposition is not straightforward for some languages. However, we believe that the general structure of our workshop can serve as a blueprint for extension to new languages. For this reason all the relevant materials are made available in a dedicated repository. The repository includes both scripts to reproduce our activity as well as a general set of insights/recommendations regarding the structure and principles of the workshop.

All of the scripts necessary to produce the materials used in the game's workflow in a different language are made available in our open-access repository[14]. To get the activity into production using the scripts provided, one only needs to create an annotated corpus in the target language.

Our specific choice of "Snow White" as a corpus is motivated by the fact that the story can be phrased in a fairly repetitive formulation, with two advantages. One is that enough bigrams are present that enable the generation of new sentences with the *bracelet method*. The other one is that the story contains recognizable characters (e.g., the dwarfs, the evil queen etc.), so that, when the unmasked text is revealed, the process results intuitively transparent. Such characteristics are desirable for the activity, and should be kept in mind when choosing a new text for a new language.

In addition to sharing scripts, we are sharing here the core structure and principles the workshop relies on, which can be reproduced when replicating the activity also for a different language.

Parts 1&2 At the beginning of the workshop (see Section 3.2) we show the limits of current technologies, in particular in terms of adaptability. To this end, we exploited diatopic variations, such as Italian regional accents, since this is an aspect readily available to Italian students. In the con-

[6] https://www.menti.com/

[7] A demo of the interface can be found at https://donde.altervista.org/

[8] http://www.festivalscienza.it

[9] https://www.bright-night.it/

[10] http://colinglab.humnet.unipi.it/

[11] http://www.ilc.cnr.it/

[12] https://www.tulliobuzzi.edu.it/

[13] https://www.sciencewebfestival.it/

[14] https://bitbucket.org/melfnt/malvisindi

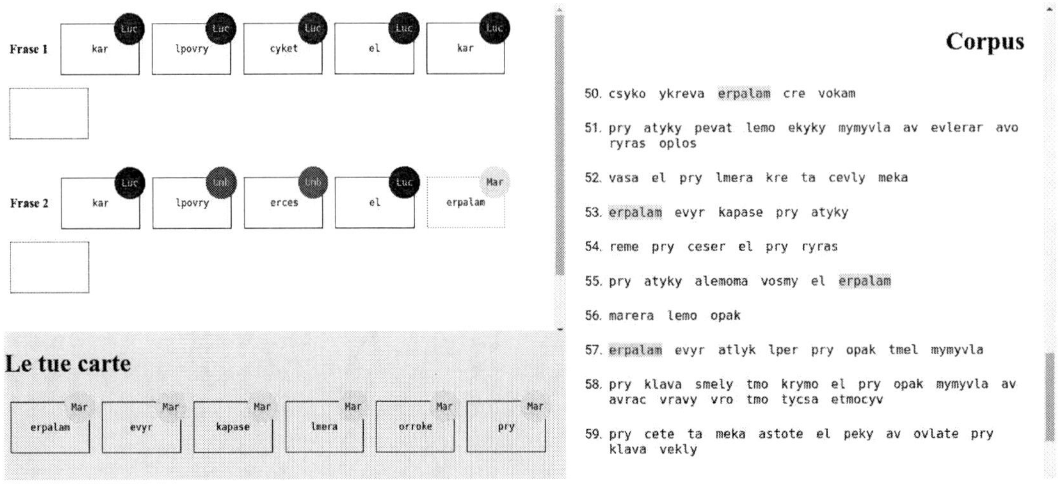

Figure 14: Interface of the online website used for the "bracelet" game (section 3.3) during the online workshops. Players can collaboratively drag and drop their card from the bottom left panel to form sentences in the top-left panel. The corpus is shown in the right panel.

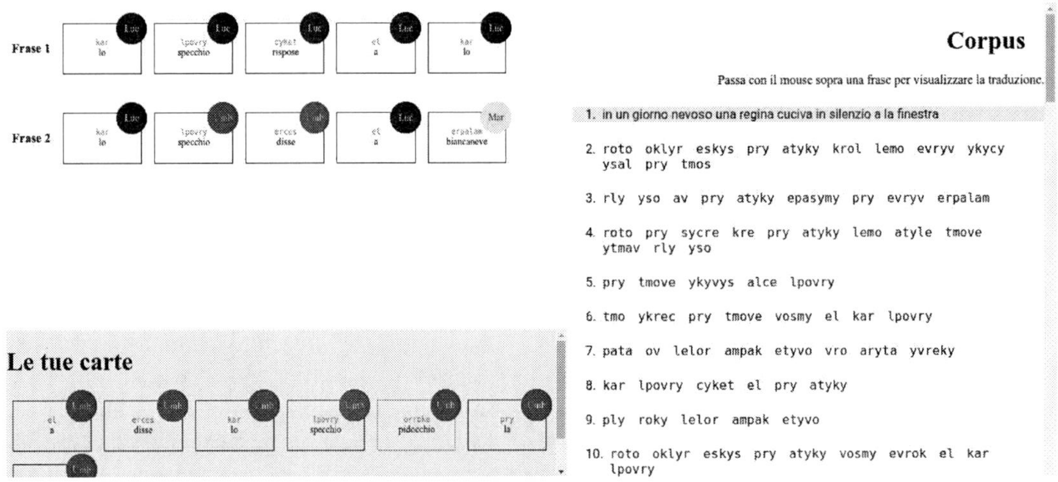

Figure 15: After the games the website shows the translation of the corpus (see for example line 1) and cards.

text of other languages, the same concept could be however shown by different means, such as the influence of jargon or minority languages, or simply differences in accuracy depending on, age or other socio-demographic and socio-cultural variables.

Part 3 The next part of the activity (Section 3.3) is the most easily reproducible in a different language as it only exploits statistical co-occurrences as a cue for linguistic structure. The only prerequisite here is the availability of a sufficiently standardized tokenization for the language of interest. As described above, we masked the language through a transliteration system: this was achieved either substituting words with sequences of symbols, or with non-words. In the case of non-words, these were generated by manually defining a series of phonotactic constraints for Italian, which should be adapted to the target language.

The main message to be conveyed through this activity is that language is a complex system; we did this disentangling semantics from the purely symbolic tier, which is the one computers most commonly manipulate.

Part 4 The following part of the activity (Section 3.4) focuses on the expressive power residing in the definition of auxiliary categories as descriptors of linguistic evidence. We achieved this by simplifying a constituent-based annotation for our cor-

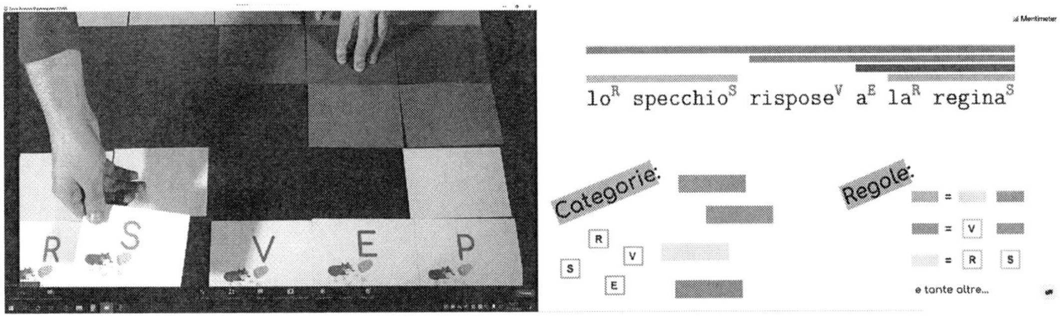

Figure 16: The picture was taken during a workshop session at "Festival della Scienza" in Genoa, in October 2020. Due to the COVID-19 pandemic, students were participating remotely. The left panel shows the tutor handling grammatical categories (colored cards for syntactic phrases and letters for parts of speech); the right panel shows a screenshot of the slides employed during the activity. Students could see both panels as slides were streamed while a webcam was capturing the tutor's movements.

pus: having continuous constituents easily allowed for the physical implementation of re-writing rules (i.e., participants had some physical constituents and tokens that could be used to simulate the generation process). We built categories in order to extract from the text a simple *regular grammar*, and we were especially careful about the fact that both the Italian and the English corpus showed a similar structure and therefore complexity level. More specifically, we restricted to five types of higher-level categories that acted as phrases (i.e., sentence, noun phrase, verb phrase, prepositional phrase, subordinate clause): this is of course a huge simplification and, for the sake of the activity, we overlooked some relevant linguistic phenomena.

We reckon that this approach might not be portable to languages that exhibit a flexible word order, so alternative solutions should be sought.

Part 5 The last section of the activity was dedicated to a discussion on the presented methods for language generation.

After that and depending on the audience, we presented some options to pursue studies in Computational Linguistics in Italy, which would of course have to be adapted to the target social context. Lay publications concerned with Computational Linguistics are also unfortunately not very common in Italy, therefore we took the opportunity to provide participants with some suggestions for further readings (Masini and Grandi, 2017).

6 Looking back and ahead

In the previous sections we described an interactive workshop designed to illustrate the basic principles of Computational Linguistics to young Italian students. It is the first activity of its kind to be designed by the Italian Association for Computational Linguistics and among the first dissemination activities in Italy for Computational Linguistics directed to young students.

The activity had the broad aim of increasing awareness towards applications based on language technology, and introduce students to the study of language as a scientific discipline.

We run the activity in both face-to-face and, due to COVID-19, online form: generally speaking, we received enthusiastic feedback both from younger participants and from the more general public. We adapted the activity to a variety of formats and time-slots, ranging from 30 to 90 minutes: the amount of time required to approach the game and get acquainted with the concepts is of course variable, and depends on the participants' background and on the level of engagement that is expected of them. Generally speaking 45 minutes are enough for a presentation including some interaction with the audience, especially in the online setting, but at least 90 minutes are needed for the participants to fully experiment with the hands-on activity.

We want to specifically stress how time is a central ingredient in the activity. While the game-related aspects remained engaging and fun even in the shortened, online versions, in order to fully grasp the mechanisms underlying the presented algorithms longer sessions would be needed. In fact, we often felt that more time would be beneficial for a deeper discussion about language as an object of study itself, and about language as data on which theories can be built. In particular, shorter time-slots or less guided activities enhance the risk of participants approaching the challenge as a puzzle that they can solve regardless of linguistic knowledge. This is because the approach to language we are presenting is entirely new to our audience, and not only to the younger students.

Although we did not have a formal system in place to collect systematic feedback, the overall response across venues and conditions has been extremely positive.[15] Curiosity and engagement of participants remained high both onsite and online, and we received many questions on several aspects of Natural Language Processing and neural networks, as well as concerning its role in Artificial Intelligence at large.

The participants' enthusiastic questions gave us many ideas for future dissemination activities. In fact, the technological world is advancing fast and we firmly believe that it is necessary to spread more awareness on the inner workings of AI-based technologies, to develop a society-level conscience to approach them in a critical way.

The activity described in this paper was targeted at middle to high-school students as well as the general public. It would be interesting to engage with a younger audience as well, as communicating the study and (computational) modelling of language to them would raise awareness towards language studies as a scientific discipline.

For our activity, we took inspiration from one of the problems proposed in Radev and Pustejovsky (2013). Puzzles such as the ones presented at the Computational Linguistics Competitions are a great way to introduce both important challenges and the methodology to solve them, as they stimulate students to investigate linguistic aspects in a bottom-up fashion. Organizing the competition in Italy would represent a bigger project for our association, to be addressed in the coming years.

Acknowledgements

The workshop has been developed with help and support from many parties. We would like to thank them all here. First and foremost, all the participants that enthusiastically played along and made the activity a success. Along with them, four tutors and science animators helped us greatly in putting our ideas into practice. We are also grateful to BergamoScienza, Festival della Scienza, Science Web Festival for hosting the activity during the festivals, to ILC-CNR "Antonio Zampolli" and ColingLab (University of Pisa) for hosting us during the European Researchers' Night, and to the Scuola Internazionale Superiore di Studi Avanzati (SISSA) and ITI Tullio Buzzi. We are also grateful to Dr. Mirko Lai, who has collaborated on the development of the web interface for the online versions of our activity. We would like to thank AILC (Italian Association of Computational Linguistics) for encouraging us to design the activity and supporting us throughout the process. Last but not least, we thank the true hero of our workshop: GingerCat. [16]

References

Federico Albano Leoni, Francesco Cutugno, and Renata Savy. 2007. Clips (corpora e lessici di italiano parlato e scritto). *Linguistica computazionale: ricerche monolingui e multilingui*.

Ivan A Derzhanski and Thomas Payne. 2010. The linguistics olympiads: Academic competitions in linguistics for secondary school students. *Linguistics at school: language awareness in primary and secondary education*, pages 213–26.

Nicola Grandi and Francesca Masini. 2018. Perché la linguistica ha bisogno di divulgazione (e viceversa). In N. Grandi and F. Masini, editors, *La linguistica della divulgazione, la divulgazione della linguistica. Atti del IV Convegno Interannuale SLI nuova serie*, pages 5–12. SLI, Roma.

Boris Iomdin, Alexander Piperski, and Anton Somin. 2013. Linguistic problems based on text corpora. In *Proceedings of the Fourth Workshop on Teaching NLP and CL*, pages 9–17.

Patrick Littell, Lori Levin, Jason Eisner, and Dragomir Radev. 2013. Introducing computational concepts in a linguistics olympiad. In *Proceedings of the Fourth Workshop on Teaching NLP and CL*, pages 18–26.

Francesca Masini and Nicola Grandi. 2017. *Tutto ciò che hai sempre voluto sapere sul linguaggio e sulle lingue*. Caissa Italia.

Harry McGurk and John MacDonald. 1976. Hearing lips and seeing voices. *Nature*, 264(5588):746–748.

Dragomir Radev and James Pustejovsky. 2013. *Puzzles in logic, languages and computation: the red book*. Springer.

Hans Van Halteren. 2002. Teaching nlp/cl through games: The case of parsing. In *Proceedings of the ACL-02 Workshop on Effective Tools and Methodologies for Teaching Natural Language Processing and Computational Linguistics*, pages 1–9.

[15]Following one reviewer's suggestion, we have implemented such a system for our latest presentation at the Science Web Festival 2021 as a Google form that we circulated among participants at the end of the presentation.

[16]`https://icons8.com/illustrations/style--ginger-cat-1`

Author Index

Association for Computational Linguistics
209 N. Eighth Street
Stroudsburg, Pennsylvania 18360

ISBN 978-1-7138-3031-3

CURRAN ASSOCIATES INC.
proceedings.com